# Oikos and Market

*Max Planck Studies in Anthropology and Economy*
Series editors:
Stephen Gudeman, University of Minnesota
Chris Hann, Max Planck Institute for Social Anthropology

Definitions of economy and society, and their proper relationship to each other, have been the perennial concerns of social philosophers. In the early decades of the twenty-first century these became and remain matters of urgent political debate. At the forefront of this series are the approaches to these connections by anthropologists, whose explorations of the local ideas and institutions underpinning social and economic relations illuminate large fields ignored in other disciplines.

**Volume 1**
*Economy and Ritual: Six Studies of Postsocialist Transformations*
Edited by Stephen Gudeman and Chris Hann

**Volume 2**
*Oikos and Market: Explorations in Self-Sufficiency after Socialism*
Edited by Stephen Gudeman and Chris Hann

# Oikos and Market

*Explorations in Self-Sufficiency
after Socialism*

Edited by

STEPHEN GUDEMAN AND CHRIS HANN

berghahn
NEW YORK · OXFORD
www.berghahnbooks.com

Published in 2015 by
Berghahn Books
www.berghahnbooks.com

**Library of Congress Cataloging-in-Publication Data**

Oikos and market : explorations in self-sufficiency after socialism / edited by Stephen
Gudeman and Chris Hann.
    pages cm. — (Max Planck studies in anthropology and economy ; volume 2)
    Includes bibliographical references and index.
    ISBN 978-1-78238-695-7 (hardback : alk. paper) —
    ISBN 978-1-78238-696-4 (ebook)
    1. Households—Economic aspects—Europe, Eastern. 2. Self-reliant living—Europe,
Eastern. 3. Post-communism—Europe, Eastern. I. Gudeman, Stephen. II. Hann,
C. M., 1953–
    HC244.Z9.C66 2015
    330.947—dc23

                                                                                    2014039961


**British Library Cataloguing in Publication Data**

A catalogue record for this book is available from the British Library


Printed on acid-free paper.

ISBN: 978-1-78238-695-7 hardback
ISBN: 978-1-78238-696-4 ebook

# Contents

# Illustrations

## Figures

## Tables

# Acknowledgments

Like its predecessor, *Economy and Ritual,* this book is the product of a postdoctoral research group led by us between 2009 and 2012 at the Max Planck Institute for Social Anthropology. We are grateful to numerous visitors to Halle during this period. Comments and suggestions on various chapters from Aliki Angelidou, James G. Carrier, Gerald W. Creed, Jane Guyer, and Mihály Sárkány were particularly helpful.

We are once again indebted to Jutta Turner, who prepared all the maps, and above all to Anke Meyer for her expert assistance in preparing the final manuscript.

SG
CH

Group Field Sites Map. Used with the permission of Jutta Turner.

# Introduction

## *Self-Sufficiency as Reality and as Myth*

### Stephen Gudeman and Chris Hann

Our comparative study of six sites in postsocialist Eurasia investigates the ideals and practices of the house economy and self-sufficiency. These two themes have a long history in European thought and custom. But we were surprised at their continuing prominence in the late twentieth and early twenty-first centuries. Our larger research project, as described in Volume 1 of this series, focused on economy and ritual; however, the economy of the house emerged so prominently in the ethnography that we felt compelled to probe more deeply into its description and analysis. Because the six study areas were reputedly in transition from socialist to market economies, we were initially surprised at the research results. Socialism supposedly integrated rural households into a wider industrial division of labor, thereby superseding the household as the basic unit of production and consumption. As for capitalist market economies, they too are supposed to promote an increased division of labor so that even where farming persists on a family basis, it becomes capitalized and the old labor-intensive forms of household production are superseded. These models are not entirely false, but in the course of our project we found ideals of household self-sufficiency to be of major importance. Studying this historical moment illuminates not only postsocialist transformations but also central features of human economy in general.

No economy, whether at the level of the house, community, or nation, can be self-sufficient. House economies always exist within a larger social and political order. The practices and images nurtured in the house are also found at other institutional levels of society, which contributes to blurring the very definition of "the house economy."

We identify a number of features of the house economy. They do not form a fixed set but nonetheless cohere as a model of activity. This contemporary existence of the house economy is provocative because it is situated at the opposite pole to the market, which is the dominating institution in almost all current economies. By focusing on the house in its many forms we are not only responding to the ethnographic data but also questioning economic theory that focuses on markets alone and applies the logic of maximization to every human activity. From an efficiency perspective, social practices, such as reciprocity, lending a hand, and sharing, either are not part of the real economy or must have some hidden functional capacity that furthers self-interest. We argue, instead, for an institutionalist approach that prioritizes social relationships, norms, and ideations and shows how needs are met at different spaces of economy. If economic activity refers to securing human livelihoods in the fullest sense, we need to emphasize yet again that a great deal of everyday behavior contradicts the model of homo economicus. Sociality and mutuality are often valued in themselves, and not merely as a means toward satisfying private preferences. Our first volume demonstrated that ritual is an integral part of these and cannot be reduced to considerations of economic efficiency or inefficiency. The long-term mutuality and solidarity highlighted in ritual are in a dialectical tension with the short-term logic of rational choice, optimization, and individualism as exemplified in markets. This tension between mutuality revealed in the house and impersonal relations cultivated in markets characterizes all human economies (Gudeman 2008).

The theme of mutuality, which we employ in the context of the house economy, has in recent years been increasingly elaborated by anthropologists in the context of kinship. Marshall Sahlins (2013) has drawn on this literature and defined kinship's quality or constitution as "mutuality of being." Our perspective is different, for we see mutuality as a broader notion than kinship alone. It is nurtured and nourished in the house through practical material activities and spreads widely beyond it and also beyond the domain of kinship (Gudeman 2001, 2008, 2012). Mutuality means commonality or connection with others as opposed to personal self-interest. It is expressed by sharing, reciprocity, redistribution, and related practices. For Aristotle "philia," which we feel for friends, family and other associates, means wishing well for them, not for one's own sake but for theirs, and the feeling is reciprocal. There is philia between lovers, cities, tribal members, and associates of the same religious group, among others (1984: 1380$^b$36–37). Philia may be viewed as one form of mutuality. Mutuality in its various forms implies a degree of empathy or the ability to see oneself in the place of the other, and perhaps to see oneself as does the other. In these implications it is very different from self-interest (unless, as some economists claim, at the risk of contradicting themselves, it is self-interested to empathize with the other). This distinction between self-interest and mutuality is typified by the contrast of calculated behavior in markets and making material life through social relationships as in the house and beyond.

## Aristotle and Self-Sufficiency

Self-sufficiency is a very old idea. It lies at the heart of Aristotle's formulation of the *oikos*, the well-ordered house that was set within the community and *polis*. Market activity was in the hands of traders (*metics*) who were external to the *polis*. Keen observer and moralist, Aristotle's conception of *oikonomia* was taken up by many others: Roman writers on the *latifundia*, the Mishnah, medieval accountants, St. Thomas Aquinas, John Locke, and Karl Marx. The Aristotelian discourse influenced the workings of the medieval manor and monastery (Duby 1969; Postan 1975), as well as the house and hacienda in the New World, where it helped to shape the rural community in relation to the state (Gudeman and Rivera 1990). More recently, its influence can be detected in the expanding interdisciplinary literature on "moral economy" (Booth 1994).

Aristotle was the first to distinguish between an object's value in use and its value in exchange. This prescient vision allowed him to separate two forms of wealth acquisition, two methods for setting exchange rates, two functions of money, and two ways of acting in the economy. He did not deny the existence of a "market mentality" but asserted the ethical superiority of the communal form: group was emphasized over individual, relationships for provisioning over the acquisition of material goods, social justice over personal greed, and plurality of values over the commensuration of goods through a monetary calculus. He well knew that goods may be exchanged in pursuit of gain, but he argued for basing an economy on excellence as opposed to efficacy. For him, virtuous activity was central in maintaining material life, because it allowed for human flourishing; the self-sufficient community that promoted excellence was the greatest human bulwark against uncertainty.

Bernard Mandeville (1970 [1714]) and Adam Smith (1976 [1776]) turned this argument upside down when they urged that an enduring economy, providing not only the greatest wealth but also the greatest freedom, and benefiting the social whole, could be founded on the exercise of what had hitherto always been considered a vice, namely self-interest. Under industrial capitalism, the Aristotelian message remains profound in its negation. Today, compared to the Aristotelian vision, everything is reversed: the market is construed as liberating, the house and community are seen as constricting. Yet twist the lens again, and the Aristotelian vision of economy becomes available as a critique of the market, with its foundations in individualism, hedonism, efficiency, and rational thought. With a well-woven argument that stretches across a number of his works, Aristotle contested exactly those features of the market that have been delineated and prioritized by economists in the last two centuries.

Aristotle recognized that self-interested practices can become dominating in life, but he set these actions against excellent or virtuous behavior. His first words in the *Politics* announce the centrality of human sociability: "Every state is a community of some kind" (1984: 1252ᵃ1). Tracing the origin of community to human nature, Aristotle urged that man is inherently a social or "political animal" (1984: 1253ᵃ2, 1253ᵃ30). The self-sufficient individual, living outside community, could only be a god or a beast. Drawing on a different analogy, Aristotle compared the single human to a playing piece on a board game, "a part in relation to the whole" (1984: 1253ᵃ26–27). Outside the state, humans lack excellence and goodness, and are "full of lust and gluttony" (1984: 1253ᵃ32–37); they look only to the endless satisfaction of material desires. Distinguishing thus between individual and community self-sufficiency, Aristotle established a vision of the human-in-community, and of community as fulfilling the totality of material and moral needs. This social perception, long anticipating the sociology of Émile Durkheim, provides the setting for his economics.

The foundation for Aristotle's arguments about economy, which are inextricable from his social philosophy, is laid in the *Ethics*, where he urges that human satisfaction is linked to the achievement of self-sufficiency in community (1984: 1097ᵇ14–15). Self-sufficiency means achieving completeness, but the wholeness to which Aristotle points is social, not individual: "By self-sufficient we do not mean that which is sufficient for a man by himself, for one who lives a solitary life, but also for parents, children, wife, and in general for his friends and fellow citizens, since man is sociable by nature" (1984: 1097ᵇ9–11). Later, in the *Politics*, Aristotle presents an origin story about the self-sufficient community. He distinguishes three forms of association: the household, the village, and the *polis*. Each is a component of what follows and each displays distinctive characteristics. Formed to meet the needs of the family, the household was the first mode of association. The uniqueness of the household was temporary, because as population and families expanded, households grew into villages. "Suckled with the same milk" (1984: 1252ᵃ18), sharing the same blood, and bound together by the morality of kinship, villagers were governed by a senior male. Eventually, the *polis* or self-sufficient community emerged. A collection of villages, the *polis* met all material needs and provided the context for the development of human excellence or flourishing.

What Aristotle considered to be the highest, best, and natural condition of a community—material self-sufficiency that combats uncertainty—is from the standpoint of modern economics the most unnatural and backward state. For him, the people of a house within a community and *polis* should not need to exchange with others from want or for gain. Aristotle offers a story that moves from inside to outside, from small to large, from origin to florescence, from self-sufficiency and community transactions to impersonal trade, from moral transaction to amoral acquisition, and from the density of the household, whose members are "companions of the cupboard," to the open space of unrestrained trade whose participants share nothing. With this narrative, Aristotle presented a platform for later community or moral critiques of the market from Karl Marx to Max Weber, and from Thorstein Veblen to Karl Polanyi. The work of the last and youngest of these critics had a strong direct impact on anthropology in the middle of the twentieth century. According to Polanyi, the formation of a "market society," in which land and labor were "fictitious commodities" separated from human life, was the key to understanding the catastrophes of modern history. The "great transformation" he called for was predicated on a revival of the Aristotelian conception of the human economy, in which economy is embedded in society, and political institutions rather than "the market" are dominant (Polanyi 1957, 2001 [1944]).

## Economics and the Anthropological Critique

In light of the Aristotelian vision, it is ironic that the modern discipline of economics takes its name from the Greek word *oikos*. Its premises are completely different, first under the impact of Mandeville and Smith in the eighteenth century, and later under that of the "marginalist revolution" that replaced classical political economy with a "neoclassical synthesis" from the 1870s onward (Hann and Hart 2011). As modern economists concerned themselves with highly developed commercial economies functioning on the basis of the division of labor and self-interest, it was left to historians and anthropologists to theorize "primitive economies" in very different, opposing terms. In the influential origin narrative of economic historian Karl Bücher (who grew up among farmers and artisans in nineteenth-century Hessen), our ancestors were originally impelled by the search for food on an individualist basis (*individuelle Nahrungssuche*). He considered this phase in human evolution to be "pre-economic." According to Bücher's typology, the first "economic stage" properly speaking was characterized by the "closed household economy" (*geschlossene Hauswirtschaft*). Taken literally, this was an easy target for twentieth century ethnographers. The most devastating criticism came from Bronislaw Malinowski, who showed that the Trobriand Islanders and their neighbors, though undoubtedly "primitive" according to the categories of that age, were capable of sustaining the complex inter-island exchange system known as *kula* (Malinowski 1922). But perhaps Bücher did not wish to be understood quite so literally. Among these Melanesian horticulturalists the gifting of surplus yams to one's in-laws, the ceremonial exchange of valuables in the *kula,* and the concomitant barter of utilitarian goods did not challenge the basic principle of maintaining household sufficiency (Spittler 2008: 225–226).

The professionalization of anthropology in the course of the twentieth century led ethnographers to amass vast quantities of data pertinent to self-sufficiency, though without necessarily bringing them any closer to resolving the definitional and theoretical issues. It was taken for granted in the "modernization" literature that a decline in self-provisioning was a measure of progress. The literature on "peasant societies" (a category invented in this era, as anthropologists gradually gave up their exclusive focus on the "primitive") tended to privilege the level of the community. The rural community formed a "part society," more or less integrated into larger societies and "great traditions" (Redfield 1956). In the later Marxist formulation of Eric Wolf, peasant households produced a surplus that was creamed off by their exploiters (1966). Where the image of the "closed corporate community" approximated economic reality, this too was the specific product of uneven development rather than an original state. Non-Marxist accounts confirmed the enduring significance of the house, sometimes deriving from adaptations to a distinctive ecological niche (Netting 1981). In other cases, such as that of the *zadruga* among the southern Slavs, strong notions of household self-sufficiency do not correspond to the realities but serve ideological and exoticizing functions during the emergence of new property systems and national identities (Todorova 1989; cf. Monova's discussion in this volume). The importance of the house as the symbolic focus of economic life has been recognized most comprehensively in Latin America (Gudeman and Rivera 1990). It is awarded a potentially universal significance in the evolution of human social organization in the late work of Claude Lévi-Strauss (see Carsten and Hugh-Jones 1996). However, this account of "house societies" and the discussions it has generated have not paid a great deal of attention either to European societies or to the economy—two deficits that we seek to make good in this volume.

Despite accelerating globalization and neoliberal markets, it is still the case in the early twenty-first century that hundreds of millions of households produce with their own labor the greater part of the staples consumed by household members. In theorizing this very literal resilience of the household vis-à-vis the market, the work of the Russian agrarian economist Alexander Chayanov has had an extraordinary influence (Chayanov 1986 [1924-5]). Chayanov was well aware that the Russian villagers whose economy he analyzed in the precollectivization era were closely involved with a new commercial economy. To that extent, Lenin was right to theorize the penetration of capitalism as a cause of social differentiation and rural impoverishment (1956 [1899]). But Chayanov argued that this social differentiation (observable in statistics recording acreage) was due not so much to new processes of class formation as to the internal processes of the household in the course of its developmental cycle. The household was caught up in a wider economy, but it did not respond to market signals in the same way as a capitalist firm. Rising prices, which would usually lead a firm to expand production in order to increase profits, might have the opposite effect on a peasant household pursuing its own notion of flourishing rather than profit. This household might be expected to curtail work (considered to be unmitigated drudgery) as soon as its cash targets had been met. So long as the household was the basic unit of both production and consumption, the dynamics of its production process (in terms of labor intensity and/or area cultivated) were thus shaped by considerations grounded in the internal ratio of workers to consumers and not by wider class struggles.

Chayanov's elaboration of a house model for the Russian countryside was a heroic achievement, especially when one considers that he spent the last five years of his life in a labor camp before being executed (Shanin 1986). It inspired Marshall Sahlins to coin the notion of a "domestic mode of production" and to explore its workings in a range of "tribal" societies (despite his distaste for the "marginalist" economic language in which Chayanov presented his arguments) (Sahlins 1972: 88). The Chayanovian model has been productive in peasant studies and economic anthropology more generally (Durrenberger 1984), as well as in rural sociology (Galeski 1972).

But this approach also has its weaknesses. Sahlins himself noted contradictions and raised the Aristotelian question of public goods in a system grounded in "anarchy and dispersion" (1972: 95–99). Marxists complained that class polarization and wider networks of oppression were blended out of the model. Feminists complained that Chayanov never engaged closely with patriarchal power relations inside the household. Indeed, he treated the house as a "black box" in much the same way that many economists have traditionally approached the firm, without paying attention to the myriad factors that lead actual behavior to deviate from what a mechanistic application of the worker-to-consumer ratio would predict. For example, instead of working harder when they had more mouths to feed inside their households, adults might seek help among kin or in wider networks of friends and cooperating partners. The principle of self-provisioning might be expanded, to include transfers of food and/or labor to those in need; or it might be infringed by sending "surplus" youth to work for patrons. But such deviations would not constitute evidence that the self-sufficiency of the house had been displaced as an *ideal*, a standard to be maintained and even vigorously asserted in the course of daily life, as in displays of generous hospitality. The members of our research group delved into these and other discrepancies. Several were struck by the seeming contradiction between a decline in "real" autarky, in terms of self-provisioning, and an emphatic assertion that the members of the household were pulling together in the cause of self-sufficiency, even when farm work had become insignificant and the resources needed by the household were gleaned in very different domains of the commercial economy and the state. In cases such as these, the researchers probed the extent to which disparate resources amassed by individuals were in fact pooled and redistributed in nonmarket ways.

## The Socialist Culture Area

Models and practices of self-sufficiency are prominent in rural ideologies throughout the world, including the ex-socialist "culture area" in which our project was based. In this section we look more closely at how these have played out materially and immaterially before, during, and after the experience of Marxist-Leninist socialism.

In the countryside of Eastern Europe in the era of imperialisms (Tsarist, Ottoman, Habsburg), self-sufficiency at the level of the household was for centuries stymied by the dominance of large estates (sometimes called the manorial economy and comparable to the *latifundia* of Latin America). Relatively complex divisions of labor at this level coexisted with production and consumption in the framework of the house. A degree of autarky was promoted at the level of the community, but markets were also important, both for local and regional commerce, and for long-distance trade. By the twentieth century, following the abolition of serfdom, the great estates were condemned as socially unjust and economically inefficient by populist movements. Alexander Chayanov was their outstanding theoretician. Ideologies of "land to the tiller" underpinned the distributive land reforms of presocialist governments.

These reforms had very limited success. Many of the new independent farms brought into existence were not viable in the prevailing conditions, which did not yet offer the rural population viable alternatives in the form of urban, industrial jobs. The consequences of this uneven capitalist development were demonstrated following both world wars. From the early 1950s socialist industrialization was designed to remedy this historic backwardness. The nationalization of industrial property in the cities was accompanied by the collectivization of land in the countryside. The socialist onslaught on the self-sufficient household was a "form of integration" reminiscent of those that Karl Polanyi (2001 [1944]) characterized in other contexts of centralized power as "redistribution." Arguably, it was consonant with the Aristotelian primacy of the political over commercial exchange. The agricultural sector became an integral part of the centrally planned economy. Where state farms were established, the members of rural households were supposed to approximate factory workers in the cities. Even where collective farms were established (a lower form of property according to socialist ideology), the requirement to work for the socialist brigade in return for receiving a more or less regular income stream ensured a sharp break with the traditional autonomy of the smallholder.

This was the theory. In fact, significant elements of household self-provisioning persisted almost everywhere. In some regions, due to the chaos that accompanied the establishment of the new socialist institutions, it gained in significance compared with the marketized economy of the presocialist era. The suppression of private property rights was almost universally unwelcome. Socialist collectives did bring significant investments to the rural sector, and in many regions they laid the foundations for an extraordinary increase in living standards (Hann et al. 2003). Ideologically, however, they were seen as destructive of a moral order, one that had its own ideology of modernization based on *embourgeoisement* or the transformation of peasants into capitalist farmers.

In a larger perspective, Soviet socialism, seen as an "alternative modernity," was the principal countercurrent to the institutions of market economy and liberal democracy as they developed in the West. The principle of the market was heavily circumscribed and, contrary to the original internationalist ideals of the communist movement, the Soviet Union under Stalin was effectively compelled to pursue "socialism in one country." When this plan was modified, central planning allowed for some regional specialization and for exchange between socialist countries. The creation of the Council for Mutual Economic Assistance (COMECON, 1949–1991) led to a limited division of labor in key industries across the Soviet bloc. In the era of détente in the 1970s, several socialist states stepped up trade with Western countries while beginning to borrow heavily (and unwisely) from the capitalist enemies. Others (notably Romania) struggled to pay off foreign debts and reassert a principle of national autarky. Even today, long after the collapse of COMECON, a principle of autarky and self-reliance, with a suspicion of markets worthy of Aristotle, is prominent in the world's few remaining socialist states (notably, North Korea).

Reliance on "rational redistribution" was the prime feature of the economies that practiced "actually existing socialism," but it was never the only form of integration, and markets never disappeared altogether. For example, while state officials determined that allocation of new apartments in cities and those rights of occupation tended to be inherited within families, village houses and dachas could still be bought and sold. Markets in consumer goods improved greatly in most countries in the last decades of socialism. As for the other key principle in Polanyi's typology of forms of integration, namely, reciprocity, it too showed great resilience in the rural sector. Reciprocity was also to be found in the under-urbanized cities where mutual prestations in the grey (or black, underground) sector were essential in dealing with the gaps and shortages resulting from the imperfect meshing of redistribution and markets.

Alongside varying combinations of socialist redistribution, limited market exchange and interpersonal reciprocity, self-sufficiency never lost its importance. What Karl Polanyi identified in his early work (Polanyi 2001 [1944]) as the principle of householding remained more conspicuous in the rural sector due to self-provisioning. In some countries, households formed a successful symbiosis with collectivist institutions. The former concentrated on labor-intensive activities on the "household plot," while the latter allowed for economies of scale and the adoption of new technologies (see Vidacs 2014; this volume, chapter 1). This householding was quite different from the Chayanovian ideal type, in which the household has no regular source of wage income. Nonetheless, socialists could plausibly claim to be implementing the Aristotelian ideal of human flourishing, or the populist ideal of the good life at a supra-household level.

In some variants of Hungarian collectivization, the most flexible in the region, the old unity of house production and consumption persisted in the sense that all members were free to remain full-time smallholders if they wished (Hann 1980). However, even here most households had at least one member earning wages or a pension, which gave scope to purchase goods with cash and eventually to produce in more specialized ways for socialist markets instead of self-provisioning. Yet the material benefits brought by the new divisions of labor of the more successful variants of collectivization could not disguise the fact that it cut deeply into cherished norms of private ownership and self-sufficiency. Idioms of the latter were nourished by the fact that household members spent a high proportion of their "leisure time" engaged in the production of commodities, using labor-intensive methods that had not changed greatly. One might buy bread in the new cooperative store rather than bake at home, but meat and vegetables still derived overwhelmingly from activities in the backyard. The first generations of socialist workers felt that, when they returned to help village kin at peak periods and in return took quantities of pickles and smoked meat back to the city, they too were still participating in the old moral economy of self-sufficiency (for the case of Bulgaria, see Smollett 1989).

The sudden disintegration of socialism brought a collapse of socialist workplaces in both town and countryside. The old ideologies of the peasant smallholder political parties were revived, but they proved to be no more viable than they had been in the 1940s. After protracted privatization procedures, capitalized family farming in the Western manner still remains the exception on the postsocialist countryside. Successful entrepreneurs (often the old power holders in new guise) depend on personal links to national elites and access to EU subsidies. Under these conditions, literal self-sufficiency in terms of self-provisioning tends to be the last resort of the dispossessed (Leonard and Kaneff 2002). The ideals of self-sufficiency have persisted and proliferated everywhere in these societies, however. As the contributors to this volume show, they can be stretched beyond the domestic realm to include the participation of household members in different branches of the new market economies.

## Self-Sufficiency and the House

The ideal of self-sufficiency may be unattainable, but it has been persuasive as a model and as a set of practices. In this it resembles its opposite, the "perfect market." Self-sufficient can mean producing what is consumed and consuming that which is produced. But we also parse the idea of self-sufficiency into further components and meanings, many of which can be found in the studies in this volume. For example, sufficiency can mean having enough or meeting one's needs as socially defined, and being satisfied with what one has. It can stand for the opposite of accumulation, as a signal of resistance to profit making in markets, and as an ethical idea. Often it is a response to both external and internal influences. Similarly, "self" can refer to a house, a collection of houses, a community, a nation, or a combination of these institutions. As an ideal, self-sufficiency is a bastion against uncertainty and instability or contingency (Gudeman 2001). In this respect, it has a broader reference than its antonym, the market, and can include the social relationships that make *life* itself sufficient. Together the two words form an oxymoron, for no self can achieve sufficiency without others (as Aristotle observed). But the imagery has been persuasive in history.

More broadly, self-sufficiency has ideological value and potency in shaping the identities of persons and groups. In some parts of the world the maintenance of a single crop or seed strain—its seeding, tending, harvesting, consumption, and reseeding—represents the durability of the social unit that holds it. Such crops may include potatoes, yams, rice, or other staples, which may have special powers of growth or vitality and provide this vitality to other crops, to animals, and to the people of a house. These identity crops may be divided when houses and other groups separate, so providing them with a continuing source of vitality. The crop (or line of animals) has the symbolic value of self-sufficiency in addition to its practical uses (Gudeman 1986, 2001, 2008, 2012; Gudeman and Rivera 1990). One of the striking findings from the studies of this volume is the resilience and resurrection of such images, and the many forms they take, which include sources of nourishment (crops, animals, land, forest, and special foods as suggested by Light, Vasile, Cash, and Monova) as well as the rituals that transform these resources into social nourishment and well-being (e.g. through protective saints and hospitality practices). The symbolization of self-sufficiency occurs at different institutional levels and includes linkages to others as ways of preserving a sense of autarky.

The second finding of our studies confirms the enduring importance of the house as an economic institution over several centuries of economic transformation. As demonstrated in our previous volume, the house takes many forms, covers different tasks, and is variously constituted in our six sites, but it is a persisting economic institution in all of them. The house has endured through many economic formations and "superstructures" from ancient times. In the culture area that we investigate it was a central institution in presocialist times. In most of the studied sites, the house approximated Chayanov's "peasant" household, being only partly integrated into quasi-feudal or market structures. The house retained an important place in most rural areas during socialism, as we have noted above, even for those who moved away from the countryside for new urban jobs. The symbiosis of house and socialist collective, which had much regional variation, was not recognized by the architects of "shock therapy" (originally devised by economists for different conditions in Latin America). Economic reforms in the postsocialist countries were directed to removing the state's role in directing production and consumption along with other institutional and legal barriers to trade and market activities. Under such conditions, the individuals within domestic groups should have "naturally" turned their energies to selling their labor and provisioning their needs and wants through market purchases. They should have pooled resources within the group, or shared with other domestic groups, only when individual interests clearly coincided. House economies should have disappeared in the face of the efficiencies and attractions of market life. Yet the house economy has endured and even gained in significance, both real and symbolic (let us note in passing that the crises of the neoliberal era have recently increased its salience in many parts of the "advanced" West). The house economy is at once a buffer against larger structures, a marginal institution in the sense of fitting within different larger structures while lying at their peripheries, and a way of making economy with its own characteristics.

Our ethnographies reveal the following characteristic processes in house economy:

1. The house economy is an incomplete but irreducible unit in economy. It is incomplete because houses are connected one to another, embedded in communities and linked to trade systems. The house economy is irreducible because it is not built out of subsidiary units, except component houses. For example, a house may contain several families who eventually separate in a developmental cycle or smaller sub-houses. The "house," thus, can be a single unit, a combination of families (usually linked by kinship), or a combination of part-houses, as in the case of affiliated elders who may help with childcare and other tasks.

2. The house economy relies on a flow of material life that underlies all economic formations. It helps constitute these flows, which link the house to its environs of the natural and social worlds, in the double sense of *oikos* as economy and ecology. This flow of material life is often symbolized by a particular food, as illustrated in Miladina Monova's study of *ajvar* in Macedonia (chapter 3).

3. In the house economy mutuality or jointness are basic social and economic acts. Productive efforts and their returns are shared, according to one or another set of values. From the house, sharing in its many forms, including reciprocity, welfare, and care, spreads into the larger social order. These processes of micro-adjustment defy any simple translation into statistics, as Jennifer Cash (chapter 2) explains with reference to her household survey in rural Moldova.

4. The house economy tends toward self-sufficiency in which significant outputs are used for inputs rather than exchanged for profit. This feature of house self-sufficiency contrasts with modern corporations, which depend on specialization, optimization, and exchange (although firms sometimes find it profitable to behave like houses and produce some of their inputs internally, in order to avoid "transaction costs" in a risky environment). The house is never autarkic, but all houses in our study are to a degree self-sufficient, even if this is limited to the opening of a homemade bottle of wine to host others, as reported by Cash. Self-sufficiency is locally defined and represented. It can mean self-provisioning in a single crop; it can mean keeping domestic animals, such as chickens and hogs, for their meat; it can be represented by herding larger animals for their products; and it can mean having free access to a resource that can be sold, as in the case of lumber in the Apuseni Mountains of Romania (Vasile, chapter 6).

In a more structural sense, self-sufficiency can be a model by which the house arranges itself—some members earn money, some members work for food, and some members raise house food so that the totality achieves a degree of independence, as in the Bulgarian case reported by Tocheva (chapter 5).

5. The house is characterized by tinkering, recombining, and inventing on a small scale—so small that it often escapes the observer's notice. Internally, handymen and handywomen "make-do" and recycle leftovers. Externally, the house adjusts to its conditions, whether a state farm or market, as Vasile reports for Romania. These dynamic adjustments are well documented for rural Hungary by Vidacs (chapter 1), even though this case stands out from the others in this volume in the extent to which the older ideals and practices of self-sufficiency have been transformed.

6. The house exercises economic functions that are only partially found elsewhere. Being parsimonious or thrifty is a typical house process. It is different from profit making. Being thrifty, which can be accomplished by restricting consumption, by saving leftovers, or by finding new ways to accomplish needed ends, preserves means for a new day. Thriftiness can be consistent with profit making, as in downsizing a corporation, but in the house thrift is not about making a profit. It is a strategy for making savings to be held, as in reusing string or carefully preserving potatoes under stairs for the winter. Thrift helps achieve self-sufficiency. House maintenance and growth occurs through saving and risk avoidance rather than the "animal spirits" of entrepreneurial investment. Savings as hoards are often put into the house itself: with savings a new room is added, or another floor is constructed, rather than directed to a venture outside the house. Similarly, a crop, meat, wine, or other product is kept at the house as a hoard to be available for meeting social needs, as is the case with animals in rural Kyrgyzstan, discussed by Light (chapter 4).

7. House economies measure their food needs and supplies, the work that has been accomplished and needs to be done, and money savings. The purpose is not to calculate a profit but to meet house needs, achieve sufficiency of supplies for communal obligations, and maintain a sense of "well-being," which may be partly accomplished through reciprocity and sharing with other houses and participating in social rituals.

No house economy in our study fits all these characteristics, and some have other important features. All the houses we studied also engage in market activities. But these are some of the qualities that we have found and investigated in our comparisons, and that have a presence elsewhere.

## Community, Nation, World

The characteristics of the house economy place it in dynamic tension with other institutions of society and their associated forms of economy. For example, the house and community are often mutually supportive. The communities studied in our project varied greatly, from the urban neighborhoods investigated by Miladina Monova in Macedonia (chapter 3) to the rather remote village studied by Nathan Light in Central Asia (chapter 4). Beyond the level of the house, all of our researchers were in one way or another continuing the venerable anthropological genre of the community study. Each one of them lived locally and experienced the "face to face" quality of social life, in many ways still the antithesis of the norms of the modern metropolis. Through participant observation they were able to show how, when the house fell short of meeting its vision of sufficiency, the deficit was sometimes made good, at least in part, through community support, for example through labor cooperation. House and community, however, may be brought into relationships of tension through the forces of the market and the state. The end of socialism placed some individuals in a position where they had no alternative but to offer their labor power to their entrepreneurial neighbors. Sometimes this was formalized as an employment relationship, but often it was disguised and represented as temporary help. Many disadvantaged villagers became dependent on state handouts, which often depended on highly personal decisions taken by the mayor or other representatives of the local state (Thelen et al. 2011).

As these examples indicate, we should be wary of romanticizing or distorting the "holistic" character of social relations in small communities (Creed 2006). The sanctions of the community may be experienced at times as harsh and unfair. Just as there can be conflict between brothers within a house, so there is potential for many kinds of conflict within communities. The settlement studied by Detelina Tocheva (chapter 5) is divided between Christians and Muslims, but this line of cleavage seems less significant than the economic differentials, which are beginning to expand following the impact of tourism and the market economy. As Tocheva shows in her contributions to this volume and its predecessor, community rituals conceal these widening gaps.

The degree to which the economies of house and community are embedded in much larger economies has changed greatly since the time of Adam Smith, and even since the age of Alexander Chayanov. According to standard economic historiography since Smith, each new epoch has been marked by the reduction of state protectionism, and the lowering of barriers and boundaries to the free movement of goods and labor. In the late eighteenth century, Smith still recognized the desirability of constraining the market principle in order to protect "infant industries." In the twentieth century, socialist economies were still highly protected to achieve ostensibly social goals. In the 1990s, this protectionism ended abruptly when it became possible to purchase new imported goods and to migrate abroad on a scale not known previously in the socialist culture area. Within each of our countries, mobility to cities increased substantially, though there was also significant movement the other way when the older established urban workplaces vanished. The houses studied by Tocheva in the Rhodope Mountains have long had close relatives in the capital and other cities in Bulgaria. Two decades after the end of socialism, more than a million Bulgarians live in Western Europe. The proportion of rural Moldovans (Jennifer Cash, chapter 2) who have migrated west and east in search of better opportunities is thought to be even higher.

This mobility of persons and goods appears to signal the transcendence of the last vestiges of the principle of self-sufficiency through the power of neoliberal markets. We have seemingly reached the dystopia of Karl Polanyi's "fictitious commodities." But what if the migrants meticulously send remittances to the rural houses that they still consider their primary affiliation, their home? What if the household members who earn cash closer to home in different branches of the national economy continue to pool their incomes and determine expenditure in old-established ways? This house may be far-removed from the old peasant ideal-type of self-provisioning, but the renewed emphasis on this institution after the collapse of the socialist institutions has also revived an ethos of resilience that knows no boundaries of space or sector. The rural house may no longer be providing its own food to any significant degree; the community may or may not continue to assert the virtues of honest manual work; the populist press may rail against the contamination of foreign goods in the new supermarkets and insist that land, the ultimate foundation of the nation, should not be sold to foreigners; but if, despite these unpropitious circumstances, or perhaps because of them, houses persist and their members continue to think and act "as if" their reproduction depended on their own more or less ingenious pursuit of self-sufficiency, the ethnographer has to take note of this obstinacy and delineate its consequences.

The house is an enduring model for the organization of economic activity, especially among domestic groups and at the community level. But when self-sufficiency is focused too narrowly on the house, society is fragile and contingent. The renewed emphasis on close kin in the practices of self-sufficiency that our group studied also implies a decline in trust, a closing-in on the part of the group that has accompanied postsocialist economic transformation. Market ideology presupposes that the sociability formerly attached to economic transactions can be relocated outside the economic domain. In the postsocialist region, this was expected to emerge with the rise of a "civil society" of free associations, which individuals can move in and out of as they please. Society appears to be alive and well in postsocialist Eastern Europe, with the expansion of many civic groups and NGOs. Yet such associations tend to be less common in the countryside, and even when they are present, as in the Hungarian village studied by Bea Vidacs (chapter 1), they do not substitute for the benefits provided by the more basic affiliation of citizenship, which are channeled by the local state. At the time of Vidacs's fieldwork, the Hungarian state had not cut back significantly on the social benefits introduced under socialism. It was, however, in the process of introducing new schemes to deal with high rural unemployment – "workfare" that is urgently needed, because many households have lost the employment security they enjoyed under socialism. In the open multi-party elections that have replaced the staged rituals of socialist elections, villagers tend to vote for parties that exploit these fears by whipping up sentiments against imaginary enemies: the distant bureaucrats of Brussels, or the impoverished Roma within their own communities. These expressions of populist politics can be theorized in terms of Karl Polanyi's model of a "double movement" (Polanyi 2001 [1944]). The expansion of the market principle provokes society to self-defense, but these mechanisms of defense are by no means benign for all citizens.

When taken up at the national level, we can expect to find the ideology of self-sufficiency prominently asserted in this double movement. Self-sufficiency underwrites protectionism as a form of self-defense from the expanding market and promotes exclusion and internal divisions, when what is needed is the consolidation at the global level of the values of Aristotle's original *oikos*.

## The Studies

The ambiguities of self-sufficiency as ideal and moral critique are captured by Bea Vidacs in chapter 1. She shows that traditional norms are still asserted by some Hungarian villagers, though the realities appear to be largely in line with the archetypal postulates of modernization theory. For example, younger villagers and newcomers in this Hungarian village are less inclined to spend many hours toiling in their vegetable gardens when the same products are readily available in the small town nearby. In the presocialist past, the villagers of Péterszeg took some of their "surplus" produce by cart to this town and the proceeds formed an important part of their income. Socialist farms eliminated this commerce but the household plot ensured a high degree of self-provisioning on the basis of family labor. Today, villagers travel by bus or by car to town and come home with plastic bags bursting from the branch of one or another German supermarket chain. Vidacs shows that the elderly Hungarian villagers who criticize newcomer neighbors or Roma for not being prepared to get their hands dirty in their gardens are themselves far from being fully self-sufficient. All exhibit forms of dependency—on neighbors, on markets, and on the state. As she explained in her contribution to our first volume, the number of households raising pigs for domestic consumption has declined greatly since the 1970s; again, the supermarkets provide easier options. Most families have one or more members earning a regular wage, drawing a pension, or receiving workfare or other state benefits, a pattern that emerged under socialism and has not fundamentally changed. The symbiosis of large and small farms in agricultural production has been eliminated; while some "losers" in the transformation have reluctantly intensified self-provisioning for the lack of any alternative, others are in a position to profit from the greater choice nowadays made available through the market. Presumably, some have a bad conscience in doing so, knowing that every bottle of imported wine purchased at "dumping" prices is a blow to the wine industry of their own country.

Wine is central to the local ideal of self-sufficiency among Moldovan villagers, as Jennifer Cash analyzed in her contribution to the previous volume. Self-sufficiency of the house, whether in crops, animal husbandry, or clothing, has dramatically decreased in the community she studied. It remains highly valued, however, as the use of home-produced wine and food in hospitality rituals demonstrates. In her contribution to this volume (chapter 2), Cash explicates the local ideal of having enough or achieving sufficiency, which implies good management of the household, regardless of whether the supplies themselves have to be purchased. Giving via hospitality is an indicator both of self-sufficiency and of good management, so much so that poorer households can achieve status by giving away what little they have. The wealthier have a greater obligation to give, while failure to do so brings loss of prestige, denigrating labels, and even God's punishment.

Miladina Monova's study of *ajvar* in the Macedonian town of Prilep (chapter 3) reveals the complexities and ambiguities of household self-sufficiency in light of dramatic economic change, invented traditions, the symbolism of self-sufficiency, and reliance on the market. *Ajvar* is prepared from peppers, oil, and other ingredients. Considered a necessity, it is preserved in order to last through the winter. Today, *ajvar* enjoys recognition as a national dish that is pure, tasty, and healthy because it is made in the home. Each housewife's recipe is different and represents her culinary artistry. The preparation of this dish requires time and physical effort as well as skill, and is often done in the street or garden, where the work is socially visible. People passing by stop and comment, and see how the entire house is involved in contributing. But almost all the ingredients of this essential national dish are purchased. *Ajvar* is itself available in shops, but few purchase it, despite the considerable inconvenience involved in manufacturing it with family labor. The domestic production of *ajvar* is relatively recent, so it is hardly a traditional dish or an embodiment of "real" self-sufficiency. Nonetheless it has become a symbol of self-sufficiency in the course of the dramatic transition to a market economy. The ideal of the house economy was resilient in this part of Macedonia before socialism, through socialism, and now under capitalism. More broadly, one can state that the house economy adapts to many different political and economic superstructures, to all of which it offers both a material and social base (Gudeman 2001). Monova's study acquires additional poignancy in view of former Yugoslavia's endeavors to accomplish self-sufficiency at higher levels (republic and socialist federation). In tracing the contemporary symbolism of *ajvar,* Monova depicts it as a creative house response to the changing faces of state power. Symbolic of house independence and sharing, it is a way of adapting to a changing economy and state that still carries conviction for the inhabitants of Prilep (though apparently less so in the capital Skopje, and not at all in neighboring Bulgaria).

Nathan Light's ethnography of a Kyrgyz village (chapter 4) takes us to a very different geographical and economic setting. Before socialism the people of this village were nomadic, but during the Soviet period they were gradually settled in collective and state-owned farms where sheep were raised, milk was produced, and some crops were sown. With the recent arrival of markets, beans have become the principal cash crop while other crops, such as potatoes and maize, are grown in domestic gardens. Although intensive breeding of high-value sheep has ceased, animal husbandry remains important, not for home consumption or market sale but for ritual giving and display on which much time is spent. These rituals, including weddings, commemorations, funerals, birthdays, and other events, represent household viability and self-sufficiency. The rituals can be small or large, and they may yield a material return to the giver because guests bring gifts that can exceed the costs of the ritual. But the monetary balance sheet is not crucial to the way household sufficiency is figured. Light's calculations show that at least a third of the year is spent in ritual activity that connects people. He terms the outcome "social sufficiency," which above all consists in maintaining a network of ties outside the household and even outside the community. These extensive ties nowadays melt into market ties, as they formerly melted into the hierarchies of the socialist institutions, but at the moment it seems that their deeper raison d'être is to keep the house viable in unstable postsocialist conditions.

The Balkan villagers studied by Detelina Tocheva (chapter 5) live high in the Rhodope Mountains of Bulgaria, close to the Greek border. This beautiful, pristine area features some agriculture and pastoralism, a few stores, some labor migration, and some hosting of tourists. Tocheva focuses on a common metaphor of the people: "working in a closed circle." It captures the ordinary meanings of household self-sufficiency, such as using local resources, drawing on household labor, and limiting dependency on external institutions. The metaphor has been used more frequently with market expansion. As Tocheva explains, the house economy (which in her main example is composed of three nuclear families) must combine different income sources, including money from tourism, with self-provisioning. The metaphor also implies pure, high-quality food that has no additives. The food, the house, and the way of life all have to be ecologically clean. To achieve this Aristotelian condition, the household draws on the work of all house members. Working in a closed circle means avoiding commercial products, such as soft drinks, and relying on local milk and yogurt. The aim is to provision the house from within, while remaining open to a limited range of market purchases. The strategy of offering domestic foods to tourists without expending much cash is profitable in the economist's sense, but more important in Tocheva's analysis is the way in which the closed circle—of provisioning from the house while drawing on the market, of coping with the latter by relying on the former—yields a sense of control. This is the other side of "self-exploitation" as described by Chayanov (1986 [1924-5]) or "debasement" in Gudeman's terms (2008). Like the Apuseni villagers described by Vasile in the following chapter, economic activity in the Rhodopes is driven by the goal of achieving mastery of a socioeconomic situation and bringing greater predictability and lower risk to material life.

Monica Vasile (chapter 6) lived with relatively remote villagers in Transylvania, Romania. Before and during socialism, they were poor for lack of resources. With the opening of markets and the lifting of state controls, they have been able to take advantage of the surrounding forests to cut trees, mill the logs, and transport the lumber for sale to the urban construction industry. The resulting boom testifies to intensified involvement in markets, but Vasile finds that people still talk about household independence and achieving self-sufficiency. Their houses are emphatically not closed units, yet the inhabitants often talk as if they were. As Vasile unfolds the situation, it becomes clear that self-sufficiency refers not to the house or to food, or even to the house and the forests on which the people depend. Self-sufficiency means being in a position to engage with changing natural and social environments, as well as the market in lumber. People are energetic, practical, and tactical in the ways they make a living. They are flexible in adjusting to their conditions. But is this a "house" or "market" practice? Making-do and tinkering usually are associated with the house, whereas innovation is the name we use for the market practices. Either way, with a sense of mastery and flexibility these villagers feel self-reliant and self-sufficient, even as they achieve this condition through their engagement with the market and reciprocal prestations with other households. Self-sufficiency in Vasile's village has to do with being one's own master, above all by possessing money and the equipment necessary to produce lumber. It also means not being in debt, being self-reliant, and being quick to take up opportunities.

* * * * *

By different paths, these studies all return us to the Aristotelian vision and amplify it for us. The Aristotelian "house economy" is the *oikos,* which is the root of both our modern terms "economy" and "ecology." Most people separate the two and think of ecology in terms of niches and a material world that is separate from the human realm. These studies show us not only that they are indissoluble but also that the social world is part of the ecology of the house. Self-sufficiency always takes place in a social context, despite many protests to the contrary. It can be a reaction to the market or a way of managing it, it can frustrate voices of free trade, and it can subsidize free trade through the costless inputs it may provide. It can be a moral ethic of different types, it can refer to mastery, control, and social respectability—but it remains always a model, an ideal, and a persuasive one at that. Would a better understanding of this impulse help us see more clearly today's pulls and counter-pulls of economy within states, between states, within and between larger configurations, such as the European Union, and within our fragile planet?

**Stephen Gudeman**, who is Professor of Anthropology at the University of Minnesota, has undertaken fieldwork in several countries of Latin America. During the period between 2008 and 2012 he was co-director of the Economy and Ritual project at the Max Planck Institute for Social Anthropology in Halle (Germany). Gudeman has published extensively in journals and written or edited eight books, the most recent of which are *Economy's Tension* (2008) and *Economic Persuasions* (2009).

**Chris Hann** is a Founding Director of the Max Planck Institute for Social Anthropology at Halle. He formerly taught anthropology at the Universities of Cambridge and Kent (Canterbury). Hann has published extensively on Eastern Europe, both before and after the collapse of socialism. He is co-author of *Economic Anthropology: History, Ethnography, Critique* (2011) and co-editor of *Market and Society: The Great Transformation Today* (2009) (both with Keith Hart).

## References

Aristotle. 1984. *The Complete Works of Aristotle*, ed. Jonathan Barnes. Princeton, NJ: Princeton University Press.

Booth, William J. 1994. "On the Idea of the Moral Economy." *The American Political Science Review* 88 no. 3: 653–667.

Carsten, Janet, and Stephen Hugh-Jones, eds. 1995. *About the House: Lévi-Strauss and Beyond.* Cambridge: Cambridge University Press.

Chayanov, A. V. 1986 [1924-5]. *The Theory of Peasant Economy.* Manchester: Manchester University Press.

Creed, Gerald W., ed. 2006. *The Seductions of Community: Emancipations, Oppressions, Quandaries.* Santa Fe, NM: School of American Research. Oxford: Currey.

Duby, Georges. 1969 [1962]. *Rural Economy and Country Life in the Medieval West.* Columbia: University of South Carolina Press.

Durrenberger, E. Paul, ed. 1984. *Chayanov, Peasant, and Economic Anthropology.* New York: Academic Press.

Galeski, Boguslaw. 1972. *Basic Concepts of Rural Sociology.* Manchester: Manchester University Press.

Gudeman, Stephen. 1986. *Economics as Culture.* London: Routledge & Kegan Paul.

———. 2001. *The Anthropology of Economy.* Malden, MA: Blackwell Publishers Inc.

———. 2008. *Economy's Tension.* New York: Berghahn Books.

———. 2012. "Vital Energy: The Current of Relations." *Social Analysis* 66, no. 1: 57–73.

Gudeman, Stephen, and Alberto Rivera. 1990. *Conversations in Colombia: The Domestic Economy in Life and Text.* Cambridge: Cambridge University Press.

Gudeman, Stephen, and Chris Hann, eds. 2015. *Economy and Ritual. Studies of Postsocialist Transformations.* New York: Berghahn Books.

Hann, Chris. 1980. *Tázlár: A Village in Hungary.* Cambridge: Cambridge University Press.

Hann, Chris, and Keith Hart. 2011. *Economic Anthropology: History, Ethnography, Critique.* Cambridge: Polity Press.

Hann, Chris, and the "Property Relations Group." 2003. *The Postsocialist Agrarian Question: Property Relations and the Rural Condition.* Münster: Lit.

Leonard, Pamela, and Deema Kaneff, eds. 2002. *Post-Socialist Peasant? Rural and Urban Constructions of Identity in Eastern Europe, East Asia and the Former Soviet Union.* Basingstoke: Palgrave.

Lenin, Vladimir Ilyich. 1956 [1899]. *The Development of Capitalism in Russia.* Moscow: Foreign Languages Publishing House.

Malinowski, Bronislaw. 1922. *Argonauts of the Western Pacific: An Account of Native Enterprise and Adventure in the Archipelagoes of Melanesia New Guinea.* London: George Routledge and Sons.

Mandeville, Bernard. 1970 [1714]. *The Fable of the Bees.* London: Penguin.

Netting, Robert McC. 1981. *Balancing on an Alp: Continuity and Change in a Swiss Mountain Community.* Cambridge: Cambridge University Press.

Polanyi, Karl. 2001 [1944]. *The Great Transformation: The Political and Economic Origins of Our Times.* Boston: Beacon Press.

———. 1957. "Aristotle Discovers the Economy." In *Trade and Market in the Early Empires*, ed. Karl Polanyi, Conrad Arensberg, and Harry Pearson, 64–94. Glencoe: Free Press.

Postan, Michael M. 1975. *The Medieval Economy and Society: An Economic History of Britain in the Middle Ages.* Harmondsworth: Penguin.

Redfield, Robert. 1956. *Peasant Society and Culture.* Ithaca, NY: Cornell University Press.

Sahlins, Marshall. 1972. *Stone Age Economics.* New York: Aldine de Gruyter.

———. 2013. *What Kinship Is...And Is Not.* Chicago: University of Chicago Press.

Shanin, Teodor. 1986. "Chayanov's Message: Illuminations, Miscomprehensions, and the Contemporary 'Development Theory.'" In A. V. Chayanov, *The Theory of Peasant Economy*, 1–24. Manchester: Manchester University Press.

Smith, Adam. 1976 [1776]. *An Inquiry into the Nature and Causes of the Wealth of Nations.* Edited by Edwin Cannan. Chicago: University of Chicago Press.

Smollett, Eleanor W. 1989. "The Economy of Jars: Kindred in Bulgaria: An Exploration." *Ethnologia Europea* 19: 125–140.

Spittler, Gerd. 2008. *Founders of the Anthropology of Work: German Social Scientists of the 19th and Early 20th Centuries and the First Ethnographers.* Berlin: Lit.

Thelen, Tatjana, Stefan Dorondel, Alexandra Szőke, and Larissa Vetters. 2011. "The Sleep Has Been Rubbed From Their Eyes: Social Citizenship and the Reproduction of Local Hierarchies in Rural Hungary and Romania." *Citizenship Studies* 15 nos. 3–4: 513–527.

Todorova, Maria. 1989. "Myth-making in European Family History: The Zadruga Revisited." *East European Politics and Societies* 4, no. 1: 30–76.

Wolf, Eric R. 1966. *Peasants.* Englewood Cliffs, NJ: Prentice Hall.

# 1

# The Ideal of Self-Sufficiency and the Reality of Dependence

*A Hungarian Case*

BEA VIDACS

One Monday afternoon in fall 2009, I attended the weekly meeting of the Folklore Circle for Women (Hagyományőrző Asszonyok klubja, literally Club of Women Upholding Tradition) in the Eastern Hungarian village of Szentpéterszeg, where I carried out fieldwork first in 1980–1981 and for a second time in 2009–2010.[1] After the business of the day had been taken care of, the women started gossiping about some young people who had recently moved into the village. The main topic of the discussion was that they did not grow anything in their garden plot. One of the women summed up the group's sentiments succinctly by stating "If she wants to cook something she first has to go to the store!" These women were for the most part in their late sixties and seventies, although they ranged in age from fifty-four to eighty-plus. Thus, most of them were born in the late 1930s or early 1940s and were raised into rural agricultural work as a matter of course. Unlike their mothers, who did not do wage work—although they worked plenty as daughters and wives of cultivators—most of these women had entered the labor force during their lifetimes, in addition to participating, alongside their husbands, in the Hungarian agricultural "miracle" under socialism (Harcsa, Kovách and Szelényi, 1998).

What they were commenting on was a radical departure from the age-old tradition of, or at least aspiration to, self-sufficiency in rural households. They were, at the same time, also hinting at tensions between the "original" population of the village (the Hungarian expression people use is *tősgyökeres*, which literally means having stock and root [in the village]) and those who have recently moved in. Somewhat more obliquely they may also have been commenting on a generational gap. Of the three, the first two are of significance for this chapter. These tensions do not often come out in the open, but they are there nonetheless. Thus, notions of household self-sufficiency in Szentpéterszeg intertwine with questions of community identity, but the picture is further complicated by at least two factors. On the one hand, the "original" population of the village is only partially capable of maintaining, or even willing to maintain, the ideal of self-sufficiency implied in the criticism. On the other hand, the village needs the in-migrants for its very survival. Like that of many other small rural communities, the population of Szentpéterszeg has been declining steadily over the last thirty years, due partly to low birth rates and partly to out-migration. Between 1980 and 2009 the population dropped by more than 25 percent and between 1989 and 2009 there were only seven years in which the number of births equaled or outstripped the number of deaths. The population loss would be even higher if it weren't for in-migration. Thus, the survival of the village depends on having enough in-migrants to make up for the natural loss.

Before turning to the discussion of this concrete case I wish to consider what self-sufficiency means as a theoretical concept and what it means to the villagers. As a starting point, I consider self-sufficiency to mean the ability of a social unit, usually a peasant household, to provide for its own material necessities, by producing its own food. In this chapter I show that in the case of Szentpéterszeg we cannot speak of economic self-sufficiency in this "classic" sense: neither households nor the village as a community is capable of this kind of self-sufficiency, nor has it been for a long time. Self-sufficiency is an elusive concept partly because it is a relational one— the question is the level on which we regard it, or what unit we consider to be economically autonomous.

Karl Polanyi (1957) distinguished between three forms of integration: reciprocity, redistribution, and the market. These he held were capable of integrating groups, providing a unity and coherence to them.[2] He did not exclude the possibility of the three coexisting in any given society. Householding was a fourth category Polanyi used some of the time (Polanyi 1944, 1957; see Gregory 2009). As Gregory points out, householding is not of the same order as the other three concepts Polanyi operates with because it is less general and thus as Polanyi himself states it is "a feature of economic life only on a more advanced level of agriculture" (1944: 53), that is to say, householding is only characteristic of certain very specific situations. What seems to be (near) universal about it is that the implied ability to fend for oneself without need for external input appears as an ideal in many peasant cultures. Certainly, it was an ideal that Hungarian peasants aspired to for a long time. Over the past half century the ideal of agricultural household self-sufficiency has, to a large degree, been replaced by the ideal of being able to provide for the household's needs through monetary income rather than self-provisioning. What remains of the ideal of agricultural self-sufficiency has much more to do with questions of identity or people's self-perception, which in Szentpéterszeg reflects responses to changing socioeconomic and demographic circumstances in the first decade of the twenty-first century.

The chapter uses examples that refer to self-sufficiency at different levels and concern different understandings of what providing for one's own material necessities entails. Through the example of bread-baking I will consider the disappearance of an emblematic form of household self-sufficiency of great symbolic significance. Discussing instances of reciprocity in the form of mutual help the villagers provided for each other during socialism, I will argue that reciprocity structured people's lives and constituted a kind of self-sufficiency at the level of the community, while also enabling the villagers to limit their engagement with the market by reducing their need for cash. This did not prevent them from fully engaging with it in other respects through consumption of durable and nondurable goods as well as producing for the market. In the last section of the chapter I will show that following 1989 these forms of reciprocity have all but disappeared and we find that the villagers now pay for (and profess to prefer to pay for) the services they previously provided each other through mutual help. People continue to help each other as individuals, but these instances of help are not instituted in the Polanyian sense; they do not structure people's lives at the level of the community. Finally, I will write about the handful of people who after 1989 have taken on commercial agricultural activities in the village, whose production is explicitly for the market and most of whom do not attempt self-provisioning at all, their spouses tending to have steady jobs. However, although they produce for the market and take advantage of EU agricultural subsidies, they define themselves as being self-sufficient and self-reliant and contrast their behavior with that of the newcomers. Thus, I argue that the ideal of self-sufficiency continues to survive in the postsocialist context, but takes on different meanings far removed from earlier notions of household self-sufficiency as an economic concept.

The chapter has four parts. The first provides a brief, historical sketch to explain the context of rural strivings for self-sufficiency in Hungary prior to the Second World War. I will argue that household self-sufficiency has not been more than an ideal for a very long time in Hungarian villages, although the degree to which households were capable of self-provisioning and self-sufficiency varied a great deal over time and according to social stratum. Although the peasantry has been part of larger political structures and participated in the market, this participation was limited to selling what was necessary in order to obtain cash for taxes and necessities they could not produce themselves. The second and third parts deal with the socialist transformation of the Hungarian countryside before and after

1956, respectively. The changes that took place led the villagers to become less able to self-provision, but with rising living standards after 1956 they became increasingly capable of providing for their own needs through engaging with the market, while also getting more and more plugged into the larger world not just economically but also culturally. This meant transformed values and attitudes toward work and leisure, but even more importantly, led to the abandonment of the villages by the bulk of the younger generation. Those who stayed behind have multiple connections to the wider world and define self-sufficiency much more in terms of a monetary income than in terms of being capable of self-provisioning from the land. The fourth part of the chapter discusses the post-1989 period, when with the end of socialism the earlier prosperity came to end. After 1989, both individual villagers and the community need to rely on outside resources to maintain themselves.

## Historical Background: Before the Second World War

The Hungarian countryside has thoroughly changed in the past sixty or so years. Even prior to the Second World War it was in turmoil inasmuch as the number of the landless was very high and large proportions of the rural population lived in almost unimaginable poverty. Many could not carry out independent farming at all; others had such small plots of land that they could not maintain themselves and their families, rather they had to work as manorial workers, or in other kinds of hired labor roles. But the rural population was diverse. While some were becoming rural proletarians, others were on the road toward embourgeoisement, following "gentry" or urban models of behavior. Most members of the rural population were actively engaged in market relations at least from the middle of the nineteenth century, albeit in a variety of ways (Szabó 1976; Gunst 1996).

While the dismal poverty of the poorest layer of the rural population was ever-present in social discourse, an idealized version of the peasantry also became part of the national imaginary. During the 1930s, the plight of the peasantry inspired the so-called Populist movement, whose members, young writers, documented the situation in sociographic writings. They were a diverse group: politically some of them leaned toward the left and some to the right. The intellectually most outstanding figure among them, Ferenc Erdei, analyzed "peasant society" in several highly nuanced works that have stood the test of time as social analysis (Erdei 1938, 1942; cf. Hann 1995; Huszár 1988). At the other end of the spectrum, some of the language that was first articulated then is coming back to haunt us now in the form of right-wing rhetoric.

Among the rural population there was an ideal of self-sufficiency, expressed partly in an almost obsessive will for land, and partly in a desire to be "one's own master" (*maga ura*), but for the vast majority this remained a desire only (Lampland 1995). For example, in Szentpéterszeg, during the first half of the nineteenth century, 33.95 percent of households had no land at all. On the eve of the freeing of serfs in 1847, of those who did have land no household had a full measure (the quantity considered to be enough to maintain a serf family) and almost 70 percent of households had as little as two-eighths of the full measure (Oláh 1987: 31–32). Following the end of serfdom, the tendency for further subdivisions of land continued and there is every indication that the inhabitants of the village had to sell their labor power or had to produce to some degree for the market in order to survive. Thus, already in the nineteenth century practically no household was able to produce its own food entirely and the majority were almost totally incapable of doing so. But even the better off, like all villagers, relied on the market for other necessities from clothing to tools.

A century later, at the end of the Second World War, villages in Hungary continued to be poor and underdeveloped, they had no electricity, and the housing stock was picturesque but poor, with no bathrooms and no running water. The bulk of the peasantry had at the most six years of schooling and very little hope of advancement. Until the end of the Second World War the country was predominantly agricultural, as shown by the fact that in 1941 49 percent of the population was still rural.

### 1945–1956

Following the Second World War, the transformation of the peasantry became one of the priorities of the new regime. A land reform, carried out in 1945 before the communist takeover in 1949, was followed by the first wave of the creation of collective farms, fashioned after the Soviet *kolkhoz* model, which in effect took back the just distributed land. It was very unpopular and largely unsuccessful, so much so that following the 1956 revolution many of the just recently formed collective farms folded and the process was restarted in 1958 on a significantly changed basis. However, the brief period of the early 1950s left a bitter taste. This was partly due to the very harsh treatment meted out to better-off peasants (referred to as *kulaks*), who were often humiliated, even deported, and their possessions confiscated; partly, however, it was due to the unreasonable delivery quotas and the severe punishments imposed on those who could not meet them. These quotas directly affected the less well-off among the peasantry as well (see Réev 1987), causing hardships for the overwhelming majority.

The regime justified the extremely harsh treatment of the peasantry in several ways. Among other things it was a practical question to them, that is, the peasantry's contribution to the economy was needed. It was also political, in that peasants had to be made part of the communist project, and it was ideological, in that the peasantry was seen as an "unreliable" element, that is to say, not being part of the proletariat they were ideologically "suspect," replete with "hidebound" ideas, such as their single-minded "obsession" with possessing land. Owning land of course was the means to feed one's family.

The other consideration that contributed to the harsh treatment of the peasantry during the 1950s had to do with industrialization. In Hungary, rather wrongheadedly, the communist leadership of the 1950s insisted on rapid industrialization, again partly following the Soviet model. Part of the pursuit of the goal of industrialization was to turn peasants into workers; the harsh treatment of the peasantry during the early 1950s outlined above contributed to peasants' moving to industrial centers and abandoning agriculture altogether. The delivery quotas forced the rural population to increasingly rely on store-bought foodstuffs. This trend became even stronger following the 1956 revolution, when collectivization became fully established in the country.

## After 1956

The success of the second wave or collectivization, following the 1956 revolution, was to a great extent due to the different tactics employed. Whereas in the early fifties the regime persecuted *kulaks*, in the early 1960s it rather wooed them and used their joining the collective farm to convince other villagers to follow suit. The reformed collectivization movement also afforded far more latitude in how production was carried out and organized. Over time it increasingly built on a combination of modernized, large-scale, collective production and a system of household plots allocated to collective farm members (Swain 1985).

The synergies thus created between the large-scale collectivized production and the household production of the members led to unprecedented wealth in rural areas in Hungary. For example, in the village where I did my fieldwork, between 1960 and the end of socialism people basically replaced (or modernized) almost the entire housing stock through the income derived from animal husbandry and considerable self-exploitation. In a village of about 1,400 inhabitants, out of 472 houses 78 were newly built between 1960 and 1969, and in the next decade 117. In 1970, only 27 houses had a bathroom, but within ten years the number rose to 168, somewhat more than one-third of the houses, and by 2010 almost every house had a bathroom. In 1980, the villagers blamed these newly constructed, "fancy" houses for the decline in casual after-work visits to each other's homes, because, as they argued, one could not drop in on someone in muddy work boots when their kitchens boasted shiny new tiles and the rooms had parquet floors instead of the earlier pounded earth.

The statistical figures could be multiplied: we could look at the number of cars in the village (the appearance of which required those who had gone to school prior to the Second World War to complete two extra years of schooling, because one could only get a driver's license if one had attended school for a minimum of eight years). We could also look at the number of children who had gone on first to secondary school and later to college or university. A side product of the rise in living standards and especially in educational levels was that in 1980 it was predictable that many of these young people would leave the village willy-nilly as there was not much for them to do there. As we shall see, this trend became much more pronounced after the end of socialism.

Much of this transformation in economic well-being and the opening up of the world to the villagers was made possible by the wealth accumulated during socialism, especially after the reforms of 1968, when increased agricultural output was further encouraged by a variety of incentives coming from the state. Different villages and regions followed slightly different trajectories, but in all parts of the country agriculture became the most robust part of the economy (Swain 1985) and the rural population thrived, all the while modernizing and becoming more and more similar in outlook and expectations to the urban population. The so-called second economy was what made this possible and the engine that drove it was increased consumerism (Gábor 1989; Hann 1990b; Sampson 1987). Even with its liberal economic policies, the Hungarian system under socialism curtailed the free market, and thus prevented people from becoming full-fledged capitalists; in addition, enterprises were hampered by soft budget constraints, which ultimately hampered the development of a truly competitive economy (cf. Kornai 1986; Hann 1990a; Swain 1992). Beyond certain limits it was impossible to reinvest profits to further develop enterprises and the regime compensated people for this and for political compliance by creating a kind of consumer paradise in Hungary through making consumer goods available to them in far greater abundance than in any other of the surrounding socialist countries (Dessewffy 2002: 52; cf. Fehérváry 2002, 2009; Hammer 2002; Nyyssönen 2006).

The collective farm and the policies of the socialist state furthered this process of integration into the larger economy and society. People relied on incomes from intensive home-based animal husbandry, but this happened with the help of the collective farm. The household plot in Szentpéterszeg, as in many settlements, was not distributed to the villagers, but rather they were assured of receiving corn for animal feed from the collective farm. The latter worked the land using its superior technology (machinery, fertilizers) and produced the corn that had to be harvested by hand by the members. I documented in my earlier study that the need to harvest the corn rather quickly necessitated close cooperation among people and gave rise to a lively system of mutual labor exchange (Vidacs 1985). Groups of relatives, neighbors, and compadres performed this task over two or three days. The harvested corn was transported to the home of the recipient by the collective farm. There were other instances of inter-household cooperation too, which I will discuss below.

Under socialism in Hungary, especially after 1958 when the countryside became fully collectivized (though there was some variability in the forms that collectivization took in various parts of the country (cf. Hann 1980; Hollós and Maday 1983; Lampland 1995; Sárkány 1978, 1983a; Swain 1985; Varga 2009; Vasary 1987)), the economic policies of the state encouraged production for the market and created synergies between state enterprises, collective farms, and the semi-private household plots of the members. Many people also participated in industry and became worker-peasants or peasant-workers (see Swain 1992: 172), often working the land in their spare time, on weekends, and during vacation time, or one member of the family belonged to the collective farm. In some places this was the wife—while the husband was commuting to industrial work. This was the case in Varsány (Sárkány 1978). In other places, for example in Szentpéterszeg, often it was the husband who belonged to the collective farm and the wife—if she did not end up working in the official workforce—"helped" him in the household production and also worked alongside with him at the collective. In such cases she did this without the benefits of membership, which in the end importantly translated into not being entitled to a pension. Thus, the collective farm itself accustomed people to a monetary income and made possible the much more important incomes gained from home-based animal husbandry. Throughout socialism people retained the gardens around their houses, which served as the basis for self-provisioning the household with fruits and vegetables as well as with poultry and other meat products. This was also the venue of their successful animal husbandry for the market.

It was in the household that the Hungarian agricultural "miracle" took place, perhaps at the cost of self-exploitation. The majority of villagers and members of the collective farms raised livestock at home in a kind of synergy with the collective farm—where they could be assured of a market for their produce, and could take it for granted that if they raised X number of pigs or bulls, or chickens for that matter, they would have a reliable source of income at a set point in time. While the state did a lot to improve the living standards of the villagers (including providing health care, and making the age of sixteen the mandatory minimum school-leaving age), it was with the money thus gained that villagers modernized their way of life.

Thus, under socialism the villagers became accustomed to monetary incomes both through what they earned from the collective (or elsewhere) and through the sale of livestock raised in the household. Although the initial purpose of the policy of introducing the household plot was to enable the members of the collective farms to provide for their own needs, i.e., self-provision, the opening up of their horizons and their ability to have access to reliable cash incomes along with the resulting relative wealth of the rural population and growing availability of consumer goods meant that people increasingly engaged with the market.

Their engagement was not complete though. They fully participated in the consumption of durable goods, but most of the food they consumed came from their vegetable gardens and from animals they raised. They almost exclusively ate home-raised meat, in the form of poultry and the products of pig-sticking. During my 1980–1981 fieldwork I often heard statements praising good home-raised chicken in opposition to the "exploded" one (*robbantott*) available in town. At the time I did not inquire what was meant by the expression "exploded chicken," which was not a common expression in Budapest, where I came from. However, it seemed to imply the difference between home-raised, free range chickens that grew gradually as opposed to the fast growth of industrially raised animals. Often these statements came at the end of casual conversations that compared the hardships of village life to the ease of urban living, and seemed to me to be affirmations of the superiority of village life.

The transition from self-provisioning to the market can be seen in what happened to bread-baking. Well into the twentieth century, for Hungarian peasants one of the main symbolic markers of being able to provide for one's family, i.e., of being self-sufficient, was having grain to bake their own bread. The delivery quotas of the early 1950s undermined this ability because often they were so high that not enough was left for the household (for use and for seed). In 1983, I interviewed a man in his fifties in a village near Budapest, who vividly recalled the humiliation he felt, some thirty years earlier, when he was forced to buy bread at the village store. He explained that he would loiter around the store until there were no other customers because he was so ashamed of *paying* for bread.

I did not hear similar dramatic stories in Szentpéterszeg, but my hosts during my 1980–1981 study, who had built their house in 1970, deemed it necessary to also build the special oven (*kemence*) that was used to bake bread in the village. By the time of my fieldwork they were no longer baking bread in it. While I was there, inspired by my presence, my hostess decided to demonstrate traditional bread-baking for me. When the neighbors heard the news, several of them nostalgically expressed the wish that they wanted to taste the "delicious home-baked" bread. Houses built later no longer included the special ovens; people even demolished existing ones as they stopped baking bread. Thirty years later, during my 2010–2011 fieldwork, I noticed that though people do not routinely bake bread it had become fashionable in the village to have brick ovens, reminiscent of the old *kemence,* built either inside the house or in the garden.

Ethnographer Mária Szalacsi Rácz Korompainé, in a 1976 article on bread-baking in the wider region in which Szentpéterszeg is located, explained that people stopped baking bread at home in the late 1960s. The article is a rather old-fashioned piece of writing on the traditional material culture associated with bread-making, but in the concluding paragraphs she also talks about the disappearance of the practice. Almost as an afterthought she devotes a paragraph to such modern developments as the introduction of factory-made bread. The passage is rather unusual in the Hungarian ethnographic tradition of the times, which often studiously avoided writing about contemporary developments in the cultural practices of the peasantry (cf. Vidacs 2005). Her statement is worth quoting here in full:

> The picture would not be complete if we did not mention that in recent years the consumption of store bought bread is spreading more and more. At present seven bread factories are in business.… fresh bread … reaches smaller villages with the help of bread trucks. The Baking Company [*Sütőipari Vállalat*] of Hajdú-Bihar county has reckoned with the fact that when private peasant production is replaced by collectivized agriculture the population's mode of life changes. For the rural population employed in large-scale agricultural enterprises [*mezőgazdasági nagyüzem*] self-provisioning, and as such, home bread-baking too, recedes. The Company, accommodating itself to changing demand, … recently introduced the manufacture of breads that resemble home-baked bread with their round shape and their greater weight [3 kg] [than what is commonly available in the stores]. At the beginning of the 1960s I still found general rejection of factory-made bread, these days it is different: they do not scorn those who buy bread from the store, they even acknowledge when the store-bought bread is good, but they still compare it to home-baked bread, that is the point of comparison (Korompainé Szalacsi Rácz 1976: 299).

Several things stand out in the quote. Her text reveals the conscious modernizing that the socialist government was undertaking by the innovation and its willingness to make concessions to tradition (in the shape and weight of the bread they were marketing). She also points out the far-reaching connections that existed between the creation of collective farms (large-scale agricultural enterprises) and the decline in self-provisioning. She only touches on the resistance that accompanied the introduction of factory-made bread in passing. Judging by my interview described above, the experience may have been quite traumatic for at least some people.[3]

Although the rural population began to switch over to a more monetized economy under socialism, in Szentpéterszeg, at the time of my 1980–1981 fieldwork, there was still a tendency to minimize outlay of cash, whenever possible. This was partly due to lack of sufficient amounts of cash and probably also to the force of tradition. Practicing reciprocity in the form of labor exchange could be interpreted as examples of keeping out of market relations whenever possible. As I mentioned above, besides harvesting maize from the household plot, there were other forms of mutual labor exchange in Szentpéterszeg. Weddings, house construction, and funerals were the most important events that mobilized the social networks of people.[4] My argument here is that these occasions of the enacting of reciprocity integrated the economy in a Polanyian sense, providing economic goods and services through the community.

Weddings were among the main events that brought together a large number of people in cooperation with each other in a form of mutual labor exchange in the village. During the 1970s and 1980s rural weddings in Hungary, reflecting the economic prosperity of villagers, became increasingly lavish and the number of guests increased significantly (Hann 1980; Sárkány 1983b). In Szentpéterszeg, as in other rural communities, the wedding meal was prepared with the help of relatives, neighbors and *komas* (compadres or ritualized best friends). An especially demanding task was the plucking of chickens, which were taken to the groom's house by a female relative of each male who had been invited to the wedding. Given that at the time of my fieldwork in the winter of 1980–1981 most weddings had about 100–120 participants and the largest I participated in had 250 guests, the task was quite taxing and required the participation of more than a dozen women the day before the actual wedding took place. These women came as help and were fed throughout the day, partly from the products of the pig that was butchered the day before. As an example of generalized reciprocity they were expected to be compensated for their labor when they needed similar help at the wedding of their child (or possibly they were returning the favor). There were other forms of reciprocity at the wedding as well, but they required a monetary contribution rather than labor. Also having to do with the food served at the wedding, women who attended the event were each expected to bring a cake along with them. These were usually store-bought at the time I did my fieldwork, and given the large quantities of cake thus received, the contributors ended up taking home a selection after the wedding (cf. Hoppál 1981).

There were also wedding gifts. Those close to the couple, that is to say close relatives and the godparents, were expected to give substantial gifts, usually in the form of durable consumer goods, such as TV sets, vacuum cleaners, or refrigerators. From those who were not so close to the couple smaller items were received, such as coffee makers (often several), which then seemed to me to be circulating, going from one wedding to the next. Even more important was the "bride's dance" (*menyasszonytánc*)— at which serious sums of cash were donated for the right to dance a few steps with the new bride, toward midnight. At the time of my research 500 forints was the minimum expected sum, averaging anywhere between 25,000 and 60,000 forints per wedding. By the late 1970s these sums went to the young couple and enabled them to start building their own house, or if they already had a house, to start furnishing it (cf. Hann 1980; Sárkány 1983b).

House construction was the other major undertaking in which mutual labor exchange played a significant part. The villagers constructed their houses with the help of relatives, friends, and *komas* with the expectation that they would have to return the favor over time. In this case too, the workers' pay was being fed.

These mutual help arrangements, in addition to creating and enacting community solidarity, also had the consequence of minimizing monetary expenses. In the case of the wedding, most of the food served, with the exception of the main dish which was either beef or mutton, was either contributed by the participants or home-grown and/or homemade. Only drinks had to be paid for. In the case of house-building too, the system of mutual help reduced the need for cash expenditures, although building materials and more specialized labor did have to be paid for.

What is of importance from the point of view of this chapter is that during the early 1980s reciprocity still served as a form of integration in the village. Mutual help was the institutionalized way of accomplishing certain tasks, be they harvesting maize, organizing a wedding, or building a house. Doing them any other way was almost unimaginable. This was all the more so as the entire village participated in these events on one or another occasion. This ensured that it was almost impossible to step out of the system, since both weddings and house-building functioned as rotating savings associations. People could be safe in the knowledge that sooner or later they would get back what they contributed in similar forms of help. Thus, the system was a form of self-sufficiency on the level of the community. Reciprocity was the organizing principle of social and economic life, which incidentally also enabled people to minimize cash expenditure and allowed them, in being reliant on each other, not to have to rely on the market too much, or perhaps it is better to say not more than necessary.

### After 1989

Following the end of socialism in 1989 the system of collective farms was dismantled in Hungary. Land was directly returned to the original owners, if they were members of the collective. Those among the original owners or their descendants who were not members received compensation vouchers. Employees of collective farms were also entitled to a certain amount of land (Sárkány 2005). With the dismantling of the collectivized system agriculture went into decline in Hungary. Pál Juhász and others describe the process, and argue that while during the 1980s some branches of Hungarian agriculture were capable of world-class production, by the mid 1990s agricultural output dropped to two-thirds of the production levels of the 1980s and incomes from agriculture did not reach even half of what they were prior to the regime change (Juhász 2006: 37; Sárkány 2005). Juhász adds that much of this income, due to the prevalence of land-leasing to entities that have nothing to do with the villages, actually gets siphoned out of the communities themselves.

In Szentpéterszeg the collective farm finally folded in 2000, but some of its lands had been returned to former owners earlier and the institution that during the 1980s was quite successful died a slow death, becoming increasingly less profitable. The gap it left in the village is still felt in that there is still nothing to replace the jobs that were lost and the synergies that had been in place between the collective and the home-production of the villagers went with the collective farm as well. In combination with the deindustrialization that has taken place in the neighboring town, the villagers find themselves in dire straits. In some ways this would be the ideal moment for self-sufficiency in the classical sense to reappear in the form of a retreat to self-provisioning, but the opposite has happened. People are more reliant on cash incomes than on their agricultural output. Partly this has to do with the aging of the population, but partly also with younger people and in-migrants most often not having the necessary knowledge or the will to engage in agricultural production.

Before turning to a discussion of people's livelihoods in postsocialist times, I will briefly discuss what happened to reciprocity in Szentpéterszeg after 1989. When I returned to the village in 2009, I found that practically all the forms of reciprocity that I documented thirty years earlier had disappeared. Once the collective farm ceased to exist and most people stopped engaging in agricultural work there was no need to help each other with harvesting. There are still weddings, although their numbers have diminished significantly; young people are more likely to live together than to marry. But when there is a wedding, it is no longer organized through the system of mutual help I outlined above. Instead, often the wedding is held at a restaurant in the nearby town or if it is held at the cultural center in the village they either hire a cook or have the occasion catered from outside the village. An important role at all weddings was that of the best man and bridesman (*vőfély*),[5] especially that of the groom. Traditionally chosen from among the relatives of the couple, his role was in part to oversee the smooth unfolding of the wedding, and in part to act as an MC. In the latter capacity he also delivered traditional, often in part bawdy, entertainment during the event. The rhyming texts that constituted the *vőfély*'s repertoire often circulated in villages in handwritten or typed form. This function is also increasingly falling on a paid "expert" from outside the community.

House-building with mutual help has likewise disappeared. With the general economic decline following the end of socialism far fewer new houses are built. When people do have the need they profess to prefer to pay for the service rather than have help. The explanation they give in both cases is that mutual help was inefficient and not everybody pulled their weight; in general, they profess to prefer the "clearer" situation of paying for a service and being done with it. In other words, the market principle has replaced the principle of reciprocity.[6]

I have argued above that the system of mutual labor exchange that I found during my 1980–1981 fieldwork acted to integrate the village as a community through the webs of relationships they created and maintained through the system. People still continue to cooperate and help each other, especially when it comes to relatives. There are also individual acts of kindness, as for example when someone had collected a very large quantity of mushrooms from his portion of forest land and gave some of it as a gift to an elderly couple with whom he had no systematic relationship. Neighbors may still help each other out, or a younger couple may "adopt" an elderly neighbor and provide him or her with material help, for example by giving him or her some food, or sending him or her a sample of the products of pig-sticking. Although some form of reciprocity may occur, it is not expected in the same way as acts of reciprocity were expected in labor exchange (despite the rhetoric to the contrary). But instead of being a form of integration in the Polanyian sense, these are private acts of goodwill, rather than something that structures people's lives or holds the community as community together.

The majority continue to have a vegetable garden, preserve and/or freeze fruit and vegetables, and freeze meat that they either raise themselves (wholly or partially) or buy at the store; however, all villagers agree that what they produce is not enough and they have to supplement what they grow from the store. Most people do not grow fruits and vegetables for sale, partly because as they say nobody is willing to buy them, and they are of the opinion that they cannot compete with the low prices of the big supermarkets. As a result, they don't find it profitable to grow to sell and often find it cheaper (and obviously less labor-intensive) to buy fruits and vegetables at the supermarket themselves. This is so even if rhetorically they disapprove of supermarkets, which they perceive as foreign multinationals that pay no taxes and stifle competition from the small producer. So it cannot be said that the economic hardships visited on them by the end of socialism and the return to capitalism have significantly turned the villagers to self-provisioning (cf. Pine 2002, who demonstrates that under similar circumstances in Poland people did "retreat to the household," but also highlights the ambiguities involved).

The one aspect of everyday life that I know of where a technological U-turn has been taken is in the use of fuel. Some years ago, during the mid 1990s, the villagers invested in having "clean" gas heating systems in their houses, but in recent years the price of gas has increased so much that those who could afford it have converted their gas heating system to a dual wood-gas system, obtaining the wood locally and only switching on the gas when absolutely necessary.

Once the collective farm disappeared, people got their land back, but often in small, noncontiguous plots, which quite a few young people and especially the elderly are not able to work. Instead, they rent out the land, either to the handful of fellow villagers who engage in agriculture or to one of two external bodies. One of these is a cooperative that was created after the end of socialism in a nearby village and the other is a private enterprise with headquarters in the nearby town. Many of those whose lands were returned or who inherited the lands from the original owners no longer reside in the village. They thus become absentee owners and generally their landholdings increase the amount of land rented out to these outside entities. Alternately, if they have siblings in the village who work the land, they let them use their land, too.

Most people live from a combination of incomes: given the demographics of the village (including the effects of out-migration by the young discussed above) there are many people on old-age pensions. Often these are widows, and a large proportion of people are on disability pensions as well. Retiring due to a medical disability has been one of the main strategies that people employed to ensure a regular monetary income when the collective farm folded. These people gain a steady income from state (disability or old-age) pensions and supplement it from a variety of sources. Those who rent their land out receive payment either in cash or in corn or other produce that can serve as animal feed or a combination of these; however, the amounts they receive tend to be rather small. No wonder that today women who had managed to persuade their husbands to allow them to work under socialism often construct their life histories around the story of how they had achieved this, and conclude with statements such as "thank God I insisted on working and have my pension now!"

Thus, it could be argued that a reversal has taken place. On the one hand, under socialism, especially after 1969, the Hungarian countryside bankrolled the economy, that is to say, the state relied on the output coming from the countryside (and its combination of large-scale, modern farming and intensive, self-exploitative home labor) to keep it going. On the other hand, following 1989, the villages, especially in such disadvantaged regions as the one where I carried out my research, cannot survive without state subsidies or the welfare system.[7] Already the functioning of the village is predicated on these.

In the case of Szentpéterszeg, state allocations to the functioning of the local Municipality outstrip the income that can be gathered locally from taxes. While earlier there was a symbiotic relationship between the collective farm and the local council, now the Municipality (*Önkörmányzat*) has to take on the mantle of both institutions. At its heyday, during the early 1980s, the collective farm was able to provide work to about 300 people but the overall number of people who were employed was more than double that number and while quite a few people were employed by the local council, a fairly large number were commuting to the nearby town or even farther away. And of course in 1980–1981 there was no unemployment. Immediately following 1989 the number of the unemployed first rose to 21, then within 10 years to 69 and according to the 2009 census figures the officially known job seekers numbered 116, while the number of inactive earners (pensioners) rose from 275 in 1980 to 473 in 2000. The village has the resources to employ 17 people on a form of social assistance that requires them to work, what I call workfare. Workfare workers get the minimum wage, but the village would be incapable of paying the entire sum. Rather, the Municipality is obliged to provide only 5 percent of this amount and the rest is derived from central state funds.

Since the number of people in need is much more than the number of those who can at any given time be thus employed by the Municipality, it rotates those who receive this kind of assistance, which of course opens up the process to maneuvering and creates tensions. In addition to the workfare workers, in 2009 there were 63 people who received a form of social assistance that required them to be available ("stand in readiness") receiving a little more than one-third of the minimum wage, also paid for by the state) should the village wish to call them to provide some kind of labor for the community. Both the workfare people and the people who have to make themselves available contribute to the overall well-being of the community, by providing necessary labor, as for example serving as a cleaning woman at the local community center or serving as a night watchman or carrying out the regular maintenance work of the infrastructure of the village, thus making it more habitable and inviting. They are also called in to contribute their labor every time the civic associations of the village organize a village-wide event (cf. Szőke 2012, Vidacs 2015).

It is hard to know how many of these workers come from the ranks of recent in-migrants to the village, because it is not always obvious who works for the Municipality in what capacity and the villagers do not openly talk about the in-migrants very often. However, at any given time during my fieldwork at least four or five of the workfare workers (out of the possible seventeen) were in-migrants. According to officials at the mayor's office, about 10 percent of the current population of the village is constituted by relative newcomers. Basically, there are two kinds of in-migrants. The first category is composed of those who seek out the village as an escape because they had fallen on hard times in the city. They still have enough resources to buy a house in the village and hope to pick up their lives there. Some of these end up on social assistance. Others are better-off people, who have steady jobs elsewhere (such as a nurse who works at the hospital of the nearby town, or a postal worker, also employed in town) and have chosen to move to the village, partly because it is more affordable to buy a house there and partly because they consider the quality of life in a village to be better than that in town. The villagers are clearly happier with the latter type of migrant and many of the mayor's policies, aimed at improving the quality of life in the village, are meant to attract these "better" type of people. Yet, they too represent a different outlook on life than that of the villagers, and among other things they are singled out by their usual unwillingness to engage in any kind agricultural activity. Some of them contradict this opinion in their behavior but in the stereotypical judgments pronounced by the villagers they are often seen in this way. Naturally, the villagers take an even more negative view of those newcomers who end up on workfare, but in both cases the criticism is muted by the need to get along and by the uniform fear of what is seen as a much worse kind of in-migrant, namely, Gypsies.

There is only one in-migrant among the handful of people who do live primarily from agriculture. These people are considered by the villagers to be independent farmers, but most of them actually have other resources. In most cases the husband deals with agriculture and the wife has a steady job—often a white-collar one. Thus, for example, one man raises bulls (he has 120 of them) while his wife is a school teacher. Another two raise cows. The wife of one works at the local branch of the savings association (a kind of bank), while the other's wife works at the local day-care center for the elderly. All these are steady jobs. Two men raise sheep. The wife of one works at the textile factory in the nearby town, an enterprise that has reduced its activities significantly in the last twenty years. For assistance with the sheep, her husband has long enjoyed the help of his four daughters, all of whom, as he proudly recounts, did their lessons in the fields while they were tending sheep. All four became (or are becoming) policewomen and while they still help him out from time to time, their lives are taking a different direction and according to their father, they will not return to the village. The other man who raises sheep alternates between being on unemployment benefits, being on workfare, and being an independent sheep farmer. He is the head of the sports association and at the same time a member of the local body of representatives, which no doubt helps him make these rather unorthodox arrangements. His wife is a secondary school teacher in the nearby town. Only one of the farmers' wives stays at home and devotes herself to the family farm. Another man owns and operates a slaughterhouse. He has slowly built up sizable land holdings and he employs his wife to do the bookkeeping. Most of these people own machinery and for a fee undertake working other people's lands, not just in the village but anywhere in the vicinity where their services are required. Interviewing them, I was struck by the fact that, like most people, they complain about the policies of the state that have led to the decline in Hungarian agriculture since the end of socialism. Many of them maintain a sense that they are upholding a tradition, which the "state" is doing everything to ruin. Amid the claims of imminent ruin, what they did not ever mention, except when I pushed them, is that each of them benefits from fairly significant EU subsidies to help them maintain their production. Often self-consciously claiming to be "peasants," they make implicit comparisons between themselves and the newcomers, saying things like "it is not the habit of the people Szentpéterszeg to go begging for aid!" Yet, the fact of the matter is that without the subsidies they would not be able to maintain their agricultural ventures.

I have tried to show above that agricultural self-sufficiency—never complete—has been thoroughly undermined in the course of the socialist transformation of Hungarian agriculture. The concept has meant different things over time, from self-provisioning to having a monetary income enabling one to provide for the needs of the household. I have also argued that while this transformation was taking place the inhabitants of the eastern Hungarian village I studied provided each other with reciprocal help in the case of important economic and social events at the level of the community. This enabled them to be partially self-sufficient in that they could in some respects sidestep the market and at the same time the reciprocity-enacted and reinforced community. As these forms of reciprocal cooperation disappeared in the postsocialist period, the villagers have increasingly turned to the market for obtaining the same services.

What remains of the ideal of self-sufficiency is just that, an ideal. This is especially the case for the handful of agricultural entrepreneurs in the village. Although they are thoroughly enmeshed in the market and rely on EU subsidies to make their enterprises viable, they use the ideal of self-sufficiency as a badge of identity. "Forgetting" in effect their involvement with the world of market relations as well as state and EU subsidies, they self-consciously claim to be self-reliant peasants. In adopting this ideal they claim the identity of being from the village, as opposed to the immigrants,

**Figure 1.1.** Map of Bea Vidacs's Field Site.

who in fact are necessary for the continued survival of the village. This identity of being from the village may in the future take on certain exclusivist characteristics but at present the comparison (and thus the identity that it invokes) remains muted, as all concerned seem to realize implicitly that they need each other for the continued existence of the village.

**Bea Vidacs,** currently a Senior Researcher in the East-West Research Center on the Ethnology of Religion at the University of Pécs, Hungary, was educated in Budapest and London and holds a doctorate in Anthropology from the City University of New York. She has carried out field research in Cameroon and Hungary and taught anthropology in the United States and in Hungary. She is the author of *Visions of a Better World: Football in the Cameroonian Social Imagination* (2010).

## Notes

1. The village is located in eastern Hungary, its population in 1980 was 1,485, and in 2009 there were 1,095 inhabitants. The nearest town is 8 kilometers away. For more background concerning my long-term research in this community and acknowledgments see Vidacs 2015.
2. In "The Economy as Instituted Process," Polanyi explains forms of integration thus: "A study of how empirical economies are instituted should start from the way in which the economy acquires unity and stability, that is the interdependence and recurrence of its parts. This is achieved through a combination of a very few patterns which may be called forms of integration" (1957: 250).
3. It is noticeable, at least for someone who was brought up under socialism and was reared on the common practice of reading between the lines, that she mentions these signs of opposition to factory-made bread (and by extension to the regime) while declaring them to have passed.
4. These differed from harvesting maize in that the return was much less immediate due to the sporadic occurrence of these events in any given household.
5. Traditional Hungarian weddings featured two representatives of the couple: a best man on the man's side and a bridesman on the woman's side. Both were called *vőfély*, but they were of unequal prestige, the best man had more prestige and a more specific set of roles.
6. The decline of house-building with mutual help is also due to changes in legislation that have nothing to do with willingness or unwillingness to engage in reciprocity. Laws attempting to curb illegal labor practices have made people afraid that if they build with the help of fellow villagers they may be fined for employing "black" labor.
7. According to the authors of a report on the economic performance of the microregion, the village falls in the third, least well-endowed zone and as such faces the greatest challenges (Szabó et al. 2005).

# References

Bodrogi, Tibor, ed. 1978. *Varsány. Tanulmányok egy északmagyarországi falu társada-lomnéprajzához (Varsány: Social Anthropological Studies on a Village in Northern Hungary).* Budapest: Akadémiai.

Dessewffy, Tibor. 2002. "Speculators and Travellers: The Political Construction of the Tourist in the Kádár Regime." *Cultural Studies* 16, no. 1: 44–62.

Erdei, Ferenc. 1938. *Parasztok (Peasants).* Budapest: Athenaeum.

———. 1942. *Magyar paraszttársadalom (Hungarian Peasant Society).* Budapest: Franklin-Társulat.

Fehérváry, Krisztina. 2002. "American Kitchens, Luxury Bathrooms, and the Search for a 'Normal' Life in Postsocialist Hungary." *Ethnos* 67, no. 3: 369–400.

———. 2009. "Goods and States: The Political Logic of State-Socialist Material Culture." *Comparative Studies in Society and History* 51, no. 2: 426–459.

Gábor, R. István. 1989. "Second Economy and Socialism: The Hungarian Experience." In *The Underground Economies: Tax Evasion and Information Distortion,* ed. Edgar.L. Feige, 339–359. Cambridge: Cambridge University Press.

Gregory, Chris. 2009. "Whatever Happened to Householding?" In *Market and Society: The Great Transformation Today,* ed. Chris Hann and Keith Hart, 133–159. Cambridge: Cambridge University Press.

Gudeman, Stephen. 2001. *The Anthropology of Economy: Community, Market, and Culture.* Oxford: Wiley-Blackwell.

Gunst, Péter. 1996. *Agrarian Development and Social Change in Eastern Europe, 14th-19th Centuries.* Aldershot: Variorum.

———. 2004. "A népi mozgalom gazdasági-társadalmi gyökerei." (The Socioeconomic Roots of the Populist Movement.) *Zempléni Múzsa.* Accessed 6 May 2012 at http://zemplenimuzsa.hu/04_4/gunst.htm.

Hammer, Ferenc. 2002. "A Gasoline Scented Sindbad: The Truck Driver as a Popular Hero in Socialist Hungary." *Cultural Studies* 16, no. 1: 80–126.

Hann, Chris. 1980. *Tázlár: A Village in Hungary.* Cambridge: Cambridge University Press.

———. 1990a. "Introduction." In *Market Economy and Civil Society in Hungary,* ed. C. M. Hann, 1–20. London: Frank Cass.

———. 1990b. "Second Economy and Civil Society." In *Market Economy and Civil Society in Hungary,* ed. C. Hann, 21–44. London: Frank Cass.

———. 1995 "Ferenc Erdei, Antal Vermes and the struggle for balance in rural Hungary" In *East-Central European Communities: The Struggle for Balance in Turbulent Times,* ed. David A. Kideckel, 101–115. Oxford: Westview.

———. 2006. "'Not the Horse We Wanted!': Procedure and Legitimacy in Postsocialist Privatisation in Tázlár." In *'Not the Horse We Wanted!': Postsocialism, Neoliberalism, and Eurasia,* 42–90. Münster: LIT Verlag.

Hann, Chris, and Mihály Sárkány. 2003. "The Great Transformation in Rural Hungary: Property, Life Strategies, and Living Standards." In *The Postsocialist Agrarian Question: Property Relations and the Rural Condition,* Chris Hann and the "Property Relations" Group, 117–141. Münster: Lit Verlag.

Harcsa, István, Imre Kovách, and Iván Szelényi. 1998. "The Hungarian Agricultural 'Miracle' and the Limits of Socialist Reforms." In *Privatizing the Land. Rural Po-*

*litical Economy in Post-Communist Societies,* ed. Iván Szelényi, 21–42. London: Routledge.

Hollós, Marida, and Bela Maday, eds. 1983. *New Hungarian Peasants: An East Central European Experience with Collectivization.* New York: Brooklyn College Press.

Hoppál, Mihály. 1981. "Elosztás és egyenlőség.—A kommunikáció rejtett csatornái a közösségben (Distribution and Equality: The Hidden Channels of Communication in the Community)." *Az MTA I. Osztályának Közleményei* 32, no. 1–2: 139–154.

Huszár, Tibor, ed. 1988. *Ferenc Erdei. Selected Writings.* Budapest: Akadémiai.

Juhász, Pál. 2006. "A falusias terek gazdasági, társadalmi és politikai gondjairól (On the Economic, Social and Political Problems of Rural Spaces)." *Erdélyi társadalom* 2: 23–42.

Kornai, J. 1986. "'Hard' and 'Soft' Budget Constraints." In *Contradictions and Dilemmas: Studies on the Socialist Economy and Society,* ed. János Kornai, 33–51. Cambridge, MA: The MIT Press.

Korompainé Szalacsi Rácz, Mária. 1976. "A bihari házikenyér (The Home-Made Bread of Bihar)." *A Bihari Múzeum Évkönyve* 1: 285–300.

Lampland, Martha. 1995. *The Object of Labor: Commodification in Socialist Hungary.* Chicago: University of Chicago Press.

Nyyssönen, Heino. 2006. "Salami Reconstructed: 'Goulash Communism' and Political Culture in Hungary." *Cahiers du monde russe* 47, no. 1: 153–172.

Oláh, József. 1987. "Fejezetek a sárréti települések történetéből (Chapters in the History of the Settlements of Sárrét)." *Hajdú-Bihar Megyei Levéltár Évkönyve,* no. 14: 29–38. Accessed 15 August 2011 at http://hbml.archivportal.hu/data/files/144710010 .pdf.

Pine, Frances. 2002. "Retreat to the Household? Gendered Domains in Postsocialist Poland." In *Postsocialism: Ideals, Ideologies and Practices in Eurasia,* ed. Chris Hann, 95–113. London: Routledge.

Polanyi, Karl. 1944. *The Great Transformation.* New York: Farrar & Rinehart.

———. 1957. "The Economy as Instituted Process." In *Trade and Market in the Early Empires,* ed. Conrad M. Arensberg and Harry W. Pearson, 243–270. Chicago: Regnery.

Réev, Istvan. 1987. "The Advantages of Being Atomized: How Hungarian Peasants Coped with Collectivization." *Dissent* 34: 335–350.

Sampson, Steven L. 1987. "The Second Economy of the Soviet Union and Eastern Europe." *Annals of the American Academy of Political and Social Science* 493, no. 1: 120–136.

Sárkány, Mihály. 1978. "A gazdaság átalakulása (The Transformation of the Economy)." In *Varsány,* ed. Tibor Bodrogi, 63–150. Budapest: Akadémiai.

———. 1983a. "Economic Changes in a Northern Hungarian Village." In *New Hungarian Peasants: An East Central European Experience with Collectivization,* ed. Marida Hollós and Bela Maday, 25–55. New York: Brooklyn College Press.

———. 1983b. "A lakodalom funkciójának megváltozása falun (The Transformation of the Function of Marriage in Villages)." *Ethnographia* 94, no. 2: 279–285.

———. 2000. "Parasztság és termelési viszonyok (Peasantry and Relations of Production)." In *Kalandozások a 20. századi kulturális antropológiában (Excursions in 20th Century Cultural Anthropology),* ed. Mihály Sárkány, 72–88. Budapest: L'Harmattan.

————. 2005. "Re-study of Varsány: Entrepreneurs and Property in Rural Hungary after 1989." In *Anthropology of Europe: Teaching and Research,* ed. Peter Skalnik, 143–151. Prague: Set Out.

Swain, Nigel. 1985. *Collective Farms Which Work?* Cambridge: Cambridge University Press.

————. 1992. *Hungary: The Rise and Fall of Feasible Socialism.* London: Verso.

Szabó, Gábor, Alajos Fehér, Béla Baranyi, Judit Kovács Katonáné, Ildikó Tikász, and Zoltán Fürj. 2005. "Strengthening the Multifunctional Use of European Land: Coping with Marginalisation: Case Study—Hungary." Eurolan Report.

Szabó, István. 1976. *Jobbágyok, parasztok. – Értekezések a magyar parasztság történetéből.* (Serfs, peasants – Essays on the history of the Hungarian peasantry). Budapest: Akadémiai.

Szőke, Alexandra. 2012. Rescaling States—Rescaling Insecurities: Rural Citizenship at the Edge of the Hungarian State. Ph.D. diss. Central European University.

Varga, Zsuzsanna. 2009. *The Hungarian Agriculture and Rural Society: Changes, Problems and Possibilities.* Budapest: Szaktudás Kiadó Ház.

Vasary, Ildikó. 1987. *Beyond the Plan: Social Change in a Hungarian Village.* Boulder, CO: Westview Press.

Vidacs, Bea. 1985. "Komaság és kölcsönösség Szentpéterszegen (Godparenthood and Reciprocity in Szentpéterszeg)." *Ethnographia* 96, no. 4: 509–529.

————. 2005. "An Anthropological Education: A Comparative Perspective." In *Studying Peoples in the People's Democracies: Socialist Era Anthropology in East-Central Europe,* ed. C. Hann, M. Sárkány, and P. Skalník, 331–341. Münster: Lit Verlag.

————. 2015. "From Pig-Sticking to Festival. Changes in Pig-Sticking Practices in the Hungarian Countryside." In *Economy and Ritual: Studies in Postsocialist Tranformations,* ed. Stephen Gudeman and Chris Hann, 75-106, New York: Berghahn Books.

# 2

# How Much is Enough?

*Household Provisioning, Self-Sufficiency, and Social Status in Rural Moldova*

JENNIFER R. CASH

The idea of self-sufficiency carries an enormous appeal for social scientists, policy makers, and local populations across a wide range of historical and contemporary circumstances.[1] The term refers to an idealized state in which an individual or collective subject satisfies all its own needs without a reliance on others. Although clearly impossible to achieve, people in many places behave "as if" self-sufficiency is a realizable goal, ordering, categorizing, and valuing social relations in ways that make self-sufficiency appear possible, normal, and desirable. The ideal may continue to govern a community's definition of itself and perception by others, long after it becomes deeply engaged with market activities (Loehr 1952). Moreover, self-sufficiency at the level of village or community, as well as the nation-state, continues to be described, with little critical perspective, as both historic reality (e.g., Salant 1987: 63) and future ideal (e.g., Yossakrai 2006) by many scholars and policy makers. In the United States, welfare reform programs of the 1990s even emphasized the goal of making individuals "self-sufficient," neglecting the intimate relations and responsibilities of family and household in most workers' lives (Morgen 2001).

The ideal of self-sufficiency is also an important one in rural Moldova. Very few households come close to producing all that they consume, and almost all rely on cash income for meeting basic needs. Nevertheless, most households insist that "we do everything" and report that the wheat and many other foods that they produce are "enough" for their annual consumption. In this chapter, I address the symbolic importance of self-sufficiency and describe some of the ways in which households achieve a reputation for "having" that is only tangentially related to the actual quantity of food that the household produces.

In rural Moldova, one of the major ways that adults achieve social status and respectability is by making the effort to be self-sufficient. The first steps to respectability involve marriage and the establishment of a new house. Householders manage their household with an eye toward achieving a closed domestic economy and producing what they will consume. This is a prerequisite for gaining social approval. However, houses that "have" are socially recognized as such only when they "give." A house may be considered self-sufficient even if it is very poor, relies heavily on cash income, engages in little direct agricultural labor, and borrows extensively from others—as long as it gives generously through displays of hospitality (and more minutely through the offering of wine), lends out its resources and equipment, or donates money, food, or labor. From this perspective, the maintenance of social relations through ritual activities like communal drinking and feasting becomes central to economic decisions regarding a household's basic "needs" and the activities that are necessary—whether working the land or engaging in labor migration—to meet those needs.

## Self-Sufficiency as Economic Model and Performance

The English term "self-sufficiency" denotes the quality of being "self-sufficient"—that is, to be "sufficient in oneself ... without aid or support from outside; (or) able to supply one's needs oneself" (Oxford English Dictionary online). The term is a calque of the Greek *autharcos,* and as the earliest references in English from the late sixteenth century suggest, it was meant to describe God's nature rather than that of individual persons or human communities. In the earliest recorded references, the application of "sufficiency" or "self-sufficiency" to individual persons carried negative connotations of arrogance, self-conceit, haughtiness, and excess. By the mid-nineteenth century, however, the terms "sufficiency" and "self-sufficiency" had extended to refer to issues of economic well-being, and especially to the production of food. It is interesting to note that the expansion of the term to describe ideal levels of household, community, and state economic sovereignty and security coincided with the development of economics and other social sciences.

The term self-sufficiency has often been coupled with debates about economic and political reform. For example, the rhetoric of "self-sufficiency" had a widespread and galvanizing impact on politics and agricultural reform in many places throughout the nineteenth century, not least in the southern United States in the decades immediately preceding the Civil War (Ford 1985: 264). Since the 1930s, popular use of the term "self-sufficiency" has flourished even more broadly, and its connotations and applications have especially expanded since the 1950s. While ordinarily coupled with nationally focused development projects, some studies of "self-sufficiency" at the beginning of the twenty-first century now also reflect the desire to expand international markets by exploiting differential patterns in household self-sufficiency. A study of Chinese fruit and vegetable consumption, for example, explains that it is important to know how rising incomes affect household self-provisioning in order to better estimate the rising quantities of food that China will need, and how those needs will affect the United States' export markets (Han, Wahl, and Mittelhammer 2001).

In most cases, the term "self-sufficiency" is used without definition or precision, and draws its power from a long history of the term's association with the discourses of rural populism, national development, and alternative communities. Yet common scholarly uses of "self-sufficiency" also draw, explicitly or implicitly, on ideal economic types suggested by thinkers such as Karl Bücher, Karl Polanyi, and A.V. Chayanov. Karl Bücher's classic model of a "closed" or "independent" domestic economy, for example, defines the household as the primary economic unit of both production and consumption (Spittler 2008: 93). Karl Polanyi defined "householding" as an economic model, or type of behavior, based on the principles of "production for one's own use" (1957: 53). Similarly, Chayanov's (1986 [1924-5]) "peasant farm" is an organizational form in which a (rural) household exploits the labor of its own members in an effort to balance total labor expenditure against consumption needs. These classic models have been criticized for their Eurocentrism (Gregory 2009), and for their evolutionary underpinnings (Spittler 2008). Nevertheless, recent scholarship on food production often reproduces the dichotomy between primitive and historic conditions of "self-sufficiency" and "modern systems" (e.g., Rose and Tikhomirov 1993: 113).

Later scholars have emphasized that neither an individual, a household, a community, nor a state is capable of producing all the goods necessary for its own reproduction (Sahlins 1972: 83; Spittler 2008: 93–94). Chayanov himself acknowledged that peasant farms participated in market activities, and he noted that a "psychology of avarice" (i.e., a desire to maximize consumption and accumulate wealth) is not incompatible with the organizational predominance of the labor-consumer balance (1986: 47). The usefulness of the classic models of closed, independent, domestic, household economies is therefore to be found in their insistence that economic principles other than those of trade, exchange, and profit making have dominated in particular societies, at particular times of history, and that they can persist and reappear within other economic frameworks. Instead, the "self-sufficiency" of a household depends on wider relations at the economic levels of community and market. As Stephen Gudeman (2008) argues, mutuality and trade are dialectically connected.

## Sufficiency and Having Enough

In Romanian, the dominant language spoken throughout Moldova, there is no exact equivalent to the compound English word "self-sufficiency." *Suficienţă*, a term that entered Romanian through Italian, denotes sufficiency and adequacy, as well as vanity and self-aggrandizement (DEX 1998). *Suficienţă*, however, only negatively references the "self" as the provider of sufficiency, much like the earliest recorded meanings of self-sufficiency in English. In rural areas, the term is not even used. In her contribution to this volume, Monica Vasile suggests that the phrase *să fii propriul tău stăpân* ("to be one's own master") comes closest to expressing the values of self-sufficiency held by ethnic Romanians in the Apuseni Mountains. I found a number of phrases, expressions, and gestures to convey the value of a closed domestic economy in which a household is solely responsible for its own production and consumption. As in Vasile's case, owning the means of production is valued in southeastern Moldova, but the similarities between the two communities do not extend much further. Although I came across the notion of "mastery" in the capital of Chişinău, it was not widely used in my field site. Sometimes, I heard *să fii stăpânul în casa mea* (to be the master in/of my own house) uttered in frustration about a perceived lack of control over one's time, habits, or well-being. When used, the expression was often directed at the state, or as a response to criticism of one's behavior or time allocation. The more usual way of representing self-sufficiency focused on the house, its reserves, and the work done to acquire them; the "master" of the house in rural Moldova is no noble lord, but manager and labor force combined.

The most common way to express a household's sufficiency is to say *noi avem* (we have), sometimes with the addition of *destul* (enough). This may be accompanied by the gesture of drawing the index finger horizontally across the throat to indicate saturation or super-saturation. People may also say that a particular item, or resources in general, *ajung* (lit. they arrive, i.e., they are enough). They say *noi facem pe toate* (we do everything) to provide their households with food and to maintain the house, and they refer to those who are perceived as succeeding in orderly house management as *gospodari* (hosts, managers). About their own attempts to provision their households, they say they want to be *în rînd cu lume* (in line with society) or *ca lume* (like people), acknowledging social pressure to conform, and even compete, in the construction and decor of one's house and garden,[2] preparation of and participation at feasts, and general social comportment. People are orderly, organized, and clean, but they also self-present as "having"—with amply decorated houses and richly dressed bodies—when receiving guests or being guests themselves (Cash 2010: 478–479). Collectively, this cluster of words and phrases describes a social world in which a model of self-sufficiency at the household level is both present and powerful, even if not easily realizable.

From the above description, self-sufficiency seems to be most importantly, and logically, about "having enough." It is this. But I will argue in the following pages that it is also possible for households to be considered *ca lume* when they have very little. Village society notices differences in the quantity and quality of what individual households "have," but there are few ways to articulate and codify such differences. For the most part, individuals are *gospodari* and *ca lume*, or they are not, regardless of actual wealth.[3] This can be explained, at least in part, by observing that "having" is logically and practically demonstrated through acts of "giving," to an extent that even households with relatively little can be seen as the social equals of those who have more. Ritual kinship relations such as marital godparenthood and coparenthood, for example, often cut across potential social, occupational, or economic divisions, as do the relations of neighborliness. The equation between having and giving is imperfect, but nevertheless demonstrable in survey data and ethnographic observation. Recognizing that "having" is made socially meaningful through "giving" has important implications for understanding the structure of economy in Moldova, and for understanding how "self-sufficiency" continues to be a shared social value even when local economies are deeply entangled with economic models of the market and finance (Gudeman 2008).

In the case of Moldova, the local economy is very heavily marked by the postsocialist transition. Ideals from the socialist period (e.g., concerning the state's responsibilities) are still present, and reputations that individuals gained during their work in the collective farm or other branches of Soviet administration still linger. The postsocialist economic transition has been especially difficult in Moldova. At one level, change and continuity in rural areas can be charted through a focus on self-sufficiency. The privatization of land and the laws regulating terms for the sale and leasing of land are said to be "fair" in ways that resonate with socialist values of social equality and state protection, but they limit the development of subsistence farming, commercial agriculture, and land markets. As villagers attempt to provision their houses, they are therefore also caught in the contradictions of the postsocialist economy that demands that villagers become small farmer-entrepreneurs, and yet effectively prevents them from doing so. At a micro-level, the changes in where and how households obtain different kinds of food can be tracked as a reflection of changes in farm and village administration during socialism, and of market opportunities after socialism.

From the perspective of household provisioning, however, neither socialism nor postsocialism is a particularly useful periodization. As informants told me, "every year is different" in the challenges that it presents to household provisioning. The Soviet period, too, was marked by constant economic change: one collective farm gave rise to two; the official designations of the farm(s) changed many times; how and when salaries were paid varied; the boundaries with a neighboring village changed, as did the regional center of administration and the administrative hierarchy of the farms and winery. Although the Soviet period is now remembered as a period of economic stability and prosperity, my questions about household economic activity in the Soviet period were never answered with clarity. People could talk in detail only about the specific challenges they faced at key events in their lives as householders: marriage, house-building, and the baptisms and weddings of their children. Thus in this chapter, the story of self-sufficiency is not really one of political or economic transition, but one about the enduring economic challenges of establishing and managing a house in a rural area that has good soil, but has never been wealthy.

## Overview: Working the Land in Postsocialist Moldova

The Republic of Moldova has the unfortunate distinction of being the poorest country in Europe. When it gained independence with the collapse of the Soviet Union, Moldova also lost the markets for its agricultural produce and wine, and much of the infrastructure that facilitated trade, with the new border regimes established with Ukraine and Russia. The establishment of an internal border between Moldova's two historic regions of Bessarabia and Transnistria made the country especially vulnerable in economic terms. Soviet Moldova's heavy industry (concrete and steel), chemical, paper, and textile manufacture, hydroelectric power production, and military-industrial complex were all located in Transnistria, a narrow stretch of territory east of the Nistru River. Moldova lost access to most of the wealth and goods produced by these factories after the region seceded during a brief armed conflict in 1992. Moldova always had substantially less industry than the other republics in the European portion of the Soviet Union, and was known primarily for its agricultural production, wine, and canning and food processing industries. In the 1990s, however, the breakdown of Soviet markets, establishment of new border regimes, and civil unrest all combined to cripple the country's agriculturally based economy.

Like most of the country, the village of Răscăieţi, where I conducted fieldwork, has fared poorly during the past twenty years. During the Soviet period, this village on the Nistru River boasted two collective farms—one focused on vegetable production for seed stock, and the other on grape and fruit production. The decollectivization of these farms provided most village households with private land, and thus the opportunity to increase self-provisioning.

Legislation facilitating decollectivization in Moldova was passed in 1991 and 1992, but most redistribution took place through the National Land Program of 1998–2000 (see Gorton and White 2003: 308, 314; Csaki and Lerman 2000: 9). The total land holdings for the village of Răscăieţi are 4,783 hectares; more than half of this amount (2,432 hectares) is zoned for agriculture. Private houses and their adjacent gardens account for 247 ha of land, and an additional 209 ha of land is devoted to gardens beyond the confines of individual houses. Until 2007, newly formed families were eligible for 0.15 ha allotments for housing and gardens, but the allotment size has been decreased to 0.12 ha in accord with national law.[4] The allotments are free to new families, but households pay an annual tax of 1 leu/sotă (i.e., 12 lei for 12 ha, approximately 1 USD); the tax goes into the village budget, but because it is set by national law, the village cannot raise or lower the amount. Other tax rates are set for different kinds of landholdings.[5] The village has a reserve of 507 ha for the establishment of new houses, but young families do not necessarily know that they are eligible for this land, and in other cases prefer to buy or rent old houses in the center of the village rather than receive new land in less favorable districts.[6]

Although some land was privatized and distributed in the mid 1990s, most was distributed in 1999–2000. At this time, the village distributed 1,433 shares of land to 1,429 eligible individuals. Full shares in arable land, orchard, and vineyard totaling 1.22 ha were distributed to all individuals registered as working on either collective farm as of 1992,[7] with more complex formulas applied to the allotments given to teachers and workers in village administration and other public institutions. Because only former farm workers received land shares, no one born after 1976 received any land; by 2009, this meant that the village's youngest families (headed by adults in their twenties and early thirties) were among those who had not received land during the decollectivization process. A more extensive study of provisioning strategies would examine these families as a separate category. Here it is important to note only that the desire to own land for the purposes of house-provisioning is strong even among these younger adults; those I surveyed had either inherited or purchased land, or expected to do so soon.

The shares in Răscăieţi are smaller than the national average of 1.56–2.0 ha, but the average landowner still owns more land than does a quarter of the national population.[8] The land shares from the former collective farms, like individual houses and the land on which they sit, can be inherited, sold, and otherwise transferred between owners. Most owners who do not want to farm their own agricultural land do not consider the option of selling it to another owner, or even back to the village, but rather rent it out to one of the village's two successor cooperative farms, which now farm 55 percent of the village's total agricultural land. Landowners who have rented their land to the cooperatives receive a quantity of wheat and sunflower seeds calculated by a government-set formula based on the size of their land.

During the past twenty years of postsocialism, Moldova has experienced several waves of economic instability and transformation. Even before decollectivization, many households turned increasingly toward self-provisioning. For example, a librarian recounted that around 1992, cow ownership in the village increased dramatically. In her neighborhood, the number of cows peaked at 360, and then declined so that in 2009, there were only 76.[9] The increase in cows, she said, was related to severe delays (up to six and even eight months) in salary payments—with a cow, one was guaranteed milk, which could be drunk or eaten as cheese or butter, sold, or bartered for other products. Cow ownership particularly increased among educated "specialists"—who had relied more heavily than others on cash salaries.

Even in the first few years after decollectivization, however, most households did not seek to use their land as an exclusive source of self-provisioning. For a few years, the continued functioning of national and export markets in vegetables, fruit, grapes, and wine meant that households could sell their excess products and use the cash proceeds to buy the remainder of what they needed. In this village, for example, grapes and wine represented major cash infusions into household budgets until at least 2005, when a Russian ban on Moldovan wines resulted in the bankruptcy of many village factories. Sales of excess grapes could bring sums in the range of 8,000 lei (roughly 667 USD) into household budgets, and still leave enough wine for the household's own needs. Through the harvest of 2007, many households still sold grapes to wine factories in nearby villages, but in 2009, only a few households succeeded in selling their grapes to private buyers, mostly from Transnistria. The reported sums from selling grapes in 2009, at 3–6 lei/kg, ranged from 175 to 350 USD.

A minority of households are determined to live off the agricultural allotments they received when the collective farms were dismantled, but most continue to purchase substantial quantities of food to supplement what they produce themselves. The public representation of most households as "self-sufficient" is so strong, however, that the degree of mixed provisioning and the importance of purchased goods (even staples like potatoes and tomatoes) only became visible through the detailed questioning of households.

## Household Provisioning: How Much is Enough?

During February–March 2010, I conducted a survey of twenty-five households using the standard questionnaire developed for the Economy and Ritual Project Group.[10] The results from the survey are suggestive, though not conclusive, about dominant patterns for household provisioning.[11] More than half (fourteen) of the households reported that they receive no salaries; ten households receive a salary, but only three of those receive two salaries; and only one household receives its primary income from owning and operating a small business. Of the fourteen households without salaries, six receive their primary income from a household member working abroad, and a seventh has recently switched from labor abroad to work in the domestic construction industry, which still requires lengthy absences from the village.[12] Another six of the fourteen households without salaries include older members who receive a pension. The lack of any salary in village households is a constant across households of all age groups. No households reported receiving unemployment compensation from the state, and only four receive social benefits. As one informant explained, only those who have no land can register to receive unemployment benefits—a reflection of the state's own expectation that people can and should meet their needs through self-provisioning before turning to the state. Yet people do not turn exclusively to self-provisioning from their land; only one of the eight households that receives neither salary nor pension has turned to working the land as its primary mode of livelihood.

Questions about self-provisioning and, more particularly, self-sufficiency emerged in the process of conducting the survey. The questionnaire was designed as a comparative research instrument to provide an overview of general patterns of economic behavior across the six field sites under study in our collective project. Questions on household provisioning, for example, were intended to stratify respondents (and field sites) according to whether they could be said to operate primarily at the "house," "community," or "market" level of economy (Gudeman 2008). We therefore asked respondents about different types of income, whether or not they self-provisioned, whether they kept reserves, what constituted their major fixed expenses, "gifts," and the kinds of things that they were likely to lend or borrow. The section on self-provisioning asked whether respondents grow food; hunt or fish; gather (herbs, mushrooms, wood); make house repairs; and sew. After having completed several surveys it was clear that all of my respondents—regardless of their purported social status, or other sources of income—were reporting nearly universal efforts to self-provision as if their domestic economy were "closed" (Spittler 2008: 93). In the final results, all twenty-five households reported growing their own food; only two households do not keep any chickens or other fowl; and in both cases their absence is reported as an interruption to the household's past and future practices. The only form of self-provisioning villagers rarely noted was sewing new clothes. Very few households acknowledged widespread or persistent forms of "help" from others.[13] In conjunction with widespread assertions that "we do everything" it became necessary to attempt some more detailed probing of the extent and limits of self-provisioning among village households.

Efforts to determine self-sufficiency are notoriously complex. From the 1960s to the 1980s, for example, historians debated a "self-sufficiency hypothesis" for the American South, disagreeing about the best ways to calculate per capita production and consumption of grains and meat across plantations and farms of varying sizes (e.g., Gallman 1970). Yet even when regions could be determined to be self-sufficient, significant numbers of individual households were not (Ford 1985: 265–266).[14] Moreover, although these calculations only address two food types, evidence from places closer to contemporary Moldova, in both space and time, indicate that households also shift the components of consumption around, especially with regard to meat substitutes (Acheson 1997: 223; Caldwell 2007: 48). Julianna Acheson's (1997) detailed study of household budgets reveals that Slovak villagers intensified their household gardening and food processing dramatically from 1989 to 1993, but could not produce more than 40 percent of their needs without becoming full-time farmers, and that most were reluctant to undertake such drastic life changes and the attendant economic risks.[15] Instead, household budgets and ethnographic observation indicate that villagers substituted cheaper food when they could, but ultimately simply ate much less during the early years of postsocialism (229).[16] Acheson observed that household consumption patterns also include substantial quantities of uncalculated and incalculable "gifts," and the possibility that household size and composition might shift in response to food constraints. It is generally agreed that expanded contextual information about available resources and other social practices is necessary for understanding whether and how households succeed in achieving self-sufficiency.

In the course of conducting the questionnaire, I gradually added questions about landholdings, whether or not allotments were rented to the cooperative farms, and whether key starches—potatoes, grain, and corn—as well as oil were "enough" for the household's annual needs.[17] Although the questionnaire included questions about the quantities of food that respondents acquired through the various provisioning strategies, my respondents were generally vague in their answers except those regarding livestock. I initially hoped that the questions I added would yield some sense of the thresholds for sufficiency. The information about a house's landholdings, number of members, and whether it has "enough" to meet their needs suggest that self-provisioning is a flexible and creative endeavor, difficult to capture in any questionnaire.

## Combinations of Land and Provisions

All households that received land claim to be growing (nearly) all of their food, but in fact, very few actually do. Most households with land, whether they farm it or rent it out, have enough wheat,[18] sunflower oil, and wine for their annual needs; tomatoes grown in house gardens, fruit from garden trees or orchard allotments,[19] and meat (mostly chicken and duck) are also adequately supplied. But potatoes, onions, carrots, cabbages, and beets— all winter staples—are almost universally reported as being purchased for much of the year. Potatoes, especially, are a point of concern for most households; only two out of twenty-five reported growing enough for their own annual consumption, and several told me that the lack of irrigation or presence of moles prevented their growth.

Data gathered by the National Bureau of Statistics in a Household Budget Survey indicate that rural Moldovan households do not normally provide all their own food. Even during good harvests, rural households purchase up to 51 percent of the food they eat, and the percentage has increased in recent years (United Nations 2012: 13). On average, rural households produce 35.8 percent of the cereals they consume; 37.6 percent of the milk; 50.5 percent of the meat; 74.5 percent of the eggs; 40.3 percent of the potatoes; 51.1 percent of the vegetables; and 72.1 percent of the fruit (National Bureau of Statistics 2010: 128). The shortfall in self-provisioning is not only a factor of land quantity, but of its use. Martin Petrick calculated that the average farming household devotes 19 percent of the harvest from its private lands to feeding livestock, 55 percent to feeding its members, and still has a remaining 26 percent of its harvest (mostly apples, grapes, and some milk) to sell (2000: 19). Petrick's calculations, which incorporate some fieldwork, differ from those of the Household Budget Survey, and agree more closely with my questionnaire results: households with an average land allotment can produce enough grain, meat, and milk for their own needs. The question, then, is why so few apparently do.

Very few households come close to supplying all of their food needs directly from the land. Of the twenty-five households I surveyed, only one actually attempts to provision itself without an external source of cash income. This couple nearly succeeds (see Cash 2015), but occasionally sells milk to neighbors and close friends to raise the small amount of cash necessary to pay "unavoidable" costs. One other household also reported coming close to supplying its own needs from a total of 83 *sote* of land with very little need to purchase food, clothes, or fuel. Unlike other households, this one even reported sewing its own clothes and repairing shoes. Nevertheless, this family had a stable income of two salaries from seasonal agricultural work, the social benefits for families with many children, and the proceeds from selling or bartering surplus milk, meat, and grapes.

The following five cases outline combinations of land and provisioning strategies. Land holdings were normally reported in terms of *sote*; there are 100 *sote* in a hectare. Also, although land claimants normally received 4 *cote* (shares) each in the 1999 distribution (see note 6), respondents reported all of their shares as a single *cotă*, and thus counted totals of 1, 2, or 3 *cote* for their household. Although the initial land distribution was equitable, current allotments vary significantly between households. Patterns of inheritance have left some households with more shares, but there are also other factors. For example, severe flooding in summer 2008 ate away at some land shares in the marshier regions of the village. While many households expected the land to dry out for the 2010 planting, many had permanently lost orchard allotments and were deciding whether to let the land lie fallow or to remove the trees and turn to vegetable production in the allotments; in a few cases, portions of the land itself had physically disappeared in the receding waters.

# 5—A young household consisting of two adults in their early thirties and one child has only 27 *sote* for their house and adjacent yard. They purchased an existing house, but knocked it down and are now slowly building a new house with painstakingly installed ultra-modern fixtures and interior design. They received no land from the collective farm, and have not (yet) inherited any. Although they have not installed a full vegetable garden and raise no animals, they plan to do both, and have already planted raspberry bushes and fruit trees.[20] They buy almost all of their food with money from the husband's work in construction, but gather some fruit, nuts, medicinal herbs, and make their own wine from vines in their yard.

#15—This household contains two adults in their fifties and supplies limited amounts of food to an adult child living in the city. They have 3 *cote*; 1 each belonging to the husband and wife, and 1 inherited from the husband's mother. In total, the household has 150 *sote*—80 *sote* of arable land, 50 of vineyard, and 20 of orchard. The household often has enough vegetables from its house garden to last an entire year, but says only the potatoes are truly reliable. They have rented all of their arable land, for which they receive enough wheat, and until 2009 had rented the orchard as well. The leader, however, has returned it to them because of the damage done by the flooding. Most of their income comes from the husband's work abroad in Moscow.

#16—Two adults in their fifties and a ten-year-old child make up this household. It has a large household allotment of 15 *sote* including the house, and an additional 35 *sote* on a hillside, which it uses for corn. They have 2 *cote*, one each for husband and wife, but the components differ. The husband, for example, has 81 *sote* of arable land (split in two locations), 20 of vineyard, and 10 of orchard. The wife has 107 *sote* of arable land (also in two locations).They have rented out all of their arable land, and receive a total of 480 kilo of wheat and 74 kilo of sunflower seeds. In contrast to household 15, which has less than half of this family's arable land, this household claims that they only receive enough wheat to last six to eight months of every year, and that they cannot grow enough potatoes or other vegetables (except tomatoes) for their own needs.

#17—In this household, there are two adults in their forties who also provide substantial amounts of food to their adult son and daughter, and the daughter's husband (all living in the capital). This household has 3 *cote* because the husband and wife have 1 share each, and they inherited a third from one of the wife's aunts. Their arable land totals only 72 *sote*, a little less than the average for one full allotment of arable, because the majority of their land is in vineyards. They have not rented out their land, but farm it themselves, and unlike any of the other families, they have their own tractor. This should not increase their yield substantially, however, as one of the benefits of renting out one's land is that it is farmed with more intensive machinery and fertilizers. On this small amount of land, the household grows enough wheat and corn for the couple and most of the needs of an additional three young adults. Some years they are able to grow enough potatoes and vegetables for their needs, as well, but not in 2009.

#24—The final example is another young family. The adults are in their late twenties and they have two children under the age of five. Neither husband nor wife received a land allotment during decollectivization. For the most part, they depend on the husband's work in Moscow six months out of every year, with additional money coming from sales of milk in the village market, and small disbursements from the state for their children, the younger of whom is an invalid. The family has aspirations, however, to produce their own food; they grow vegetables in their home garden, but still need to buy potatoes, onions, carrots, and beets. In the recent past, they received 1 ha (100 *sote* or approximately 1.5 times the normal allotment from decollectivization) of arable land from their marital godfather, which produces enough wheat for the family's needs. The husband has purchased 1 *cotă* (22 *sote*) of vineyard, so that the family will have its own wine.

From these five household examples, it is clear that there is no single threshold for the basic staples of wheat, corn, and oil to demarcate sufficiency. In terms of wheat alone, three households produce "enough" wheat on plot sizes ranging from 72 to 100 *sote* to feed two adults and various combinations of minor and adult children living in the city; but a fourth household can feed two adults and a child for only six to eight months on the wheat that it produces on a plot of 188 *sote*. If the wheat is recalculated in terms of the average yield of 2.8 kg/*sotă*, the situation is no less confusing; even if we only consider how the wheat is used to feed the two adults that are in every household. In this case, three households succeed in feeding their members with average quantities of 100.5 kg, 112 kg, and 140 kg per person. In other words, since each of these households also feeds additional dependents, semi-dependents, and livestock, per capita consumption among the adults of the household is actually lower than the regional average of 114 kg/person. Yet household 16 does not have enough wheat with 240 kg/person at its disposal—more than double the regional average of consumption. How can these differences be explained? The difference is not with livestock holdings: household 16 has one cow, but so do the households that do have enough grain, except 17 (which prefers to raise pigs); household 24 has two cows. Household 16 is clearly pursuing very different strategies of household provisioning than the others, but it is not clear whether its members are eating differently from the others, or giving more food away to their younger and poorer neighbors or to their five adult children (all reported as having their own household budgets).

A more detailed questionnaire would help to clarify some aspects of household consumption patterns, but it might also distract attention from the immediate conclusions borne out by this small sample in combination with ethnographic observation.[21] Part of the art of household management is concerned precisely with balancing different combinations of resources. Moldovans themselves often cannot articulate how they allocate resources to "make ends meet," and identify this as one of the major differences between their "economy" and that of Americans and Western Europeans. In the case of provisioning, village households eat bread baked from their own wheat, store-bought bread, home-grown potatoes, purchased noodles, rice, and potatoes, gifted ritual breads, and—as a last resort and special treat— *mamăligă*.[22] *Mamăligă* is associated with poverty because it is a bread substitute, but it is also associated with childhood; its very name evokes associations with *mamă* (mother), and adults, especially men, appreciate it as a special treat. During the 2009–2010 winter, the household I stayed with ate progressively more *mamăligă* as the winter progressed, much to the delight of the husband and unexpected visitors, who wondered aloud to each other, "why don't we eat *mamăligă* more often?" There was never an answer, but probably the explanation is quite similar to why the household's cows ate progressively more pumpkins as the winter progressed, but then had their rations switched in order to leave "enough" pumpkins for the household's remaining needs. Cows, like people, eat a variety of foods, and their owners keep track of the approximate balance of hay and dried grasses, corn, and pumpkins that are available over the winter months, knowing that each food type also has different nutritional components. Household heads also keep track of, and adjust, their own consumption patterns in an ongoing balance, so that "enough" is a quantity relative to other supplies, whether home-grown or purchased.

The importance of balancing available resources is not specific to the postsocialist period, but the privatization of land has introduced new variables to household budgeting and management strategies. The households that are now most vulnerable to crop failures, food price increases, and economic uncertainty are those who have "continued" their membership in collective farming by renting out all their land (United Nations 2012). The government sets rental terms that are more favorable to owners than lessors, so those who rent are guaranteed a set quantity of the harvest (or less commonly, a cash price) regardless of the season's yield or market prices. They must either purchase or otherwise acquire all the remaining food that they cannot grow in their house garden. Households that have not rented out their land, however, can diversify and shift the crops they grow to better match their own consumption patterns.

## Working, Having, and Giving: The Meanings of (Self-)Sufficiency

Achieving sufficiency does not require fixed quantities of any one type of food, but rather a constant adjustment of consumption to the available resources. Moreover, because "having" is ultimately about social status and respectability, houses only achieve self-sufficiency when they account for the needs of others, as well as their own. The relationship between having and giving was first brought to my attention by one of my informants, and borne out by other sections of the questionnaire. Self-sufficiency, it turns out, depends on generosity; having is signaled by giving. Feasting and serving guests with wine signals adequate food supplies, regardless of the reality.[23] On the questionnaire, amid the variability recorded about food supplies, consistent figures were given for how much wine a house needs (200–300 liters per year) and for how much an average feast costs (100

USD or EUR).[24] In the remainder of the chapter, I consider the differences between two neighboring houses; one house belongs to Vera and her son Petrica, and the other to Vasia and Maria.

Vasia and his wife, both trained teachers in their early fifties, have also farmed since decollectivization. Initially, they had one allotment between the two of them, but they later inherited an additional allotment from an elderly neighbor. By 2009–2010, they lived relatively comfortably with two teaching salaries, one medical pension, a garden, two allotments of land (used for corn and vegetables), and the majority of oil and flour that one of their friends, who had moved to the capital, received for the land shares that she had rented to the successor cooperative. At home, they had one cow and a calf, and roughly 100 ducks and chickens from a surprisingly good hatching season. Managing these extensive resources was hard work, however, and the couple had long days beginning normally at 6 A.M. and lasting until 10 P.M., with few breaks except those brought by visitors, phone calls, or mealtimes.

In contrast, their neighbor, Vera, also in her early fifties, lives alone for most of the year. Her husband is deceased, and her children grown; the son works irregularly in Moscow, staying with his mother when he returns to the village. She has had a variety of jobs, at various points having been a brigade leader on the collective farm and also a beautician. Now she receives a single medical pension, rents her share of land to the successor collective for oil and flour, and occasionally cuts hair at home. Her strongest social relations are with her grown children and her neighbors, many of whom are *cumetrii* (coparents); she rarely visits with former co-workers who live, for the most part, in the village's newer neighborhoods, which are at least a twenty-minute walk away. Her home garden is barely tended, and she lives largely on rotating store credit between her pension disbursements. Yet Vera reads and relaxes regularly, and claims not to feel the degree of stress felt by her neighbors, Vasia and Maria, as they try to accomplish herculean quantities of work.

Despite their differences, both houses are considered respectable. Although her neighbors may claim that Vera does not "work," somehow she manages to avoid being labeled "poor," or "lazy," and although she is known to enjoy a drink, she is not considered a "drunkard." Houses like Vera's, that are respectable without being able to provide for their own needs through self-provisioning, reveal the importance of social relations at the heart of self-sufficiency.

Over the past decade, the composition of Vera's household has changed significantly: her husband died, as did a younger son, and a grown daughter married and moved to a nearby village. The family's friends and neighbors often tease the remaining 32-year-old son about his unmarried status, but he has a number of ongoing and casual relations in the village and else-where, and seems to feel little pressure to marry or establish a separate house. The son's continued presence in his mother's house follows a tra-ditional pattern in which the youngest son remains in his parents' house, even after marriage, to care for his parents in old age, and eventually inher-its their house. The mother and son lead separate adult lives; the mother lives alone while her son is working in Russia, and when he returns she often goes to stay with her daughter for extended periods—but they still re-port themselves as a single household, noting that they "share everything" when it comes to money, food, and other resources.

The first time I entered Vera's house, I was shocked by what I saw—bare floors, little furniture, undecorated walls. The house stood in stark contrast to the house owned by Vasia and Maria, with its recently installed indoor toilet and shower, well-appointed rooms, and carefully hung curtains. Vera pointed to her own indoor bathroom as I entered, noting that the family used to have running water as did all the houses in the village center. Now that the central pipes are only opened once per month, however, she has to carry in buckets of water from her holding tank each time she wants to bathe, heating it on the stove. She laughed off the difficulties of the situation, and continued the tour of the house, explaining as we went that she and her husband had begun to furnish their house, as all couples did, but that one of her three children had been an invalid from a young age. The family had put all of their money toward seeking his cure, and never furnished the house. But, she concluded, bare floors are healthier anyway!

Compared to other households, this one produces relatively little of its own food. It currently raises no animals, and also produces no cereal crops for animal feed. Although its garden is smaller and weedier than others, the household proudly reports that it grows vegetables, fruit, and grapes; both mother and son also gather fruit and herbs, while the son fishes but does not hunt. They receive wheat and sunflower seeds as rent for their land shares, and report that they maintain a reserve of vegetables, potatoes, on-ions, garlic, carrots, jam, pickles, compote, racchiu, and wine. On the sur-face of things, the household appears as self-sufficient as many others, and certainly self-reports as such. Like almost all other households, this one also reports that it does not receive gifts, food, or assistance from others. Yet neighbors insist that the appearance of sufficiency is deceptive. Much of the reserve was purchased from local stores on credit, and the household's production levels are quite modest. In fall 2009, though the household col-lected 1 ton of grapes, like many other households, they only produced 50 liters of wine. The wine may have met the ordinary needs of two adults, but the household also used it to pay workers on several occasions, and by early spring 2010 had already depleted their supply. Without wine of their own, the son turned several times to his neighbors for wine to host visitors; the neighbors gave, though not always very happily.

Despite the many ways in which this household diverges from an "ideal" household, its generosity redeems it. Other villagers often make positive remarks about the family's devotion to its handicapped child, acknowledging the financial strain that it placed on the house. The family is not considered to have been particularly pious or frugal. They did not "scrimp and save" or restrain from feasting, drinking, and other pleasures, but they gave, often to their own detriment. The household's tendency to give was marked even on questionnaire results. Very few households reported that they made financial donations to others, while this one said that it "often" did. On another question that asked respondents what they would do if they received 50,000 EUR unexpectedly, this household immediately responded that half of the sum would be given to sick children, and did not designate a use for the remaining half. The sum of 50,000 EUR corresponds to the cost of a small apartment in the capital, and most respondents said they would use the sum to purchase housing for their children. Other common responses focused on household improvements, educating children, or receiving medical treatment for chronic health problems. Only four other households indicated that they would donate even a small portion of the sum. Interestingly, three of these households are headed by women who have confronted social marginality through divorce. All households demonstrate the status of having by giving, but those that actually have less often give in more publicly visible forms to achieve and maintain respectability. By giving to others, those who have suffered misfortune (especially if it prevented them from establishing or maintaining an ideal house) publicly perform gratitude for the gifts they have received in the past and recognize the suffering of others.

## To Have Is to Give; To Give Is to Have

Vera's case reveals how status and respect are premised on a house's demonstrated commitment to self-sufficiency and not on its actual success in achieving a closed domestic economy. Vera and her husband achieved the threshold of social respectability early in their marriage. The couple married in 1968, began to build their house shortly thereafter, and had three children. When Vasia and Maria arrived in the neighborhood in the early 1980s, Vera and her husband helped them to construct their house, and accepted the invitation to baptize the new couple's two children. Through the baptism, Vera and her husband became *cumetri* with Vasia and Maria. Several other families also requested that the couple baptize their children, serving as social recognition that Vera and her husband had achieved the basic level of social status in the village. They were *ca lume*. In the intervening years, Vera and her husband upheld their part of *cumetri* relations, especially with Vasia and Maria, through "respect," and by providing help and assistance on many occasions.

Today, Vera and her son continue to honor the household's social relationships, giving help and assistance, mostly through labor, but also material. Vera, for example, often appears unbidden to help Maria with tasks such as killing and plucking chickens, preparing jams, and battening covers on crops in impending thunderstorms. A woman who "had" a more extensive household of her own to manage, like another neighbor with whom Vasia and Maria are also *cumetri,* would not be able to "give" such extensive impromptu help. Petrica also appears, unbidden, to help Vasia and Maria finish large-scale projects. For example, when Vasia and Maria hired workers to cut wood for fuel, Petrica appeared to sweep brush and branches from the street when they had finished. Even when Vera and Petrica help for long periods of time, they are not paid, nor is their help calculated and remembered as a specific quantity; it is simply subsumed under the general line of "being neighbors." By the same token, Petrica and Vera are always fed when they appear near mealtime; the family sometimes seeks them out to offer them specially prepared dishes; and they are given wine for the asking when their own runs out—all also under the general rubric of "being neighbors." Most of the time, the unequal flow of food and wine from one neighbor's house into another goes unremarked and is therefore unrecordable on questionnaire forms.

## Give, But Don't Borrow ... The Obligations of Self-Sufficiency

The status accorded to Vera's household is based on a combination of three factors. First, the household has always aspired to be self-sufficient; it embarked on the initial step, symbolized prominently by house ownership, and continues to self-represent itself as self-sufficient by maintaining reserves of food and wine (even when they are purchased), and by denying high levels of assistance from others. Second, the household's early efforts to achieve "self-sufficiency" were recognized by others who extended and accepted offers of ritual kinship; the household has maintained these relations. Third, the relations of ritual kinship, like those of neighborliness more generally, are premised on relations of generosity and giving; Vera's household gives generously, and is recognized for giving "beyond its means." Older adults, for example, frequently despair of Petrica ever establishing his own household—not only because he seems so disinterested, but also because he is "too good" and likely to give away, rather than amass, any resources that he might gather.

Households that meet the basic threshold of self-sufficiency must give in order to maintain their social respectability. To a large degree, giving accompanies ritual activities in the guise of lavish hospitality, extravagant spending (on hospitality), and gifts. All households, for example, reported observing an extensive annual ritual cycle of religious holidays and life-cycle events, including six holidays recognized by national law (Cash 2011b). Respondents often tired of enumerating the number of feasts they hosted during the twelve months of 2009, but most reported at least nine occasions, and some listed up to fifteen. When we consider that the absolute minimum cost for preparing one of these feasts (for eight to ten people) was calculated by several respondents at 300–400 lei (roughly 25–33 USD), and that more common estimates were given in the range of 100 USD or EUR, it becomes clear that the observation of ritual occasions is an expensive undertaking relative to household incomes. Much of this cost is not absolutely necessary. The only socially obligatory feast foods (stuffed cabbage or grape leaves, chickpea stew, and wine) only require the purchase of rice, and women acknowledge that they know how to make most of the other purchased foods from household reserves. The appearance of purchased foods—dishes heavy with mayonnaise, hard cheese, smoked meats and fishes, brightly wrapped chocolates, and champagne—all signal that a house has gone beyond its means to sponsor the feast.

The positive values associated with giving also appear in questionnaire responses. The questionnaire included two questions about borrowing and lending. As with the questions about provisioning, they provide a much better picture of what households ideally do, than what they actually do. In my observations, households borrow frequently from neighbors and relatives. My host's family, for example, regularly lent objects to at least seven other households, and the relationship was largely reciprocal. Something was borrowed or lent at least once per day. When I visited other houses, there was invariably a phone call or a knock at the gate, with a neighbor requesting to borrow something.

Yet in survey responses, a full ten of the surveyed households deny that they ever borrow anything. Those that acknowledged borrowing claimed to borrow primarily work tools, household appliances, or dishes for special occasions. The second question on lending was phrased in the negative, asking whether there were some items that a household would never lend. Twelve households reported that they would lend anything, often underscoring their own generosity by setting the limit at their health, life, children, or spouse. Another ten households claimed that they do not lend precisely the items that people report borrowing most often—household appliances and work tools. These tools are considered costly and essential to the house, and their owners fear that they will be broken or not returned. Nevertheless, it is clear that they do lend these items when asked. Often, one person in a household is considered more generous, so the household can maintain the position that it does not lend important tools, and yet continue to do so anyway. As the head of household 25 explained, "Neighbors come and ask, and if I have it, I give, even though my wife says not to."

The consequences of a household having and refusing to give are potentially severe. One of the village's two leaders, for example, has a reputation for being stingy and greedy. His reputation stems, in part, from the way he formed the village's second successor farm, taking advantage of a moment when the first leader seemed to be on the brink of retirement and "stealing" many of his contracts. By his own account, and that of people close to him, the second leader has taken on high debt loads to the detriment of his own family to farm the contracted land, all the more so because he has engaged in the higher-risk cultivation of orchards that the first leader does not farm. I was befriended by the man's wife and daughter, who took an interest in my research project and invited me to their house on a few occasions. On the first visit, following accounts of the man's rapidly increasing wealth, I was surprised to discover that the family's house was finished very simply. With the exception of a newly redecorated bedroom, it was not much more well-appointed than Vera's house, and it also had no running water. The house itself hardly lent proof to claims that the leader was getting rich at the expense of other villagers. When I volunteered this opinion in response to one of his critics, however, the woman immediately countered my assertion that he had nothing to give, by saying that God had already taken everything away. The refusal to give, even when one is "poor," can be punished by divinity by taking away one's health, family members, or luck.

## Conclusions: Having Enough to Give

In the 1930s, budget studies among peasant households in Romania (including Bessarabia) concluded that landholdings under 3 hectares were insufficient for supplying a household's basic food needs (Hitchins 1994: 341). To survive, "households had to limit their consumption of food and be satisfied with inadequate clothing and substandard housing" (341). This reduction of "needs" was clearly the response of the great majority of peasant households. At the same time, households with landholdings between 3 and 10 hectares also appear to have had difficulty "making ends meet"; though they produced "enough" food for themselves, the costs of doing so outstripped the value of their production. Across interwar Romania, even the 5 to 20 percent of villagers whose landholdings of 10 to 50 hectares enabled them to comfortably self-provision usually supplemented their incomes with nonagricultural activities, suggesting that even 50 hectares of land did not provide "enough" to achieve an idealized vision of self-sufficient peasant life (339)!

Today, households that attempt to self-provision in Moldova must do so with an average of 4.21 ha (see note 6). In the village where I conducted research landholdings are smaller, and the average household that received two plots during collectivization has only 2.56 ha, including its house garden. Remarkably, the great majority of households reports that this small allotment yields "enough" wheat, oil, animal fodder, fruits, vegetables, meat, and wine to fill their cellars with an annual store of food and wine, and to meet their annual cycle of social obligations, including both expected and unexpected occasions of hospitality, celebration, and mourning. How is self-sufficiency possible on such small landholdings when it was apparently impossible on larger holdings in the past?

In the preceding pages, I have interrogated my informants' reports of self-sufficiency, and come to five conclusions. The first conclusion is that it is possible, but rare, for an average-sized household to produce its annual supply of food, with a staple of wheat supplemented by some corn, on 2.56 ha. The second conclusion is that there are no absolute standards for what constitutes "enough" of any food item except wine. Having enough food means, to a large extent, that one shifts and balances consumption over the year so that reserves do not run out before the next harvest. The third conclusion is that most households do not actually attempt to produce all of their own food, but rely on money from waged work, state pensions, or remittances to fill in the gaps that self-provisioning leaves. In some cases, especially among younger households, most reserves are purchased in any given year. Even when the land does not yield "enough," a household can have enough by stocking its reserves through other means. The fourth conclusion is that even households that purchase substantial quantities of food consider themselves self-sufficient (i.e., both "having" and "doing everything") if they are engaged with self-provisioning at any level. Fifthly, and most importantly, a household's status is gauged by others on two principles: what the household has (in terms of house, reserves, and land), and what it gives.

These findings are important for producing a better picture of the local economy because they call attention to the art of household management and the importance of sharing. All of the existing data for production and consumption in Moldova focuses on either the individual or the household. It assumes that everything that is purchased or produced is consumed by the purchasing unit, and does not track what is given away. Other anthropologists have already called attention to this weakness in standard assessments of economic well-being. Jane Guyer (2004: 131–151), for example, succeeded in explaining the "inconsistencies" that have consistently been found in household budget surveys of Ghanaian households. In contradiction to Engel's Law, by which households spend proportionately less on food as their incomes increase, Ghanaian households at all but the very highest income levels spend roughly similar percentages on food. Guyer's ethnography revealed that this is so because richer households feed poorer ones, in a flexible and descending scale. Because the food is offered as hospitality appropriate to diverse occasions and social relationships, it goes unrecorded by census takers who assume that only household members consume the household's resources. In Moldova, as in Ghana, households give substantial portions of what they have to relatives, neighbors, and ritual kin, and—in rural areas—much purchased food is specifically designated for giving to others at feasts. Who gives to whom and how much is difficult to track, however, because people do not publicly acknowledge how much they have given to others, or how much they have received. While people may not fully know what they give or take, the art of "having enough" nevertheless incorporates an ongoing assessment of what is given and taken through social relationships.

At a broader level, my findings reveal that self-sufficiency is primarily an ideology about how individuals and households should obtain and demonstrate social respectability through economic activity. Self-sufficiency does not refer to a single set of economic behaviors, or even principles, that ensure a household's independence from market relations. It does not even refer to behaviors that ensure independence from other households, although people often wish it did. Instead, the cluster of words, phrases, and gestures that can be glossed as "self-sufficiency" convey the centrality of social relations in economic activity. In rural Moldova, economic activity is imagined as ideally centered on the house; household members should provide for their own needs. The commitment to pursuing a house economy constitutes the threshold of social respectability, and is symbolized by the display and outlay of material resources in the form of house construction and furnishing. Yet socially respectable persons are also expected to recognize and bear responsibility for the needs of others outside their house. They do so by giving: lending tools, offering hospitality, and hosting feasts. Self-sufficient households are worthy of respect not because they succeed in cutting themselves off from wider social relations, but because they are committed to balancing their own needs and desires against those of others. How they do so is a delicate art, but erring on the side of generosity gains greater social approval.

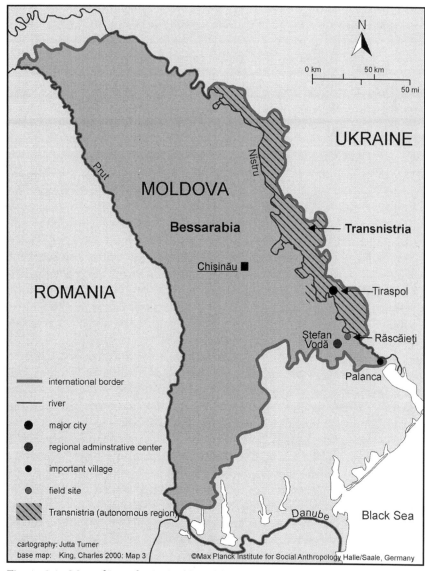

**Figure 2.1.** Map of Jennifer R. Cash's Field Site.

**Jennifer R. Cash** received her Ph.D. in Anthropology from Indiana University. Before joining the Economy and Ritual project she held teaching positions at Indiana University, Franklin College, the University of Pittsburgh, and University College London. She is the author of *Villages on Stage: Folklore and Nationalism in the Republic of Moldova* (2011).

## Notes

1. The fieldsite and fieldwork featured in this chapter are described in more detail in Cash (2015). As for that chapter, in addition to the collaborative work of the Economy and Ritual group, comments from Christoph Brumann, Virgiliu Bîrlădeanu, Varvara Buzilă, Ludmila Cojocaru, Jane Guyer, Eeva Kesküla, Patrice Ladwig, and Mihály Sárkány have greatly improved my analysis. I, of course, am responsible for any shortcomings or misinterpretations that remain.

2. This includes even how one hangs laundry out to dry in the yard, or—in urban areas—on balconies.

3. Studies of rural social structure throughout Romania during the interwar period revealed several levels of distinction between peasant households based on their ownership of land, animals, tools, patterns of hiring workers, and ability to meet their own needs from working their own land (see Hitchins 1994: 339–340). Some villages in Moldova maintain social distinctions involving land ownership that date to the Ottoman period (Cash 2011a: 141, 143). I did not encounter either type of historic distinction in the village where I conducted fieldwork, but rather heard a moral discourse about households and their self-sufficiency that reflects some Soviet influence on the rural social structure. Other adjectives used to distinguish households include saying that a rural family consists of *oameni simpli* (simple people) in contrast to *intellectuali* (intellectuals); and individuals can be *muncitor* (hard-working) or *leneş* (lazy). Households can be *nevoiţi* (needy) but still have the moral qualities associated with being *gospodari*; and they can be *mai saraci* (more poor) or *mai bogaţi* (more rich) without differences in their moral evaluation. Normally, people avow that *noi nu suntem oameni bogaţi* (we are not rich people), and disparage individuals and families that think they are *mai sus* (above) others. In many cases, adults over forty have retained the social reputation they gained during the Soviet period (e.g., accusations of illegitimate gain still hang around the reputations of some people who worked in farm administration). This complicates social judgment of the household, but the spouses of greedy, stingy, or corrupt individuals may still be judged a *gospodar/gospodină*, and (if a woman) as being in her place (*la locul ei*).

4. In the 1980s, the parcels were even larger—at 0.25 ha (25 *sote*), which may account for some of the appeal to young families of buying existing houses, rather than accepting the free allotments from the mayor's office. In some years, as well, families received additional allotments for each child.

5. The taxes for an average share of vineyard, for example, amount to 24 lei (about 2 USD) and 11 lei (less than 1 USD) for orchard.

6. Houses in the center of the village are within 15 minutes walking distance to all public buildings (school, kindergartens, mayor's office, medical center, post office, culture house, church, and bus stop); they also have easy access to water, which is pumped from the main aquifer into private holding tanks at least once per month. Houses in outlying regions of the village must arrange to have barrels of water delivered to their holding wells.

7. A share of land, referred to as a *cotă* or *parcelă*, is not a fixed quantity. In this village, 1 *cotă* is 0.22 ha of vineyard, 0.11 ha of orchard, 0.27 ha of arable land in the

swampy section of the village, and 0.62 ha of land on the village's hillside. Most people received a total of 4 *cote*—1 each of the above categories. As evident in the following descriptions, current allotments vary. In other locations with larger collective farms or smaller populations, shares were larger—up to 3 hectares per person for nearby villages in Moldova, and of up to 50 ha/person in Ukraine.

8. The low figure of 1.56 ha is provided by a paper published by cadastral experts in the Ministry of Agriculture (Guțu, Gorgan, and Guțu 2009: 2), who were advocating for a new land redistribution program that would overcome the process of excessive plot fragmentation in many locales. A United Nations report (2012: 7) calculates the average as 1.8 ha, but notes that a full 25 percent of private owners hold less than 1 ha. This report records an average garden allotment of 0.21 ha, which is slightly smaller than the allocations made in Răscăieți during the 1980s, but nearly double the 0.12 ha currently available to new households. Yet another study (Petrick 2000: 12) indicates that the median size of a private plot is 2 ha. Although all three sources use official data, the differences arise because there is no formal differentiation in official statistics between the private landholdings of large agricultural firms, individual commercial farmers, allocations to former farm workers, and the holdings of people who have land but did not receive shares during decollectivization. Petrick (2000: 12) provides the best discussion.

9. As far as I can tell, these cows were not privatized from the collective farms. Even though 1992 marked the beginning of one phase of privatization in Moldova, most farms did not issue entitlements to either land or assets until at least 1998 because high levels of debt made it difficult to calculate the actual assets (including livestock, grape vines, and trees) that were available for privatization (Csaki and Lerman 2001: 5). Interviews with former farm workers and administrators did not reveal any variations from the national trend. Instead, the proliferation of village cows in the 1990s was described as a result of "gifts" from neighbors, relatives, or friends that were valued as a response to the hardships of economic uncertainty and the conflicts in neighboring Transnistria. Cows must be bred yearly to continue milk production, so a house that owns a milking cow is faced with an annual decision of whether to slaughter the calf or to raise it. The number of cows in the village in any given year thus reflects a household's efforts to balance its resources (labor and access to fodder) against its needs for milk and meat, a cash sale of the animal, and pity (*jele*) for calves (especially the female ones).

10. All interviews were conducted in Romanian; Corina Rezneac translated the questionnaire.

11. Respondents were selected through snowball sampling. Despite the possibility for bias, this approach was unavoidable since villagers were unwilling to complete the questionnaire unless I had been recommended to them. I did take care, however, to explain to respondents the need for a representative sample, and a key informant periodically reviewed the list of households I had interviewed to identify points of over- or under-representation based on the head of household's age, neighborhood, and employment status.

12. In each of these cases, a man works abroad in construction. There are many households where the worker is a female, but none of these households were willing to be interviewed. My host family suspected that it was "shame" that kept men with

wives working abroad from speaking with me, but there is also an important socio-logical dimension to the lack of male respondents in the survey. In general, when I asked to speak with the head of household, I was referred to an adult woman. In ethnic Moldovan families, both husband and wife share the role of head of house-hold; the man is ordinarily considered the "higher" head (as in the expression, "the man is the head, and the woman is the neck"), but the woman has primary respon-sibility for money and household provisioning.

13. The questionnaire distinguished four types of possible help—gifts, food, assistance, and borrowed tools or equipment. The question about gifts was almost universally interpreted as referring to presents on special occasions (e.g., birthdays), which fif-teen households acknowledged. As a more abstract category, only three acknowl-edged "gifts" coming from friends and relatives in better material situations. Only five households acknowledged receiving food from others; two acknowledged "as-sistance" in the form of babysitting. Several acknowledged borrowing tools, but made it clear that they paid for the use of tractors (the most common "borrowed" item), and usually also paid the owner of other specialized electric tools (like weld-ing torches).

14. Lacy Ford (1985: 265–266) reapplied Gallman's calculations (that demonstrated the self-sufficiency of southern cotton plantations) to a smaller sample of South Carolina upcountry farms, and found that farms with 25 acres or fewer could not achieve self-sufficiency in grains or meat, but bought the surplus products of local farms with higher yields. Farms of 26–50 acres had varying success, with some producing significant grain and meat surpluses, but only 59 percent of total farms achieved sufficiency in meat, and 80 percent in grains. At the highest levels of self-sufficiency (51–100 acre farms), only 87 percent of farms achieved self-suffi-ciency, even as the most productive farms in this cohort produced surpluses of well over 30 percent of their needs.

15. Household gardens in Acheson's study were quite small, in the range of 7 to 15 square meters. Vegetables and fruit produced from these plots could meet the household's needs for a maximum of six to eight months. Households produced a limited quantity of their own meat (fowl), eggs, and occasionally milk, but pur-chased supplementary quantities, along with all bread and grains. The few farmers who had taken advantage of land privatization succeeded in full self-provisioning with 16.5 ha of land, and only needed 1.5 ha to grow potatoes and other vegetables (1997: 262–265).

16. Melissa Caldwell's study of a Moscow soup kitchen in the late 1990s also reveals how quantitatively low supplies of food can be rendered as "enough," and the use of strategies to "stretch" key meal components—tea, soup, and bread, for example—thus rendering a meal normal, even when it may be deficient in taste or nutrition (2004: 41). Importantly, meal recipients also appear to be diverting the income they do have toward social obligations rather than food (86).

17. I used the verbal phrase most commonly used by my informants in discussing food reserves, *a ajunge pentru un an*—do they last an entire year?

18. Households that reported an actual quantity of wheat received, by their own re-port, approximately 250 kilos per allotment when the land was rented out. The average household size is 2.08 individuals, yielding 120 kg/year/person—enough to

satisfy the regional individual consumption of 114 kg (National Bureau of Statistics 2010: 123), and leave a little leftover.

19. Fruit is also often gathered (from "untended" orchard allotments) and gifted from close relatives.

20. The combination of activities undertaken by this family is an interesting one because it concentrates on three important symbols: a newly built house, (fruit) trees, and wine. I have previously discussed the importance of wine (Cash 2015); as for the importance of the other symbols—there is an expression that, during his lifetime, a man should "build a house, dig a well, and plant a tree."

21. In his (2000) assessment of the viability of Moldova's "peasant farms," based on a sophisticated calculation of average land holdings, labor input, expenditures, and market value of surplus crops, Martin Petrick determined that small-holdings were not viable in market terms. Even reliable cash income from other sources did not enable the average rural household to cross the official poverty threshold. Yet, as he found, numerous rural households still managed to survive. How they did so, he concluded, "is a challenging question that deserves further research" (2000: 22).

22. In the decades preceding socialism, an increasing number of peasants could not afford to eat wheat bread as their staple carbohydrate. Bessarabia, like Romania more generally, was an important granary at the turn of the twentieth century, and much of the annual wheat harvest was exported, even at the expense of domestic consumption (Kaba 1919; Hitchins 1994). Lacking wheat, peasants boiled corn meal to make *mamăligă*, a kind of polenta. Increased corn consumption was accompanied by rising rates of pellagra; between 1888 and 1906, recorded cases of pellagra across Romania increased nearly tenfold from 10,626 to 100,000 (Hitchins 1994: 170).

23. In his study of Slovene settlements, Robert Gary Minnich (1979: 62–72) found a similar situation in which host/guest relations transform relations of mutual assistance and labor exchange into proof of self-sufficiency.

24. At the time of fieldwork, the rate of exchange between the Moldovan leu and the US dollar was 12:1; it was 16:1 with the euro. The rates were similar enough that people often referred to dollars and euros as if they were equivalent currencies.

## References

Acheson, Julianna. 1997. "Traversing Political Economy and the Household: An Ethnographic Analysis of Life after Communism in Kojsov, a Rural Village in Eastern Slovakia." Ph.D. Dissertation, Department of Anthropology, University of Arizona.

Caldwell, Melissa. 2004. *Not by Bread Alone: Social Support in the New Russia.* Berkeley: University of California Press.

———. 2007. "Feeding the Body and Nourishing the Soul: Natural Foods in Postsocialist Russia." *Food, Culture, and Society* 10, no. 1: 43–71.

Cash, Jennifer R. 2010. "Moldova." In *Berg Encyclopedia of World Dress and Fashion,* Vol. 9, East Europe, Russia, and the Caucasus, ed. Djurdja Bartlett, 473–480. New York and Oxford: Berg.

———. 2011a. *Village on Stage: Folklore and Nationalism in the Republic of Moldova.* Berlin: Lit Verlag.

———. 2011b. "Capitalism, Nationalism, and Religious Revival: Transformations of the Ritual Cycle in Postsocialist Moldova." *Anthropology of East Europe Review* 29, no. 2: 181–203.

———. 2015. "Economy as Ritual: The Problems of Paying in Wine." In *Economy and Ritual: Studies of Postsocialist Transformation,* ed. Stephen Gudeman and Chris Hann, 31–51. New York: Berghahn Books.

Chayanov, A. V. 1986 [1924–1925]. *The Theory of Peasant Economy.* Manchester: Manchester University Press.

Csaki, Csaba, and Zvi Lerman. 2001. "Land Reform and Farm Restructuring in Moldova: A Real Breakthrough?" Discussion Paper 5.01, Department of Agricultural Economics and Management, The Hebrew University of Jerusalem. Accessed 28 February 2001 at http://departments.agri.huji.ac.il/economics/en/publications/discussion_papers/2001/index.htm.

DEX. 1998. *Dicționarul Explicativ al Limbii Române* (Romanian Dictionary), 2nd ed. Bucharest: Univers Enciclopedic.

Ford, Lacy. 1985. "Self-Sufficiency, Cotton, and Economic Development in the South Carolina Upcountry, 1800-1860." *The Journal of Economic History* 45, no. 2: 261–267.

Gallman, Robert. 1970. "Self-Sufficiency in the Cotton Economy of the Antebellum South." *Agricultural History* 44, no. 1: 5–23.

Gorton, Matthew, and John White. 2003. "The Politics of Agrarian Collapse: Decollectivisation in Moldova." *East European Politics and Societies* 17, no. 2: 305–331.

Gregory, Chris. 2009. "Whatever Happened to Householding?" In *Market and Society: The Great Transformation Today,* ed. Chris Hann and Keith Hart, 133–159. Cambridge: Cambridge University Press.

Gudeman, Stephen. 2008. *Economy's Tension: The Dialectics of Community and Market.* New York and Oxford: Berghahn Books.

Guțu, Vladimir Gh., Maxim Gorgan, and Dumitru Guțu. 2009. "Privatizarea—Premisă obiectivă a creării sistemului cadastral (Privatization—The Objective Premise for Creating a Cadastral System)." *Studia Universitatis,* seria Științe sociale 8, no. 28: 50–67. Chișinău, USM revistă științifică. Citations are from publication-ready ms. in author's possession.

Guyer, Jane. 2004. *Marginal Gains: Monetary Transactions in Atlantic Africa.* Chicago: University of Chicago Press.

Han, Tong, Thomas Wahl, and Ron Mittelhammer. 2001. "The Effects of Self-Sufficiency on Fruit and Vegetable Consumption of China's Rural Households." *Review of Agricultural Economics* 23, no. 1: 176–184.

Hitchins, Keith. 1994. *Rumania 1866–1947.* Oxford: Clarendon Press.

Kaba, John. 1919. *Politico-Economic Review of Basarabia.* Hoover Commission for Roumania.

Loehr, Rodney. 1952. "Self-Sufficiency on the Farm." *Agricultural History* 26, no. 2: 37–41.

Minnich, Robert Gary. 1979. *The Homemade World of Zagaj: An Interpretation of the "Practical Life" among Traditional Peasant-Farmers in West Haloze—Slovenia, Yugoslavia.* Occasional Paper 18. Bergen: University of Bergen.

Morgen, Sandra. 2001. "The Agency of Welfare Workers: Negotiating Devolution, Privatization, and the Meaning of Self-Sufficiency." *American Anthropologist* 103, no. 3: 747–761.

National Bureau of Statistics of the Republic of Moldova. 2010. "Household Budget Survey." Accessed 28 February 2013 at http://www.statistica.md/pageview .php?l=en&idc=263&id=2206.

Petrick, Martin. 2000. "Land Reform in Moldova: How Viable are Emerging Peasant Farms?" Discussion Paper #28. Institute of Agricultural Development in Central and Eastern Europe (IAMO). Accessed 28 February 2013 at http://www.iamo.de/ dok/dp28.pdf.

Polanyi, Karl. 1957 [1944]. *The Great Transformation. The Political and Economic Origins of Our Time.* Boston: Beacon Press.

Rose, Richard, and Yevgeniy Tikhomirov. 1993. "Who Grows Food in Russia and Eastern Europe?" *Post-Soviet Geography* 34, no. 2: 111–126.

Sahlins, Marshall. 1972. "The Domestic Mode of Production: The Structure of Underproduction." In *Stone Age Economics*, 41–100. New York: Aldine de Gruyter.

Salant, Katharine Blair. 1987. "Marpha Architecture: The Effects of Economic Self-Sufficiency and Development." In *Architecture, Milieu et Societe en Himalaya,* ed. Denis Blamont and Gerard Toffin, 42–76. Paris: Editions du Centre National de la Recherche Scientifique.

Spittler, Gerd. 2008. *Founders of the Anthropology of Work: German Social Scientists of the 19th and Early 20th Centuries and the First Ethnogaphers.* Berlin: Lit.

United Nations. 2012. "Rapid Food Security and Vulnerability Assessment—Moldova." Accessed 28 February 2013 at http://www.un.md/drought/2012/RapidAssess mentMoldova2012Final.pdf.

Yossakrai, Kanokrat. 2006. "Community Power and Integration for 'Sufficiency Economy': Cases of Buddhist, Muslim, and Akha Communities in Thailand." In *Tai Culture: Interdisciplinary Tai Studies Series,* vol. 19, Special issue on Women and Gender in Tai Societies: 197–199.

# 3

# When the Household Meets the State

Ajvar *Cooking and Householding*
*in Postsocialist Macedonia*

MILADINA MONOVA

In this chapter I explore self-sufficiency as ideology and practice through examining the relations of the household with outside forces, mainly those of state and market.[1] The household is a social institution shaped and reshaped through constant interactions with these larger institutions. I illustrate the ideology of self-sufficiency (*samoizdržuvanje*) in Macedonia through focusing on a red pepper dish known as *ajvar*.[2] The story of the preparation of this staple cascaded down from the ideology of state autarky, to regional (republican) autarky, and to the household in the socialist era. I argue that in claiming the superiority of the "homemade" (*domašno*), the antiquity of the tradition, and the pure, healthy quality of its *ajvar*, the household is "domesticating the state" (Creed 1998; Hann 1990). This new tradition appropriated by all ethnic groups (Macedonians, Albanians, Roma, Turks) was made possible by a combination of market forces and state policies, especially those pertaining to self-sufficiency. *Ajvar* is a staple of the winter diet in both towns and villages. In the villages, families may grow their own peppers, but in towns urban dwellers need to purchase a significant quantity in order to meet the needs of the house and to fulfill wider obligations.

I pursued fieldwork among urban households, in the medium-sized city of Prilep. As in many other cities in South-East Europe, in Prilep, houses with gardens prevail over apartment buildings, which facilitates activities relative to domestic economy. I also made direct observations and conducted interviews in the capital, Skopje, where despite distance from family land and the predominant apartment setting *ajvar* cooking remains widespread.

The concept of economic autarky was elaborated at multiple levels in Soviet-type, centrally planned economies. Above the level of "state autarky" there was "block autarky," a concentration of trade within the alliance known as COMECON (Lavigne 1991: 16). An affinity between planning and the maximization of self-sufficiency is also to be found in Western states in which capitalist markets are the dominant principle of economic organization (Holzman 1974). Autarky ideologies are never fully realized. When the Yugoslav state ostensibly promoted autarky at the level of each constituent republic, foreign loans were soon necessary to maintain the fiction; self-sufficiency remained a chimera. We can see exactly the same at the level of the household. To make *ajvar*, industrial peppers are purchased on the market from producers able to offer their commodity at a low price thanks to subsidies. In processing those peppers at home and promoting the meal to the status of a national dish, households respond creatively to the state's social and economic engineering.

In contemporary Macedonia, homemade *ajvar* is considered to be a staple, an indispensable food providing household members with the vegetables and vitamins they need to get through the winter. It is the most important element of the winter supplies (*zimnica*), which include other pickled and conserved products stored by every household in its basement. *Ajvar* is highly valued both in terms of nutritional quality and in terms of the work invested in preparing it. It is said to be "delicious," "pure," and "healthy" precisely because it is homemade and guaranteed by the culinary skills of the *domakjinka* (housewife). In hard times it is said to replace meat, which many people today consider to be too expensive; it is most commonly eaten as an accompaniment to store-bought bread and white cheese. Homemade *ajvar* is commonly contrasted with what people contemptuously call "industrial" or "chemical" *ajvar*. The homemade dish has to be made of "good products," "without additives," in order to extract the best from the pepper. For my informants, the best evidence of the superiority of the *ajvar* over any other homemade dish is that is "exhausting," "time- and work-consuming." The process of making it is said to be "difficult" and "complicated," comprising a series of "tedious," "repetitive," and "physical" tasks. It can only be performed by a team working together, often based on neighbors' mutual aid (*ispomoš*). This, I was told, explains why a house does not offer even small quantities for sale. Every self-respecting household is supposed to cook its own *ajvar*. It is consumed so quickly that by March there is seldom any remaining in the basement. So, my informants told me when I offered as much as 40 EUR for a jar: "You don't understand. It is not to be sold, it is for us to eat the entire winter. What are 40, even 100 EUR? It will pay a few of the bills. But what am I going to eat during the winter?" Another informant told me: "There is too much work in each jar. If you want to eat *ajvar*, come and cook it with us. We can transport the peppers for you, prepare the stove, and provide good company."

The process of preparing winter preserves can take several weeks. *Ajvar* attests to a household's wealth because the peeling, cutting, sorting, cooking, and sealing of vegetables and fruits is a public performance. Most of the time, canning takes place on the street or in the garden, closely monitored by neighbors, friends and passers-by. The bigger the quantity of vegetables, the more diverse a housewife's (*domakjinka*) recipes, the more she is respected, and the more the family is considered to be doing well. A household without *ajvar*, buying things that can be produced at home, is stigmatized as "lazy" or "not worthy of regard" (*ne čini*) because household labor is the most valued ingredient of the *ajvar*. When people explain why homemade *ajvar* is better than the purchased product, they say it is "our work" and that it is made by the "whole house." Labor is the effort and time the family group employs in the complicated undertaking that leads finally to the cherished dish in the jar. The work includes collecting dry branches in the countryside over many months for the fire; collecting and cleaning glass jars; finding the best quality peppers from the most reliable trader, setting out a suitable place for the summer kitchen on the street or in the garden; and making contacts with those with whom one shares cooking equipment. The housewife also invests time refining and re-creating her recipes, remembering past successes and adjusting to new tastes.

To illuminate relationships among household, state, and market I draw on Karl Polanyi's concept of householding through different authors—Rhoda Halperin and Stephen Gudeman—who make somewhat different use of his ideas. Polanyi defined householding as one of four "forms of integration" (the others are reciprocity, redistribution, and market exchange). In contrast to the other forms, householding refers to a "closed group" that is a "self-sufficient unit," "producing and storing for the satisfaction of the wants of the members of the group" (Polanyi 2001 [1944]: 53). Scholars who have subsequently used the concept of householding have differed in the degree to which they prioritize the household as an actual social unit, corresponding to a domestic group, or as a theoretical formulation of a type of economic behavior. In other words, do households always practice householding? Both Halperin and Gudeman conclude that they generally do, and elaborate additional dimensions of householding as a strategy. Halperin considers householding in relation to the market and state, while Gudeman provides the conceptual lead for investigating whether the state itself can sometimes pursue householding.

Halperin follows Polanyi's definition of householding as a strategy of self-sufficiency and family autonomy. She adjusts the concept to contemporary industrial and post-industrial societies in order to introduce a more dynamic and processual approach to the study of the household. Householding is a particular "form of integration," with the capacity "to deal with complex economic processes and combinations of economic processes; articulation of different institutional arrangements, organizing units of production and consumption in stratified, state-level societies" (Halperin 1994: 143). Extending Polanyi's definition, Halperin insists on "the various non-capitalist forms of economic organization that persist and grow in the midst of capitalist and post-capitalist economies" (1994: 143). She puts the household into an institutional context combining state and market, showing how household members draw on nonmarket opportunities in order to make a living. Halperin's emphasis on the ways in which state and household shape each other's strategies is particularly fruitful for my case. While Polanyi understands the household as a unit of production, and assumes that production "for its own sake" has nothing to do with the motive of gain or with the institutions of the market, Halperin focuses on a more abstract principle of householding that helps to delineate "the limits of households as provisioning units" (1994: 149). Household ideology is autarkic, but its practices reveal a more complex picture. Most of the time, the household is "embedded in market relations" (Gregory 2009: 143). Halperin sees householding as a "form of resistance to capitalism and to dependency upon the state" (1994: 164), but I follow a different line.

The story of *ajvar*, born in socialism and persisting in postsocialism, shows that market, state, and household mutually reinforce each other; they are not constantly in opposition. The persistence of *ajvar* cooking as a householding strategy suggests that some logic other than resistance is practiced by the household; it has to do with ideology. Gudeman and Rivera (1990) analyze the house as a model radically different from that of the profit-oriented corporation. They depart from Polanyi's emphasis on householding as one of four "forms of integration" (the others are reciprocity, redistribution, and market exchange). Focusing on the house as a unit, Gudeman and Rivera see two prongs to its distinctive economic logic: one is "to maintain" or "support" itself, and the other is "to augment or increase" its resources, which they call "the base" after a local Colombian model (1990: 39). But are these components specific to domestic economy, or can the principle of householding also be found in other institutions including the state itself?

I argue that the interaction among the household, the state, and socialist and postsocialist markets has another dimension that has previously been neglected. Logics of keeping, holding, increasing, and storing resources are part of a general logic of self-sufficiency and can also be seen at the level of the state (Gudeman 2001, 2008). We can also infer from Polanyi's argument that not only the family but also larger entities such as the settlement and the manor can function as self-sufficient units (Polanyi 2001 [1944]: 56). The common feature is the principle of producing, storing, and redistributing inside a closed group, as well as the state, which can be added to the list when it organizes redistribution according to the exigency of self-sufficiency at regional or at national level. The state may even elevate self-sufficiency to be a dominant ideology; when this happens we can say that it is following the logic of householding.

## The History of *Ajvar*

Peppers were introduced into this part of the Ottoman Empire from the sixteenth century onward. Before the appearance of *ajvar*, the traditional pepper meal in Macedonian villages was *tolčeni piperki* ("smashed peppers"). It was prepared on a daily basis during the season and not preserved. Red peppers were preserved by drying, typically in garlands suspended outside the house during the entire winter. These red peppers are small, their thin skin is very difficult to separate from the flesh, and they were principally employed to add some flavor to other meals based on beans, potatoes, or rice.

Before it reached the status of a staple and became a key component of household self-provisioning, *ajvar* emerged as a component of urban festivities within the Kingdom of Yugoslavia (1918–1941). Inspired by different peasant recipes, it was a creation of the modern state and its high culture, promoted and spread in restaurants, official celebrations, religious feasts, and other festivities. Before socialism, *ajvar* was sometimes known as a Serbian specialty, *srbski ajvar* (Burr 1935; Slabey 1949; Edwards 1954. In the Slavonic encyclopedia of 1949 it is defined as "Serbian salad of crushed peppers and egg-plants, grilled" (Slabey 1949: 338). In the Kingdom of Yugoslavia the dish was cooked on the base of green peppers, sometimes accompanied with a sauce of red hot peppers. The famous entomologist and writer Malcolm Burr (1935) mentioned *srbski ajvar* as one of the most delicious meals he tasted in Serbia. He described an encounter with a hotelier in the town of Zajčar, "a gourmet at the table and a genius in kitchen," who was preparing *ajvar* for a big reception with Serbian officers (Burr 1935: 165). Born from the dismantlement of two empires, the Ottoman and the Austro-Hungarian, Yugoslavia developed its high cuisine by drawing on both (Slabey 1949: 337). By the early socialist years, *ajvar* seems to have been introduced in restaurants throughout the new Federation. Lovett Fielding Edwards noted sarcastically that this "local salad" called *ajvar* "is sometimes sold by pretentious hoteliers as Serbian caviar to which it bears not the slightest resemblance" (Edwards 1954: 79). During the next decade, recipes became available in all Yugoslav languages in cookbooks, although green peppers seemed still to prevail (Zakonjsek 1966).

Today's *ajvar* requires two basic ingredients that became items of mass consumption after the Second World War—the industrial hybrid pepper known officially as *kurtovska kapija* and sunflower oil, which displaced other fats in domestic cooking.[3] *Kurtovska kapija,* known informally as *ajvarka,* is a Bulgarian hybrid named after a village near Plovdiv where it was first hybridized in 1960. The pepper's hybridization was the result of a deliberate effort to respond to the new needs of socialist mass consumption: high yields were needed for processing factories with standardized year-round production predicated on greenhouses. The Bulgarian hybrid quickly spread throughout the socialist block (COMECON), including the USSR, where it was called the "Bulgarian pepper." It reached Macedonia in 1966. Throughout Yugoslavia, the Bulgarian hybrid was taken up for industrial production by the *kombinati,* which were the main state institutions controlling food production within each republic (Alcock 2000: 135).[4] It only became a staple for domestic consumption in the winter months, however, in Serbia and Macedonia. By 1983, agricultural agronomists had noted its importance in household processing (*domašno proizvodstvo*) in Macedonia.[5]

Reflecting on the history of food supply systems in African urban contexts, Jane Guyer has refuted the notion that urbanization necessarily leads to a decline in self-provisioning. For some urban households, self-provisioning "seems rather to be an option jealously maintained where possible, and resorted to intermittently by all sectors of the urban population except for those who are totally deprived of access to land" (Guyer 1987: 23). Either households produce their own food, or kin living in the countryside make substantial contributions. There are parallels in Macedonia, where many urbanites continue either to work their own land or maintain relationships of reciprocity and mutual help with parents in the village from which they are partially provisioned, supplementing what they purchase on the market. But *ajvar* as a reflection of modern householding and as a creative response of the household to the state's social engineering is also rooted in a persisting conception of the domestic group as a self-sufficient unit.

## Self-Sufficiency and the State

The Macedonia term *samoizdržuvanje* literally means "self-sustainability," but it is the closest rendering available of the English "self-sufficiency." During socialism, at a more formal level in the media and in political discourses the Serbo-Croatian term *samodovoljnost* was often employed. Questioned about self-sufficiency, my informants tended to give descriptive definitions rather than employing either of those concepts. For example when describing life in villages in the past they would say "We ate what we produced; what the land gave; we worked hard not to buy; the house had everything and we did not buy much from outside."

Within the Kingdom of Yugoslavia, economists discussed the concept of household self-sufficiency in the framework of two major preoccupations: the "modernization" of a state in which almost 80 percent of the population was constituted by peasants living from the "subsistence economy," and the fragmentation of peasant property resulting from household division in accordance with traditional rules of inheritance. These two issues were discussed together under the general heading of "agricultural overpopulation" (Tomashevich 1955: 303).[6] The new state had to deal with very complex ethnic and religious diversity. In the north (Croatia), Austrian social democracy had already introduced an encompassing pension system and the premises of a welfare state (Grandits 2010). In the South (Macedonia, Kosovo) the Ottoman system of semi-servitude, bonding landless peasants to their landlords, was far from entirely dismantled. To combat unequal development and rural overpopulation, the authorities undertook ambitious land reforms. In addition to redistribution and the "colonization" of territories previously occupied by other ethnic groups, a campaign was mounted to encourage cooperatives (called *zadruga* in reference to the old Slavic model of the extended family) as a way to develop commercial agriculture. However, these measures had little success in the poorly developed southern regions. After 1945, the communists set up a federal system, combining one-party hegemony with far-reaching administrative autonomy. This model was shaped by experiments with local self-government and regional economic self-sufficiency during the war years, when partisan committees implemented the principle "each household provides for itself from its own land." These policies derived in large part from what was known as the "Slovene model" in communist ideology from 1934 and reasserted by the Slovene National Liberation Front in 1944 (Woodward 1995: 59).

Within the socialist Federation, this economic conception of self-sufficiency was translated at the political level into republican autarky at multiple levels. Although the federal state was supposed to be autarkic vis-à-vis the USSR and the rest of the world, individual republics were conceived as self-sufficient toward the center and toward each other (Kardelj 1976; Cichock 1985: 216). The Constitution of 1971 strengthened this autonomy still further. Edward Kardelj, Marshal Tito's deputy and the main architect of these changes, emphasized the need to diminish the role of the central government in Belgrade and to increase the autonomy of the republics, leading eventually to full sovereignty. He also sought to strengthen the workers' self-management system, both within individual enterprises and throughout the state. Somehow the leading role of the working class in the

Federation was to transcend the separate interests of the republics (Stan-ković 1971). These policies to encourage self-management and "domestic autarky" (Bićanić 1973: 7) were supposed to encourage local manufactur-ing,[7] but they were contradictory and eventually contributed to the disinte-gration of Yugoslavia (Şuster 2000: 717).

## Self-Sufficiency: Persistence and Change

Self-sufficiency and the minimizing of participation in the market sphere characterized the Yugoslav household until the Second World War. "The basic motivation in the economic activity of the overwhelming portion of Yugoslav farm households was to provide food and other necessities for the family ... by direct production of goods and services ... by members of the family, rather than the maximization of total money revenue from farming for the market" (Tomashevich 1955: 431). In Macedonia we can follow dynamics of persistence and change in household self-sufficiency thanks to foreign ethnographic accounts from the 1930s (Obrębski 2002 [1932], 1977) and 1960s (Rheubottom 1971, 1996). In a chapter on "[t]he economic aspects of matrimonial exchange," the Pole Józef Obrębski dis-cussed the *šema na ekonomja na samoizdržuvanje*, "scheme of economic self-sufficiency," as a principle governing over the totality of peasant life (Obrębski 2002 [1932]: 5 8–63).[8] Rural households were not cut off from market relationships. They raised cash crops and sold animals for money, which they needed to pay taxes. Peasant credits were also widespread in the presocialist Kingdom. At the level of the house, in Obrębski's survey, a typical peasant household also required money to purchase tools, crockery, and "necessities" such as gas, sugar, salt, oil, and coffee.

The relationship among the ideology of self-sufficiency, labor, and social prestige is clearly attested in Obrębski's ethnography. Economic success and capital accumulation depended on labor performed collectively over sev-eral generations rather than on property and landownership. For villagers in the region of Poreče, "wealth and success cannot derive from property and before anything else they stem from work" (Obrębski 2002 [1932]: 9). A household's local reputation and an individual's authority as well as the allocation of power within the community were a function of material wealth. For a given house, the essential condition for good economic per-formance was the capacity to achieve a high level of self-sufficiency and to accumulate surplus goods that could be exchanged for money. This de-pended on a complex division of labor that could occur only in extended families. Small families with no male children or deceased members were considered incomplete and "constituted by definition the rural poor."

(Obrębski 2002 [1932]: 10). To succeed one had to rely on a large labor force. The joint household, according to the Polish ethnographer, was the basic "socio-economic unit of the rural society" as well as "the principal mechanism of cultural filiation" (Obrębski 2002 [1932]: 23). Kinship ideology emphasized the "ideal of the big family."[9] The typical extended family was composed of three generations. The oldest was represented by the conjugal unit of the head of the household and his wife (*domakjin* and *domakjinka*), the middle by the sons, their wives and unmarried daughters, and the third by the grandchildren.

The local cultural model did not reveal practices of concentration of capital and wealth that could be transmitted from generation to generation. Wealth was maintained and increased through common effort in the course of working together as a family. If those conditions were absent, wealth was depleted and what remained was "the private, father's land that could be the base of future accumulation of wealth but not its equivalent ..." (Obrębski 2002 [1932]: 9). A wealthy household was one that managed to accomplish self-sufficiency relying on family labor and continuing various economic sectors—including animal breeding as well as agricultural activities, but also cash-oriented activities and the specialized domestic work performed by women and men when they produced clothes and household equipment.

In the 1930s, Macedonian households produced not only their food but also their clothes, as well as many household items, some of which were included in the bride's dowry. Little was sold, even when a surplus was available, because each family was producing for itself and there was no effective market. Wealthier peasants making a living primarily from animal husbandry, particularly sheep breeding, considered money the same way as they saw their flock. Money was a good to be exchanged for other goods when the working capacity of the group did not allow further development of the livestock. Moreover, money had specific uses. It represented the earnings of the labor force hired in the agricultural season or for dwelling construction (Obrębski 2002 [1932]: 16). Money was a durable and productive good. The money secured form surplus production was kept separate from cash earned otherwise, which was used for ongoing expenditures. When the stock of cash grew, peasants preferred to convert it to gold coins. When one possessed gold, one was likely to lend some to relatives or friends without charging interest, following the same rule as for lending a flock (Obrębski 2002 [1932]: 17–18).[10] A high level of self-sufficiency required cash. "In this scheme of economy of self-sufficiency, the continuous exchange of the household surplus production for money is necessary. The surplus is made of those goods that exceed internal needs of consumption and therefore go to the market" (Obrębski 2002 [1932]: 59).

Departing from household size and its economic performance, Obrębski distinguished three social classes in the village: "the rich, the middle, and the poor." The richest were those families counting at least ten members, those in the middle had five to six members, and the poor had smaller families. The rich could be found in all economic niches in the village and provided work for the poor. The main difference between the rich and the middle was that the first were predominantly breeders (*stocar*) with a large number of livestock (*stoka*). The word *stoka* means commodity, capital, and goods for exchange. Middle-ranking families also had animals, but they were fewer in number, and the predominant occupation of these house-holds was agriculture for self-consumption and exchange. These middle peasants could not accumulate wealth, their balance sheet did not reckon profit, and they could "just make a living" (*možet da životarit*) (Obrębski 2002 [1932]: 11). Their production did not suffice for self-consumption. For example, they could not produce enough wheat for their bread and had to buy some on the market. The cash needed to pay for additional food and for taxes was obtained from charcoal produced from the local forest, which was the main commodity exchanged for money. The poor were com-posed of small families who had "more people who eat than who work." They could not produce even their bread, nor could they process wood for charcoal as they did not have mules to transport it to the market. They also lacked livestock, apart from a few goats. Their plots were small or of poor productivity, as they did not produce manure. They depended on "village philanthropy and the generosity of the richest families" (Obrębski 2002 [1932]: 10–11).

The fundamental characteristic of village social stratification in Obrębski's study was the instability of status and the high potential for social mobility both up and down the scale. A middle-ranking family could become rich if it enlarged its number of members and vice versa. A rich household affected by illnesses or wars could lose working members and become middle-ranking or even poor. A family's status could change from one generation to the next. The principal cleavage was between the interests of the rich family and the interests of the middle-ranking family. The poor, according to Obrębski, were the "natural ally of the rich" as they depended on the generosity of the latter. This process constantly menaced "social cohesion" within the community and weakened "group solidarities." This variable class structure created differentiations within the lineage and pitted kin with different interests against each other. There was no such a thing as a "peaceful village community," concluded Obrębski. He considered such an image to be the creation of anthropologists' imagination and not a social reality (Obrębski 2002 [1932]: 12).

More than thirty years later, in the mid 1960s, the American anthropologist David Rheubottom observed shifts in the self-sufficiency ideology of Macedonian village life following urbanization and the expansion of factory work. In the region of Crna Gora, very close to Skopje, he found that "a proper peasant is self-supporting. Crna Gorci shy away from becoming enmeshed in the market economy" (Rheubottom 1996: 4). Crna Gorci grew all crops important for their diet, including cereals, beans, tomatoes, peppers, grapes, and melons.[11] Most food produced by the household was consumed, while any surplus from agriculture, shepherding, and viticulture was sold in Skopje's markets. Rheubottom saw the peasant household as striving toward self-sufficiency. Like Obrębski, he noticed that a head of household gained social prestige and authority from it: "Their local reputation depends in large measure on their ability to manage the household so that this group can support itself on what it can grow and produce" (Rheubottom 1996: 4). During his fieldwork in 1966–1967 in the largest village of the region, there was only one shop selling processed food. The most frequently purchased item was school notebooks.

In contrast to Obrębski's observations in the 1930s, Rheubottom found that households were intensely involved in wage labor. They purchased clothes and household items in the market. However, self-sufficiency ideology remained strong. Although the younger generation wanted city clothes, shoes, and watches, older people "prided themselves on being relatively self-sufficient and able to satisfy most of their needs through their own efforts or those of local craftsmen" (Rheubottom 1971: 23). In a survey of fifty-one households, he juxtaposed households' per capita landholdings with the number of members working outside the village for wages. Families with more land were less engaged in wage labor, although the difference in the total number of individuals was not very important (Rheubottom 1971: 261). In rural districts, during socialism wage labor provided resources, but not enough to meet household needs and land was valued as an insurance against unemployment. This maintained interdependencies within the patriarchal family between household members living in the village and those in the city, who all remained subordinate to the head of the household.

Self-sufficiency and wage labor maintained the balance of the household within a Yugoslav socialist economy that was afflicted by high inflation and urban unemployment. Working together or *zaednica* (literally "togetherness") was vital to a household's growth and prosperity. "The principle of operation is very simple. Those who work on behalf of the household have the right to be maintained by it; and those who are maintained have the obligation to work for it." Those who worked for wages had no claims over their money and did not make decisions about how to spend it. This money was a common good (Rheubottom 1996: 6). What maintained the household as an autonomous unit of production and consumption was labor and the complex system of task allocations (Rheubottom 1971: 30).

## Remembering Self-Sufficiency in the Past: Mitre's Family in the Village of Bayr near Prilep

Prilep is a city predominately inhabited by families originating from nearby villages. People often refer to the past in the village where domestic economy comprised a high level of self-sufficiency. I take the example of Mitre's family originating from the region of Borovo to illustrate both the persistence of the ideal of self-sufficiency and changes in the new urban context.

Before most of its inhabitants migrated to the town of Prilep, a similar economic structure prevailed throughout the region of Borovo until 1970 (Monova 2015). Mitre, in his late seventies at the time of my fieldwork, migrated to Prilep from the biggest village in the region in 1969 with his wife.[12] His household was the biggest and the wealthiest in the village. According to his recollection, when the domestic group was at the peak of its growth before division, it contained thirteen individuals. They lived in *zaednica*—a community, sharing all assets and governed by the head of the household. The group was composed of the head of the household and his wife, the head's parents, his wife's brother and family, the head's two married sons and their families, and the head's unmarried daughter. The domestic group lived in two houses; one had two floors and the other had three floors. Mitre's count of household members spans the 1960s and early 1970s; he counts himself and his brother as the married sons with families, even though both men moved to the city early in their marriages.

The family contained in-marrying men, which often occurs when a well-off family comprises only female children. The head of the household, Mitre's paternal grandfather, joined his bride's family because she was one of five daughters of Milos, the wealthiest farmer in the village. Mitre's great-grandfather Milos was called *čorbadžija*[13] because of his imposing stature and his "big capital."[14] He married off all his daughters—three "went away with a piece of land to get rid of them for good" and two brought their husbands home (*domazeti*). Only one of the daughters that returned home bore a male child, Mitre's father. To continue the family, Mitre's father recruited the help of his wife's brother, and the whole family worked together until socialism arrived. At that time, the household's assets comprised 32 hectares of land, two water mills, 500 sheep, and 150 cattle. Between 1944 and 1952 the process of collectivization left the family with little land and few animals. Some of the arable land was later returned, but most of their animals were distributed to poor peasants. Within ten years, the family managed to rebuild the stock of sheep they had before socialism. Then, in the early 1960s, Mitre's brother decided to take his part and sell it to pay his land taxes before moving to the city. Mitre's father argued with him: "How can you run away from this capital (*sermija*)? Why do you want to divide, to become a poor man? This capital and land require working people, a collective (*zaednica*) that stays together and remains rich. If you divide you will have nothing." But Mitre's brother divided and left for good.

The family cultivated various cereals for feeding livestock, horses, and chickens. According to Mitre, "being well-doing in Bayr does not mean saving money." Their land was just enough to nourish the animals through the winter. They also grew sunflowers, corn, wheat, rye, barley, and vegetables for house consumption. They sold some of the sunflower seeds, and also grew opium and a small amount of tobacco as cash crops. "Since Turkish times" the traditional cash crop in the region had been opium, before the socialist regime replaced it with tobacco. From sales of the tar obtained from the milk of opium poppies, households paid their taxes and had cash savings. Opium oil from the seeds was also of nutritional value for people, and cattle and sheep grazed on the field after the harvest. Through the early years of the socialist period, Mitre's family took their sunflower and opium seeds to a mill in a neighboring city and sold them for some 7,000 denars— nearly four months' wages in a cooperative. Once the taxes were paid and necessary goods purchased, the remaining cash was minimal. "The only way to earn money was to sell a calf, a lamb, a sheep and sometimes cheese." Wool was kept for making dresses, carpets and blankets. Sizable quantities of meat were conserved in salt and fat for winter consumption. "We worked big, we produced big. The whole family. We worked hard to have enough to eat without buying."

According to Mitre's recollections the men in his family "resisted" state employment as long as they could. The timber processing company started recruiting in the village in 1947. Only "the poorest went working for wages" recalls Mitre, and no one from his family left for Prilep until 1967. Mitre married soon after and followed his brother to work as a bus driver in the city. When Mitre's father died, the farm was left in the hands of a cousin and Mitre's sister who, in the years following her brothers' departure to the city had married-out and then returned to her family of origin after being widowed. For nearly three decades, the farm was still not formally divided: sheep and cattle were left in the care of a local shepherd paid by the family. The children raised in town had no interest in taking over the farm. In the mid nineties Mitre and his brother sold the remaining animals and part of their land. In 2009 Mitre was living with his wife in their two-story house sustained by one pension and by remittances from their son and his family in Australia. Throughout the three decades in town, self-provisioning from the village declined continuously for lack of a labor force. The family had divided and without a large domestic group working in *zaednica*, market relationships had taken over practices of self-sufficiency.

Peppers were not an important crop when Mitre was still living in the village.[15] But "somewhere in the sixties" he remembers families starting to grow red peppers for the market. The majority of villagers still preferred raising tobacco, which had higher returns. Mitre's family first started cooking *ajvar* from purchased peppers in Prilep, where in the early 1970s it became a major component of the city dwellers' diet. The former villagers were now factory workers, and this led to diversification of consumption and transformations of the pattern of self-provisioning. The winter preserves responded to the needs of the nuclear family; meat and vegetables were increasingly purchased, and *ajvar* became a surrogate for the lost world of village abundance.

Rheubottom (1996) found that in the 1960s, participation in wage labor was an indicator of a village household's incapacity to achieve self-sufficiency. By contrast, in contemporary Prilep wages are indicative of well-being while agricultural work, to which many families have returned, indicates unemployment and impoverishment (Monova 2015). However, in the Borovski district of Prilep where I did my fieldwork, the ideology of self-sufficiency while persisting has taken new forms. Borovtsi moved to the city in large numbers in the early 1970s and became fully dependent on waged labor, and the nuclear family replaced the joint household. The preparation of winter preserves, however, is now the incarnation of the self-sufficiency ideology. At the end of the summer, families preserve tomatoes, peppers, green beans, peas, carrots, zucchinis, eggplant, cabbage, and cauliflower, even if they did not grow them. Most of the vegetables are boiled or blanched before being placed into plastic bags in the freezer, a key component of the material culture of the Yugoslav house since the 1960s. Green tomatoes, part of the red and green peppers, cauliflower, and cabbage are pickled in brine and stored in large plastic receptacles. Fruit is typically transformed into compote and marmalade and stored in the basement. The better-off hire the butcher or a relative in a village to slaughter a pig or a lamb. At home in town, the family gathers to prepare sausages and preserve cooked meat in jelly. In the people's representation, consuming what one has produced is connected to a contemporary discourse of ecologically clean food. It represents a household's self-esteem. As in the past, consuming what one produces yields social prestige even as market participation is needed to sustain the practice.

## Household *Ajvar*: A Creation of Socialism

The three most valued components of a household's winter reserves are the *ajvar*, brandy (*rakija*), and wine. Many younger households do not prepare brandy and wine because they do not have the conditions or the time to prepare all three components at home. In this case, the younger people give money to their retired elderly relatives who buy the grapes and make *rakija* and wine for all. In contrast, regardless of household size, status, or financial situation, almost all participate in preserving some food, especially *ajvar*. Even households composed of a solitary individual link up with others to share resources and labor. In the capital, Skopje, families often associate through friendship and neighborhood rather kinship.

Every year in mid September the preparation of *ajvar* is featured prominently in Macedonian newspapers, television, and the internet. Journalists report the intensive activity around mobile kitchens set up on the street. Producers complain about low prices for peppers while consumers complain about the growing price. In the capital, Skopje, people are gradually withdrawing from the production of *ajvar* for lack of time, family labor (small households), available space for outside cooking, rising prices of peppers, oil and wood; and, finally, because a law was passed in 2008 prohibiting *ajvar* cooking in public areas. The ban reclassified an activity that people had previously considered to be clean and healthy as one that is dirty and dangerous. It extends to cover the cutting and stacking of wood, the dust and smell of roasting peppers, the use of coal, wood, or other forms of fire, and public gathering around stoves that impede street traffic. The police were generally lenient with families that responded to the ban by removing their summer kitchens to cul-de-sacs and abandoned squares, but the possibility of fines of up to 2,000 EUR is a frightening sanction that deters many from continuing *ajvar* production altogether. To quote a participant in internet forums: "the main question now is whether or not homemade *ajvar* will lose the battle with the industrial variety."[16]

Ilona Jakimovska, an anthropologist from the University of Skopje, claims that Macedonian citizens are now faced with the dilemma of choosing between homemade *ajvar* or membership in the European Union.[17] According to Jakimovska, the law amounts to an attack on the "community relationships" that makes *ajvar* cooking possible. She argues that if homemade *ajvar* were to disappear from the table Macedonians would "stand to lose not only [*ajvar*'s] unique taste but also the whole culture of neighborhood relationships that forms part of the traditional culture." Of course *ajvar* is "of recent origin," but Jakimovska holds that the social prestige of the household (*domakjinstvo*) as a distinct Macedonian institution is at stake. Householding requires knowledge, skills, and work that are inseparable from sociability with kin and neighbors. If Macedonians purchase *ajvar* instead of making their own, they will sacrifice all that is invested in women's everyday comparisons of quasi-secret recipes and the sharing of wood purchased by two or more families and cut with a common saw. Jakimovska thus condemns a law that "limits social interactions among individuals and impoverishes social life. It banishes *ajvar* socialization into the domain of illegality."[18]

In the capital *ajvar* cooking now is differently appreciated along class lines. Well-off families with high level of education criticize the traditional recipe. "*Ajvar* is overcooked, there is no single vitamin remaining." They prefer roasted red peppers during the season for immediate consumption and this is not called *ajvar*. When they miss the taste of the "traditional *ajvar*" they occasionally buy some from a reliable contact on the "green market" who has the reputation of cooking "healthy." The housewife's reputation in Skopje in educated milieus is not formed through reproducing the family recipe. "Why should I waste time and energy to cook *ajvar* when I can buy it?" I was told. Although in this case families prefer to buy it, they still value the notion of the "homemade" (*domašno*). The so-called "industrial *ajvar*" is rejected as both "unhealthy" and "cheap." However, the industrial *ajvar* is present in supermarkets, and different segments of the population purchase it in the seasons when they cannot find either homemade *ajvar* or jars leftover from their own production.

In Prilep, in contrast to the capital, nothing seems to presage the disappearance of *ajvar* cooking. Visitors between September and October are likely to be overwhelmed by the flavor of the grilled red bell peppers and the pall of grey-black smoke covering the whole city. Here, the start of the red peppers' processing is delayed a little due to the tobacco harvest, which may last until late September (Monova 2015). After the last tobacco leaves have been stripped and aligned on their wooden frames in gardens and on the streets, the green and yellow shades of the tobacco leaves meet the bright red of the peppers. For a couple of weeks the flavors of peppers and tobacco mingle. Streets, squares, parks, and courtyards between old socialist apartment buildings, as well as private gardens are invaded by people who leave their apartments to cook the precious dish for days on end. Each family is equipped with two types of stove, one for roasting the peppers and the other (1 meter in diameter) for boiling them in a big casserole with oil and, sometimes, a small quantity of eggplant, carrots, or tomatoes.

The preparation of *ajvar* is expensive and time-consuming. To prepare a minimum quantity for a family of parents and a child, at least 100 kg of peppers, and 2–3 liters of sunflower oil, plus coal and wood are needed. This is enough to produce about twenty-six medium-sized jars for the winter. Glass jars are saved from store-bought foods or purchased new. The two handmade barbecue stoves require a lot of space, so neighbors and relatives often agree to share them. They also share the labor because it takes at least two adults to execute the parallel tasks of roasting, peeling, chopping, and boiling peppers over several days. Most of the work is done by women, but men also participate, especially during the strenuous period of boiling.

To make *ajvar*, peppers are constantly turned over charcoal fires so that they roast evenly. The baked peppers are then placed briefly in a closed dish or plastic bag to cool, before the skin is peeled and the seeds are removed. The cooks' hands become sticky with pepper skins, but they cannot wash them because water damages the quality of the peppers. The roasted peppers are left to drain overnight, and then ground in a mill or chopped into tiny pieces. The resulting mush is then boiled slowly, and stirred continuously for a minimum of four hours, in an immense casserole on the second stove with oil and other vegetables. Salt is added right before the hot mush is poured into jars that are immediately sealed.

For me, it was curious that, unlike other preserves that either come from family-owned land or *might* have been grown by the family, the red peppers for *ajvar* (as well as the grapes for *rakija* and wine) are purchased entirely on the market. Why are the three most highly valued components of household production so strongly tied to the market? Here I restrict myself to *ajvar*, which has a distinctive status as a food and an identity marker. Of the twenty-two households I surveyed, only one grew peppers. This was the only household engaged in commercial agriculture; it sold most of the peppers it produced to friends, to acquaintances, and at the local market place. The rest of the peppers were used for their own *ajvar*. The other twenty-one households had never grown any peppers, either during socialism or after, which contradicts what people generally say about *ajvar*—that it is a very old tradition, that Macedonians have always cooked *ajvar*, and that its making was transmitted between generations from mother to daughter. In reality, the custom of making *ajvar* at home is no older than the industrial production of red bell peppers.

Homemade *ajvar* is said to be ecologically clean because it is ideally made with a household's homegrown peppers. Some people are conscious of the fact that peppers are grown industrially, with the help of pesticides, but this is overlooked. The peppers purchased on the market are considered good enough because of their local origin. They are rendered healthy as well as delicious thanks to the recipes and the know-how of housewives, who are always developing their skills in convivial contestation with each other. The same applies to the purity and perfection claimed by men when comparing their homemade wine and brandy, which in most cases also comes from purchased grapes. When I asked why they did not grow their peppers, people cited "practical reasons." First "*ajvar* needs too many peppers." To grow so many would be "another job." Besides, to cultivate on family land they would need a car to reach the countryside, and even then the fuel costs would exceed the cost of buying peppers on the market.[19] Another reason given is that "it's not worth the effort" (*ne se izplakja*). "Why should I toil working the land when the peppers are cheap? I can buy them and just cook them." Peppers of local origin, however, are highly valued. When men go to the market to purchase peppers, they ask after the producer, his name and his place of residence. Many have personal relationships with a grower from whom they buy directly every year. Everyone agrees that times have changed since "grandparents" time: "in the past, for peasants the rule was that you ate what you had sown. Now you just buy it." In Skopje most people rely on *ajvar* cooked by the family but even though they buy it they seek to find *ajvar* produced in similar conditions to the past. The so-called "industrial *ajvar*" of low quality nevertheless responds to needs of urbanized families living in apartments who have a more diversified diet and no relatives in the countryside to support them with staple food.

## Conclusion

In this chapter I tried to shed light on household self-sufficiency as changing practices connected to state politics that shape ideologies and markets. Through defining human economy as "embedded and enmeshed in institutions, economic and non-economic," Polanyi (1957: 148) opened a space to recognize the role of political institutions. I have explored the articulations between household ideologies of self-sufficiency and the state and argued that in preparing *ajvar*, households continue to adhere to the principle Polanyi identified as householding. The making of *ajvar* is an encounter between family, the state at various levels, and even supra-state institutions such as COMECON and the EU, which have both had an impact in different historical eras. Making *ajvar* is a recently created "need" that shows how the institutions of householding are shaped and reshaped by new forms of political economy. *Ajvar* exemplifies contemporary householding as a strategy of self-sufficiency and family autonomy.

In valuing the homemade and their family relationships, households do not thereby reject the socialist and postsocialist market relations that provide them with the materials for self-provisioning. We rather see a striving for balance between involvement and distance, a line of multi-leveled relatedness, which begins within the house, within small groups of kin and friends, and moves outward to supra-local networks. The peppers used for *ajvar* emerged as the result of socialist policies to provide industrial food for a post-peasant, urban population. Macedonian households responded creatively by using what the market made available to achieve a new form of self-sufficiency. Of course, this cannot be understood economistically. *Ajvar* is an identity marker because it represents continuity with a much older ideology of self-sufficiency, an ideology which was able to sustain itself vigorously in Macedonia due to the distinctive features of the socialist Federation of Tito and Kardelj.[20] I have shown that households do not much care for industrial *ajvar* (most of which goes for export) but they gladly purchase industrial peppers in large quantities to produce their own *ajvar*. This household demand was a creative response to socialist economic planning, and an interaction between an ideology of self-provisioning and market relations in urban contexts transformed by industrialization and rural exodus. The household production of *ajvar* partially compensated for socialist-era food shortages, but not only. If *ajvar* was still enthusiastically prepared in Prilep two decades after the fall of socialism, something of the former complex embedding of culture and economy has been maintained.

In reinventing new practices of self-sufficiency households demonstrate the plasticity of this form of integration. *Ajvar* is a way of reinvigorating self-sufficiency ideology that values the homemade and work that is performed together. The product is a sign of wealth, and its public performance generates local reputation and prestige. *Ajvar* has shifted from the status of a peasant salad to a national "specialty" elaborated for urban elites, and during socialism to an item of mass consumption bridging domestic and industrial production. The encounters of households with different forms of market and state institutions have not eliminated the idea of the household as a closed group, working for its own benefit, producing for internal consumption a product which is not to be exchanged. When they make *ajvar* households are not just coping with or resisting the market and the state. They are finding a way to creatively engage in self-sufficiency through converting resources stemming from the market and from state policies to support locally produced crops to serve their own interests.

People get peppers from the market, but it is not an impersonal market, since the producers and suppliers are often known to the buyers. The ingredients have to be "local" and "ours," not imported. Their local origin makes them part of the wealth of the larger community to which the household belongs. If we follow Stephen Gudeman's metaphor of the house and its connections with outside, the purchased crops come from outside (the market) and move into the house where they are transformed into wealth. *Ajvar* is meant to keep (*krepi*) and sustain the family throughout the winter and it is considered central to the daily menu, regardless of its actual nutritional content. At the end of the production process *ajvar* stays in the home and belongs to those who have produced it.

**Figure 3.1.** Map of Miladina Monova's Field Site.

**Miladina Monova** holds a doctorate in Social Anthropology from the École des Hautes Études en Sciences Sociales, Paris, based on a study of refugees of the Greek civil war in Yugoslav Macedonia. She has taught anthropology at the University of Lille 1, and held Fellowships at Collegium Budapest, the École Française d'Athènes, and the Center of Advanced Studies in Sofia. She has published extensively in the fields of refugee studies and ethnicity and nationalism in the Balkans.

## Notes

1. Further details concerning field research in Macedonia in 2009-2010 can be found in Monova 2015. I am extremely grateful to my informants in the town of Prilep and in the capital Skopje. Households in different ethnic and religious communities were extremely collaborative in providing the most detailed accounts of their budgets for the cooking of winter preserves. Throughout my research Ljubco Risteski and Ines Crvenkoska, both anthropologists in the Department of Ethnology of the Ss Cyril and Methodius University in Skopje and themselves preparers of *ajvar,* helped me step by step to grasp the intricacies both of budget computation and oft he symbolic dimensions of *ajvar* togetherness.

2. *Ajvar* shares the same Turkish etymology as "caviar." In former Yugoslavia as well as in Bulgaria, where the dish is known as *lyutenitsa*, the main ingredient is roasted red bell peppers. Within former Yugoslavia the second ingredient is eggplant, while in Bulgaria roughly one-third is made up of tomatoes. Another difference lies in the technology of home processing. In Bulgaria, urban families use electricity rather than wood and rely heavily on an electric utensil known as the *chushkopek.* This is a double-sided grill into which the peppers are inserted, making the roasting easy to carry out on the balcony of an urban apartment.

3. Sunflower oil was a luxury available primarily through itinerant traders until sunflower cultivation was introduced on a large scale by the Germans during the Second World War. Sunflowers were cultivated as an industrial crop with greatest intensity between the early 1960s and the early 1980s to meet the demands of rapidly growing urban populations (*Zemjodelski Kalendar* N.5, 1983: 56).

4. At the time of my fieldwork in 2009–2010, 90 percent of the output of food processing factories in Macedonia was directed toward export. Pepper was the main product of the country's forty-five mills, followed by the tomato (*Dnevnik*, 24 August 2009). The mill owners complain of a lack of peppers on the local market, as growers prefer to export to Bulgaria, where they can obtain higher prices (*Nova Makedonja*, 29 September 2009).

5. *Zemjodelski Kalendar* N.5, 1983: 120.

6. According to the census of 1921, 78.9 percent of the total population depended on agriculture. In 1931, the year of the last prewar census, the agricultural population was 76.5 percent of the total.

7. For the most part, Yugoslavia's agriculture was not collectivized. The census of 1971 recorded that 80 percent of cultivated land in Macedonia was devoted to "individual agriculture" (*individualno zemjodelie*). Various policies and incentives were introduced in agriculture to improve productivity, further rural development, and integrate peasants into the welfare system of the country (*Zemjodelski Kalendar* N.1, 1978: 21). For example, the new pepper hybrid featured on the list of subsidized "quality crops" that were eligible for low-interest federal credits; by lowering the cost of the new seeds for individual producers, the state hoped peasants would replace their cultivation of the traditional red peppers with the hybrid.

8. Obrębski's 1932 manuscript was never published in English. For the Macedonian translation published in 2002, Tanas Vražinovski (translator from the Polish and an

ethnographer himself) drew on original field notes in which Obrębski mixed Polish and Macedonian.

9. In trying to give a definition of the large patriarchal joint-family, on occasion Obrębski employs the concept of *zadruga*. He refers to scientific definitions, rather than to local usage of the word or the actual existence of the institution. In his survey, the biggest household had eleven members. However, the ideal of the joint family, located somewhere in an ideal past when the village was rich and peasants prosperous, was still strong and widespread in the 1930s.

10. The shepherd who was given a flock kept for himself the newborn animals, the milk, and the wool but had to give back the flock to its owner with the same number of animals as at the moment he got it, in the same physical condition.

11. One of Rheubottom's informants reported that a household of eight or nine people required over 3,000 kg of wheat per year. This quantity could be produced on one or two hectares of good land because yields averaged 2,000 kg/ha, and very good fields could yield up to 4,000 kg/ha in an exceptional year. People tried to work more land than the minimum in order to ensure the necessary production (Rheubottom 1971: 234).

12. The village of Bayr had 1,091 inhabitants in 1948, but only 664 in 1981, and 376 in 1991 (Bunteski 1998: 11–14; Koneski 2004: 97).

13. In several predominantly Christian areas of the Balkans, as well as in many parts of Eastern Anatolia, the term *čorbadžija* is used as a title for Christian members of the rural elite—rich peasant heads of villages and other rural communities. In vernacular Macedonian the word means "boss."

14. During the interview Mitre employed the two terms—the modern "capital" and the Turkish-derived *sermija.*

15. Whereas the last prewar census (1939) figures does not mention peppers as an industrial crop in Macedonia, by 1978 peppers and tomatoes dominated the production of all other crops. See *Zemjodelski Kalendar* N.1, 1978: 15.

16. In internet forums some participants proclaimed "the beginning of the end of homemade *ajvar*" (http://forum.idividi.com.mk/forum_posts.asp?TID=15169). The difference between industrial and household *ajvar* is that the first is made of peppers cooked with the skin while the latter is made from roasted peppers from which the burned skin has been removed.

17. Interview, *Utrinski vesnik*, 12 September 2012.

18. Ibid., Jakimovska.

19. In the Prilep region, almost all public transport has ceased since the collapse of the federal republic and the market has yet to provide any replacement.

20. A comparison with Bulgaria makes this point clear. Here, there is a similar dish made from red peppers and tomatoes called *lyutenitsa*. *Lyutenitsa* was also of key importance in the Bulgarian winter diet during socialism, and summer kitchens between apartment blocks or on balconies were also common in urban life. However this tradition gradually disappeared after 1989 and people now prefer to purchase industrially produced *lyutenitsa* because the homemade version is considered too expensive. See *Sezonut na lyutenitsa ne uhae na lyutenitsa (The lyutenitsa season doesn't have the flavor of lyutenitsa)*, *Nov Zhivot*, Istochni Rodopi, 12 September 2012. Pepper production in Bulgaria has declined; they are mainly

imported from Macedonia and Turkey and their high prices make *lyutenitsa* a luxury. See "Lyutenitsata si e bulgarska, makar I s kitajsko pure," *Noviat Glas*, 17 September 2009.

## References

Alcock, John. 2000. *Explaining Yugoslavia*. London: Hurst and Co.

Bićanić, Rudolf. *1973. Economic Policy in Socialist Yugoslavia*. Cambridge: Cambridge University Press.

Bunteski, Riste-Bunte. 1998. *Materialnata položba na naselenieto vo Prilep I Prilepsko, 1870-1940*. Prilep: Društvo za Nauka i Umetnost.

Burr, Malcolm. 1935. *Slouch Hat*. London: George Allen & Unwin.

Cichock, Malcolm A. 1985. "Re-evaluating a Development Strategy: Policy Implications for Yugoslavia." *Comparative Politics* 17, no. 2: 211–228.

Creed, Gerald W. 1998. *Domesticating Revolution: From Socialist Reforms to Ambivalent Transition in a Bulgarian Village*. University Park: Pennsylvania State University Press.

Edwards, Lovett F. 1954. *Introducing Yugoslavia*. London: Methuen.

Grandits, Hannes. 2010. "Kinship and the Welfare State in Twentieth-Century Croatian Transitions." In *Family, Kinship and State in Contemporary Europe, Vol. 1: The Century of Welfare: Eight Countries*, ed. Hannes Grandits and Patrick Heady, 249–254. Frankfurt: Campus.

Gregory, Chris. 2009. "Whatever Happened to Householding?" In *Market and Society: The Great Transformation Today*, ed. Chris Hann and Keith Hart, 133–159. Cambridge: Cambridge University Press.

Gudeman, Stephen. 2001. *The Anthropology of Economy: Community, Market, and Culture*. Hoboken, NJ: Wiley-Blackwell.

———. 2008. *Economy's Tension*. New York: Berghahn Books.

Gudeman, Stephen, and Alberto Rivera. 1990. *Conversations in Columbia: The Domestic Economy in Life and Text*. Cambridge: Cambridge University Press.

Guyer, Jane. 1987. *Feeding African Cities: Studies in Regional Social History*. London: International African Institute.

Halperin, Rhoda H. 1994. *Cultural Economies. Past and Present*. Austin: University of Texas Press

Hann, Chris. 1990. *Tea and the Domestication of the Turkish State*. Huntingdon: Eothen Press.

Holzman, Franklyn D. 1974. *Foreign Trade Under Central Planning*. Cambridge, MA: Harvard University Press.

Kardelj, Edvard. 1976. *The System of Planning in a Society of Self-management*. Belgrade: Socialist Thought and Practice.

Koneski, Metodi. 2004. *Ekonomski i opštestven razvoj na Prilep i Prilepsko po osloboduvanjeto: (1944-1990)*. Prilep: Društvo za nauka i umetnost.

Lavigne, Marie. 1991. *International Political Economy and Socialism*. Cambridge: Cambridge University Press. [Maison des Sciences de l'Homme (first edition in French, 1985)].

Monova, Miladina. 2015. "'We don't have work. We just grow a little tobacco.' Household Economy and Ritual Effervescence in a Macedonian Town." In *Economy and Ritual: Six Studies on Postsocialist Transformations,* ed. Stephen Gudeman and Chris Hann. New York: Berghahn Books.

Obrębski, Józef. 1977. *Ritual and Social Structure in a Macedonian Village,* ed. Barbara Kerewsky and Joel M. Halpern, Issue 1 of Occasional Papers Series. Amherst: Department of Anthropology, University of Massachusetts.

———. 2002 [1932, 1934, 1936]. *Etnosociološki studii,* vol. III, ed. and trans. from Polish T. Vražinovski; trans. from English L. Guševska. Skopje, and Prilep: Institut za Staroslovenska Kultura, Matica Makedonska.

Polanyi, Karl. 2001 [1944]. *The Great Transformation. The Political and Economic origins of Our Times.* Boston: Beacon Press.

———. 1957. "The Economy as Instituted Process." In *Trade and Market in the Early Empires. Economies in History and Theory,* ed. Karl Polanyi, C.M. Arensberg, and H.W. Pearson, 243–270. New York: Free Press.

Rheubottom, David. 1971. *A Structural Analysis of Conflict and Cleavage in Macedonian Domestic Groups.* Ph.D. Thesis, University of Rochester, published in Ann Arbor, MI.

———. 1996. "Land, Labor and the Zadruga: The Economic Viability of Peasant Households in Macedonia." *Manchester Papers in Social Anthropology* no. 3. Manchester: Department of Social Anthropology.

Slabey, Joseph, ed. 1949. *Slavonic Encyclopaedia.* New York: Philosophical Library.

Stancović, S. 1971. "Constitutional Changes in Yugoslavia—Part One: Meaning of the 21 Amendments." *Radio Free Europe Research Reports* No. 0922. http://www.osaarchivum.org/files/holdings/300/8/3/text/79-4-252.shtml.

Şuster, Zeljan. 2000. "Self-Management in Yugoslavia." In *Encyclopaedia of Eastern Europe. From the Congress of Vienna to the Fall of Communism,* ed. Richard Frucht, 717. New York: Garland Publishing.

Tomashevich, Jozo. 1955. *Peasants, Politics and Economic Change in Yugoslavia.* Stanford, CA: Stanford University Press.

Woodward, Suzan. 1995. *Unemployment: The Political Economy of Yugoslavia, 1945-1990.* Princeton, NJ: Princeton University Press.

Zakonjšek, Pavla. 1966. *Praktična Kuharica: Slovenian Cookbook.* Zagreb: Znanje.

*Zemjodelski Kalendar,* N1. 1978. Skopje. Published annually.

*Zemjodelski Kalendar,* N5. 1983. Skopje. Published annually.

# 4

## Self-Sufficiency is Not Enough

*Ritual Intensification and Household*
*Economies in a Kyrgyz Village*

Nathan Light

Household self-sufficiency in the village of Beshbulak in northwestern Kyrgyzstan is less valued for itself than for the *social* sufficiency that self-sufficiency supports.[1] The village moral economy links people and households in relations of mutual responsibility, including long-term social networks and mutual aid alliances. Concern for reputation and desire for close ties lead people to use resources produced at home to support activities in the social groups to which they belong. Subsistence production, thrift, and disciplined consumption conserve household resources and enable people to make better contributions to feasts and other events. Household members help each other participate in events and maintain positive reputations. Rather than promoting distinction and separation from village economic life, Kyrgyz ideals about self-sufficiency mean people rely on efficient household subsistence production and limited consumption to uphold their responsibilities to kin, allies, and community. Household sharing also helps individual members pursue education, invest in productive resources, and even pay for defense against legal prosecution or other threats.

While Aristotle suggests that autarky allows households to provide subsistence without market interactions, self-sufficient subsistence practices of Kyrgyz in Beshbulak maximize responsible participation in community economic life and the many exchanges that take place in social rituals. Kyrgyz social rituals in the village I describe constitute a distinctive sphere of economic activity in which there is a complex accounting for contributions, both symbolic and material, but in which people are not competing to maximize material returns because mutual recognition for generous participation is also valuable (Robbins 2009). In effect, this social economy converts material participation through gifts and hospitality into symbolic value in an economy of recognition. I suggest that this is particularly effective within the bounded and stable groups characteristic of Beshbulak social life: there is close attention to carefully balanced reciprocity within the looser and less enduring groups such as rotating savings associations, while more enduring groups, especially agnatic kin and households, are more willing to support less productive members and be less calculating (see Light 2015).

This chapter presents an account of Kyrgyz social orientation in which production is managed by the household but involves some mutual aid between households. Ritual consumption takes place in larger groups, under a moral principle of reciprocal sharing and egalitarian transfers, and the only overtly recognized hierarchy is that of status based on age. Wealthier people have larger rituals, but gain little by these: they have larger obligations as well and end up with little effective power or authority. I begin my discussion with an overview of how domains of production, consumption, and circulation interact, and of relevant theoretical models, and then discuss ethnographic examples to illustrate variations of practice in relation to this broad community pattern of economic life.

People in Beshbulak come together socially for work and ritual within a variety of solidarity groups—patrilineal kin, affines, neighbors, rotating savings associations, classmates—and generally invest more in these relations than in productive resources or personal savings. Mutual aid and exchange relations are ways to accumulate trustworthy allies and a good reputation that are at least as reliable as bank accounts or property. Resources put into social circulation create interlocking relations and solidarity in multiple groups. Strong social ties can respond flexibly to changing needs in ways that banking and other contractual economic relations cannot.

The important relations of production, circulation and consumption in Kyrgyz communities such as Beshbulak can be understood in terms of interlocking cycles. Jonathan Parry and Maurice Bloch (1989) contrast long-term exchange relations to shorter-term cycles of market exchange. Other economic anthropologists turn to Karl Marx's distinction of non-expansive domestic commodity production in the commodity-money-commodity cycle and expansive capitalist accumulation of profits in a cycle of money-commodity-money (e.g., Sahlins 1972: 84). But nuanced analysis of the specific cycles of Kyrgyz socioeconomic life suggest that these abstract categories lack explanatory power because different products of domestic work have different uses in economic life, and people enter into a wide variety of relationships that expand their access to needed material, labor, and symbolic resources. Kyrgyz produce and transform resources within social events and create dense networks of relations linking individuals and their households in ways that align the forces of self-interest and community interest. Kyrgyz productive strategies revolve around a variety of options, most of which produce social relations through locally defined material transactions, and cannot be reduced to simpler, universal categories such as money and commodities. Most Kyrgyz in Beshbulak do conceive of social transactions as having some characteristics of investment or savings that yield future returns, but they do not pursue profit so much as security through their relationships (Werner 1998). Ongoing trust relations that aid in the reproduction of social and material life are more important than monetary or material profit, and yield instead the benefit of reliable social ties. Economic profit attained through extracting material returns in excess of one's contributions to social events introduces the self-interest related to market transactions and thus is kept out of most village social relations.[2] The diverse kinds of production, exchange, and consumption in Beshbulak cannot be reduced to the simpler economic cycles of domestic production or of subsistence and commodity production suggested by Sahlins and others, nor to short- and long-term cycles as suggested by Parry and Bloch. In fact, these reflect narrow economic thinking that villagers tend to avoid because it reduces the social benefits that result from feasts and rituals. The variety of productive and consumptive activities bring community members together in many different kinds of events that create a more interdependent, efficient, and secure socioeconomic community life.[3] Self-sufficiency is not enough because people and their households benefit from reciprocal responsibilities within social groups beyond the household, including kin, classmates, friends, colleagues, neighbors, and community as a whole.

In order to sustain this valued social sufficiency, people generally subscribe to a number of moral principles (Light 2015): it is best to be generous when possible, and one should always avoid the appearance of being cheap. One should not be boastful or competitive about generous acts. Participants in ritual events should receive equal treatment except for differentiation based on age and relationship to hosts (affines are the most respected guests). People should preserve balanced reciprocity as much as possible and not try to profit from local transactions. They follow general norms about contributions or gifts in events and in reciprocity for previous gifts. If someone initiates a purchase of something such as an animal, they should not bargain over the price. A local seller should set a reasonable price but is not going to offer items at a discount except to friends.[4] Local morality also obliges people to help preserve the capacity of all members to survive in the community, or in the terms of James Scott, the "right to subsistence" (see Light 2015 for more discussion). Household subsistence is valued for its own sake and for cultivating families and individuals that participate successfully and responsibly in the community, as well as for producing material surpluses that make community ritual life possible. If a household has trouble maintaining self-sufficient subsistence, others encourage and help it, even giving or loaning resources to conduct life-cycle rituals and feasts.[5] Even if a household can barely afford subsistence, ritual events maintain community ties and mutual respect; a household should offer hospitality to its allies no matter how limited its resources. Household reputation includes community perceptions about whether household members are doing their best despite adversity, misfortune, or limited productive capacity. However, there are usually people in the community willing to make loans, and although most households manage to repay them, some remain impoverished and eventually come to rely more on gifts, i.e., charity. Unfortunately a few money lenders in the village do charge exorbitant interest rates that make some debts difficult to repay, but these are unsecured loans so ultimately the lenders cannot collect.

My argument in this chapter is that ritual events, including feasts and gift exchanges, are social responsibilities that involve costs but also provide benefits, and motivate accumulation and expense of important resources. Kyrgyz villagers feel socially obliged to support events, but also want and enjoy them, and their commitment to such social events stimulates production beyond subsistence needs. They earmark domestic animals for consumption in feasting and avoid everyday household consumption of meat, reserving the best foods for ritual events and hospitality (cf. Gudeman 2001: 38). In addition, villagers raise and prepare ceremonial foods (preserved fruit and salads, butter and cream) used in providing hospitality, and sell cash crops to obtain the funds necessary to hold celebrations, feasts, and commemorations.[6]

Widely shared expectations for participation in social groups and events, including giving hospitality and gifts, contributing resources and work for others' events, engaging in mutual aid or paid transactions, and making and taking loans, provide for an organized social economy with clear obligations to family, agnates, affines, classmates, neighbors, and so on. Shared expectations, recognition of personal autonomy, avoidance of direct conflict, and desire for a good reputation facilitate participation. Numerous differentiated relationships mean people have to limit their commitments to each one. Some groups include fairly rigorous accounting to make sure members contribute equally and fulfill their obligations. People have to balance their obligations and exclusive commitment to a single group is uncommon. People generally retain personal autonomy except when working within a strongly hierarchical structure such as a patrilineage. Thus we have the slight paradox that no commitment to a group takes precedence over duty to the household, but the combined effect of many obligations to groups means that the household should be self-exploiting and thrifty.

Self-disciplined thrift and self-sufficient subsistence enable responsible participation in social relations, and it is in community social life that a household's self-sufficiency and responsibility are assessed. Self-sufficiency is recognized as the basis for household contributions to the community and shapes the reputations of the household members. Subsistence production sustains people, but their lives are valued and recognized through responsible participation in social groups. Socially sufficient management of responsibilities maintains ties and reputation; rituals and feasting are the most important contexts for performing social sufficiency for audiences of friends, kin, and allies. A priority on self-sufficiency emphasizes subsistence production with limited exchange, while pursuit of social sufficiency involves managing resources to participate effectively in social exchanges.

## Animals, Domestic Production, and Intensification

Beshbulak household production can be divided into three partially overlapping categories with limited conversion of products from one category to another: domestic consumption, market exchange, and ritual consumption or exchange. Ritual exchange and consumption or feasting are social obligations for which Beshbulak households maintain a separate "ceremonial fund" (Wolf 1966) that is accumulated alongside production for domestic subsistence and for market exchange.[7] Kyrgyz animal stocks are part of their "ceremonial fund" and most villagers resist exchanging animals for non-ceremonial resources. Kyrgyz thus relegate animals to a distinct economic sphere (Bohannan 1955; Barth 1967).[8] Raising animals is basic to household economic activity but meat is rarely part of household subsistence consumption except in well-off households. The cows, sheep and goats kept by 80 percent of households are sold or exchanged only when a household has accumulated more than enough for foreseeable ritual obligations. Kyrgyz villagers who run short of money or incur debts avoid selling animals, but try to rely on loans or charity for subsistence needs while earmarking their animals for ritual activities. Although accounting for animals and calculating equivalences among those of different species, ages, and qualities can refer to widely recognized monetary values, the animals themselves are rarely brought to market (Light 2015). The reluctance to sell animals contrasts with Eric Wolf's characterization of peasants as readily shifting resources among different "funds."

The Kyrgyz case thus challenges the common idea that subsistence needs must take priority over production for other purposes, and shows how circulation of resources within the community provides for paths outside of the closed household economy that serve to link its ceremonial and subsistence funds. Sahlins (1972) and Wolf (1966) both argue that a subsistence fund dominates in the household economy unless political hierarchy leads to intensified production for ceremonial purposes.[9]

Animals are a familiar and efficient means for Beshbulak villagers to convert labor into living resources that gradually increase in value and can be reserved for ritual hospitality and gifts. Daily care of animals generally takes precedence over maximizing crop production through weeding, cultivating, or fertilizing. Cows provide milk, fowl provide a limited number of eggs, and dung serves as fuel and fertilizer, but the strongest motivation for raising animals is to provide meat for ritual feasts. Sheep can be served at one's own feasts or given as gifts and contributions to feasts of others, while cows and, less commonly, horses are often earmarked for gifts or rituals that may be planned several years in advance. Animals can also be loaned to others who need to hold a feast. Such loans should be repaid with an identical animal (i.e., an animal born at the same time: after a year, the loan of a two-year-old sheep should be repaid with a three-year old; see Light 2015).

In order to reserve animals for feasts, Kyrgyz households consume little meat and subsist on milk products, flour, potatoes, oil, vegetables, and fruit. Along with thrift and self-discipline in food consumption, they also earmark other resources for rituals and hospitality rather than household use: rooms where guests eat, furniture, cookware, platters, cups, tablecloths (*dastorkon*), mats for sitting and sleeping, and samovars for preparing tea. Such equipment can be loaned among households for major events, but most households have sufficient equipment to offer hospitality—both food and overnight accommodations—to at least ten or fifteen guests with little advance planning.[10]

Beshbulak household economies thus offer a clear contrast to the "antisurplus tendency" that Marshall Sahlins finds characteristic of the domestic mode of production (1972: 86). Beshbulak villagers do generate a "surplus" or cash crop, generally beans, potatoes, and/or fruit that is sold to buy household subsistence needs that they do not produce, such as wheat flour, oil, and consumer products. Most Kyrgyz animal production is isolated from subsistence needs and used instead to produce social relations through feasting. Sahlins argues that households only produce a surplus beyond subsistence needs when political hierarchies compel intensified production and extract this surplus for redistribution and accumulation. He does not leave room for sources of intensification such as the nonpolitical feasting through which Beshbulak inhabitants create community social life.

For Kyrgyz, as for many other Central Asians, Sahlins's model of domestic production should be adjusted to recognize other motivations for intensification besides politics and markets: Beshbulak Kyrgyz do produce surpluses, but much is reserved for ritual activity and they generally limit their animals to those needed for feasts they will host and for gifts they will offer to others. Only a small number of households attempt to accumulate wealth through raising animals for market trade, and even these generally spend considerably more on feasts. Few households abstain from local rituals. For major events such as marriages or funerals, people try to hold large feasts but without exceeding the animals that they have available or can reasonably borrow from others. Hosts try to offer a feast at least as large as what people in the community expect, thus ensuring recognition of the event as appropriate to the hosts' means.

Land is relatively evenly distributed and most crops can be sold or consumed for subsistence, while animals are kept largely for ritual needs, not sale or consumption. Only 15 percent of Beshbulak households produce a surplus of animals beyond what they need for rituals, while more than 80 percent of households produce a cash crop surplus beyond subsistence needs. Cash is a necessary part of contemporary subsistence because most people have to buy oil and flour, and it is also needed for ingredients for feasts. Animals are more inconvenient to buy and sell than crops and are vital for holding feasts. Unlike crops, animals usually continue to increase in value over time, while crops must be harvested and then begin to lose value. Animals are thus more readily reserved while crops should be sold or consumed. The one distinctive case is that of dry beans, which keep well after harvest and which are readily sold to local buyers, so people tend to hold part of their harvest and sell beans when they need the cash.

Sahlins makes restrictive assumptions about the economic and political role of rituals and feasting. He repeatedly mentions rituals as impediments to production (1972: 56, 63, 65, 74, 86), but identifies feasting as a more functional activity that serves the quest for political influence and the creation of hierarchy and followers. He does not consider the role of feasts in interactions among kin and other solidarity groups as found in Kyrgyzstan but only in relation to the intensified production that he claims is stimulated by political activities (1972: 130).[11] For Beshbulak villagers, however, most feasting is part of creating and maintaining the reciprocal and affinal ties that are central to collective recognition of life-cycle rituals, and most have an explicitly spiritual intent because sociality is understood to produce spiritual effects. Feasts are seen as opportunities to show mutual respect and appreciation, and cultivate positive feelings among community members, rather than to promote individual interests. Life-cycle feasts do not give special recognition or respect to political figures or their activities, and even death commemorations for local notables have no overt political content. Some community celebrations offer opportunities for wealthier villagers to make publicly acknowledged contributions. Similarly politicians may show up as part of the middle-school graduation ceremonies. There is thus a political dimension to some public local events but in most events age provides the only overt hierarchy. Feasts that are sometimes held to garner political support are carefully framed within prevailing cultural models of honoring local elders and seeking their *bata* blessings, which are more moral encouragement than political endorsement (cf. Beyer 2009).

In Beshbulak, feasting for both happy or sad occasions generates mutual recognition and sociality under the banner of shared community spiritual goals and adds to solidarity among kin and friends, while material and political instrumentalities threaten solidarity with potential conflicts. This contrasts with the more common political feasting in other parts of Kyrgyzstan where big men hold feasts for clients and allies (Radnitz 2010: 84–86; Ismailbekova 2012; cf. Kushner 1929). In these cases Sahlins's model of intensification in service of and as a result of political organization is more relevant.

To summarize, the Kyrgyz "domestic mode of production" is rarely restricted to subsistence alone, but also supports participation in community and in building and maintaining ties with allies through rituals. Households produce a surplus above subsistence needs, particularly in the form of animals that are reserved for ritual consumption. In addition, households produce cash crops—some of which, such as dry beans, are never eaten at home—and use the money for subsistence needs, ritual activities, and other household goals. The antisurplus tendency that Sahlins identifies is indeed present, but only in the sense that most households do not save or invest to increase material capital, but use "surplus" instead to participate in the community to sustain ties and reputations within largely egalitarian exchange relations. Some households do accumulate money for particular purposes. After fulfilling subsistence and ceremonial needs, including the cash and animals needed for feasts and gifts, the most common investment of surplus is in education for children. Surpluses are also used to establish small-scale enterprises such as shops or to purchase vehicles that can be used to provide income through transportation services.

## The Buryat Comparison: Intensification for Socialist or Ritual Economies

Caroline Humphrey tested Sahlins's ideas about self-sufficiency and the domestic mode of production in her ethnographic study of a collective farm in Buryatia. In her comparison of Soviet and post-Soviet periods she describes the complex organization of production and the distribution of authority, respect, and rewards among workers and managers. Although the herding camps known as *otara* preserved more self-sufficient modes of Buryat kinship-based work and life, the overall collective farm system involved extensive interdependence among different work units with products circulating among them. Workers could double their wages through producing animals to sell to the farm. Collective farm households also depended on services and material resources they received through the farm, including feed for sheep and cows (Humphrey 1998: 241–242, 290–294). Finally, Buryat collective farm workers in the Soviet system also maintained ties to kin living elsewhere, particularly in towns, for access to goods and services and as a reserve labor pool for harvesting hay, in exchange for which town-dwellers usually received food products. In the post-Soviet period these ties became even more important as collective farm resources and services were curtailed (1998: 296–297, 456–459). Humphrey concludes that self-sufficiency has expanded dramatically in the post-Soviet period, but it cannot become a general ideal because some basic material inputs—wheat flour and concentrated animal feed—cannot be produced by households, and because people are accustomed to both "lateral reciprocity with kin and neighbors" and "vertical inputs from the farm and the state" (1998: 460). Postsocialist households also cannot be self-sufficient because they depend on external providers of electricity, fuel, and services such as education.

In another study Humphrey (2002: 164–174) considers redistribution and political authority in the context of collective harvesting: a postsocialist farm chairman was unable to enforce labor discipline in the collective effort to harvest hay because the political and economic system no longer adequately supported his authority. Instead he had to motivate workers with gifts within ritual activities. Humphrey finds that this does not conform to Sahlins's idea that leaders command resources from "independent households" that otherwise remain within the domestic mode of production. Instead the households remain within collective social relations: when the farm chairman manages to heighten solidarity through appropriate ritual acts and gifts then people are drawn into production as part of the ritual event.

Humphrey also attends to the ways that Soviet and post-Soviet hierarchical management intensify production through division of labor, planning, technological innovation, resource and job allocation, and distribution of products (Humphrey 1998: 228–266). Intensified production supported the growth of the integrated Soviet economy: by division of labor and "rational" management Soviet planners sought to maximize production of high-value farm products such as sheep wool through new technologies and work processes (Jacquesson 2010). Scientific management was applied to workers' lives as well, attempting to shift medical practices, beliefs, and rituals away from kin and community activities toward socialist principles (Lane 1981; Michaels 2003).

Humphrey supports my own observations about the Soviet economy as an example of political power intensifying production and extracting surplus: intensified Soviet production allowed the state to both increase foreign exchange earnings and offer more consumer products to workers. Government planners could direct new goods and services to rural areas, although economic development, production, and consumption were also conducted as symbolic performances in which the state converted economic activities into demonstrations of the state's own success. Prestige products were distributed as rewards for heroes of Soviet labor: Kyrgyzstanis remember automobiles and televisions being given in the late 1960s to the most productive shepherds.

Intensified production in the service of state economic, political, and social goals was a central feature of working life in Soviet-era Beshbulak, but with the loss of centralized planning and integrated production and distribution, post-Soviet Beshbulak household economies have changed radically. Specialized production of commodities continues, but is oriented toward market sales, and households spend much more time on production for their own subsistence. In addition to the crops that provide domestic subsistence and market commodities, animals produced in the household provide a surplus used for social sufficiency: these are primarily consumed in ritual feasts among people who are important within the household's social networks, including agnates, affines, neighbors, classmates, and friends.

In postsocialist Beshbulak there is widespread discussion of—and occasional efforts towards—intensifying production through investment and entrepreneurship, but most households tend to be successful only as independent operators and have limited cooperation even with close allies: the only businesses based in the village with employees are the few herder-families who have hired a laborer to help with herding sheep, or the one household that hires people to process commodity crops. Otherwise, every local enterprise consists of a single household that rents additional fields and hires occasional day laborers, operates equipment and vehicles to provide farming and transport services, or runs a shop selling consumer goods or gasoline. The managerial roles and hierarchically organized workplaces and brigades of the Soviet period are gone, and even if households are not economically self-sufficient, they are largely independent in organizing and managing their economic activities and hence decisions about intensification and redistribution of surpluses are made within the household. Economic decision-making now occurs almost entirely within households and local government only manages communal resources and collects taxes and fees for water, pasture, and veterinary care.

In the rest of this chapter, I describe the social organization of Beshbulak, focusing on the ways that self-sufficiency and sharing emerge in social relations.

## Beshbulak in Soviet and Post-Soviet Kyrgyzstan

The village of Beshbulak is one of several small communities along the course of the Karatash River in northwestern Kyrgyzstan, with roughly 4,000 inhabitants in 700 households. The nearest market town has a population of 13,000 and is one hour away by road, while the *oblast* (province) capital with 33,000 inhabitants is roughly two hours away. The large city of Taraz (Jambul) is 80 kilometers away in southern Kazakhstan, but has become more difficult to reach in the post-Soviet period because of the time and documents required to cross the border.

Until the beginning of the twentieth century, Beshbulak and surrounding river valley areas served as winter quarters for transhumant pastoralists who took their herds of sheep and horses to mountain pastures as much as 60 kilometers away. During the early Soviet period these Kyrgyz were organized into small cooperatives (*artel'*) that shared basic farming equipment and animals, although most of the community continued to join the summer migration to the mountains rather than farming over the summer. Between the 1930s and 1960s the number of families who made the summer migration to distant pastures steadily decreased and more people remained in the village tending fields and animals over the summer. Small cooperatives were gradually combined into larger collective and state farms.[12] Beshbulak was converted first to a state farm and then to a pure-breed state farm (*plemsovkhoz*) in the early 1960s when it began to specialize in raising sheep with high quality wool to be sold on Soviet and international markets. Locals proudly describe how the 3.5 kilos of wool produced from one adult sheep would be taken to Moscow and made into a high quality suit worth over 100 rubles. In addition to commodity production of wool and tobacco intended for Soviet and international markets, the Beshbulak state farm raised horses and pigs (and even yaks for a brief period), maintained a small dairy, and produced fodder crops, apples, and wheat that were for its own subsistence and operational needs, as well as to sell in nearby state-run shops.

The shift toward large-scale state managed wool production points to increasing state-organized intensification of agricultural production through specialization and technological innovation. Soviet-era intensification of large-scale, specialized animal husbandry in Kyrgyzstan required intensive pasture use that resulted in over-grazing (Jacquesson 2010). Ecological damage was somewhat mitigated by intensive production of fodder and concentrated feed.

Increasing efficiency, intensification, and technology meant that farms grew in size and state farms became more numerous. Between 1940 and 1983, collective farms in Kyrgyzstan shrank in number from 1,700 to 180 but the average size increased by a factor of five from 160 to 870 workers. The state increased its management of production by converting many collective farms into state farms: in 1940 the Kyrgyz Republic had 36 state farms with an average of 500 workers each, while by 1983 there were 256 state farms employing an average of 770 workers each. By 1983, the 86 sheep-breeding state farms held nearly half of Kyrgyzstan's total sheep, while collective farms held 40 percent and private ownership accounted for around 12 percent. State and collective farm sheep produced most of the wool while privately held sheep accounted for one-third of the meat production.[13]

Socialist ideological policies designed to limit economic hierarchy and exploitation, facilitate equal access to services and resources, and provide full employment meant that Soviet-era Kyrgyz were not able to maintain traditionally self-sufficient production nor produce adequate domestic surpluses for social rituals. The disruptive transition to collectivized ownership of animals, fields, and equipment during the first two decades of Soviet rule led to reliance on shared resources controlled by the political regime. After the relaxing of the strict controls of the 1930s and 1940s, household control over their own animals, land, and other resources grew somewhat in the 1950s; the state relaxed its fixation on collective production and allowed households to own a small number of animals: five sheep and one cow or one horse was the rule for the period after Stalin's stricter controls were relaxed. These animals were important for consumption and exchange during life-cycle feasts.

For most of the Soviet period people in Beshbulak maintained private production of some household subsistence needs, but depended heavily on income and services provided by the collective farm. Locals like to comment that Soviet-era market prices were low and made it largely unnecessary to produce subsistence products such as vegetables, wheat, or milk for oneself. As Humphrey pointed out for Buryatia as well, selling animals to the collective farm was an important source of income. Some Kyrgyz managed to keep more animals by mingling them within the collective herds, while others accumulated surplus in cash or through loaning animals to people who owned less than their official quota. The rural-urban interdependence described by Humphrey (1998: 296–297), in which urban dwellers provide extra farm labor in exchange for rural produce and animal products, was and continues to be important for Kyrgyz as well.

## Changing Division of Labor and Socialist "Rationalization"

A fundamental goal within Soviet economic rationalization was eliminating the economic uncertainty felt to plague unplanned markets for labor and goods. Under Soviet rule, full employment, reliable incomes, fixed prices for staple goods, and free or affordable services (medical care, childcare, education, utilities, transport, irrigation water, veterinary care) provided people with more secure lives and budgets as well as opportunities for social mobility. Economic development and planned production, as well as the expanding availability of consumer goods, helped Soviet citizens see themselves as modern citizens of a multiethnic, industrialized state. Kyrgyz households produced less of their own fuel and food than in the pre-Soviet period and obtained foodstuffs, coal, and electricity through the state farm and its shops.

Although many products were relatively affordable, households with surplus labor did produce some items such as vegetables, bread, or clothing at home to increase savings. Soviet-era Kyrgyz relied on domestic garden plots of 0.15 hectares for growing vegetables and fruits that they preserved for the winter. Many baked their own bread and most other everyday foods, such as fried dough and noodles, were always homemade. People raised animals for dairy and meat but these also could be sold to the state. Domestic production of animals and other foods that could have been bought in shops marked a distinctively Kyrgyz sense of self-sufficiency. One villager compared the ways Russians and Kyrgyz in Soviet-era Beshbulak spent their Sunday breaks from collective farm work, saying that Russians would go on excursions and have picnics while Kyrgyz would work in their gardens and care for their animals. Kyrgyz set themselves higher domestic production goals because their frequent feasts and domestic ritual celebrations required intensified production of valued foods.

Even in the Soviet period when much of a household's subsistence resources could be obtained through the state farm, feasting remained an important part of Kyrgyz social labor and considerable time was invested in producing ritual events and being a guest at them. Feasts were limited by both economic constraints and political policies in the 1930s–1950s, but as prosperity increased there was more official tolerance for such events. Nonetheless, most ritual feasting had to remain outside of "rationalized" collective farm life and wedding feasts and animal gift exchanges took place at night in order to avoid observation and restriction by authorities, especially the all-important *nike* (from Arabic *nikah*) Muslim ritual which makes the marriage licit: even now the local *moldo* (mullah) usually conducts *nike* around midnight. In the Soviet period Muslim death rituals were more acceptable and were conducted during the daytime.

Soviet social policies attempted to limit the time and resources that Kyrgyz expended on feasting, but domestic production was encouraged for much of the later Soviet period because it supplied additional food resources to the economy. Although Soviet versions of life-cycle rituals were promoted (cf. Lane 1981), and those with a university education or who belonged to the Communist party organized smaller "Komsomol-style" weddings among friends, most Kyrgyz merely hid the fact that they continued to hold large feasts and exchange bridewealth and dowry, including large gifts of animals, during the Soviet period (cf. Humphrey 1998: 398–399).

The discourse of socialist rationality included commitment to individual choices in love and relationships, and arranged marriages and bridewealth were attacked as involving unacceptable parental control and market transactions that treated women like property (Keller 2001; Northrop 2004; Edgar 2004; Kamp 2008; Loring 2008). Soviet ideologues interpreted exchanges around life-cycle rituals to be akin to market exchange, involving contracts and property relations that were unacceptable in human relationships. The importance of material exchanges within social ties and life-cycle rituals was condemned as exploitation of people within market-like economic hierarchies, but in fact the larger problem was that the power of ritual exchange created conflicting loyalties.[14]

The Soviet ideal was to replace village systems of particularistic social and economic exchange with bureaucratically defined relations within the collective farm and with the state beyond it. Economic practices were to be managed according to plans, while symbolic exchanges were to occur within approved institutions. Material exchanges among households linked through kinship and alliance were disrupted in order that household loyalties would not interfere with providing labor to and acquiring resources from the state and its institutions. Soviet rituals displayed ideological links of citizens and the larger society and connected people to Soviet systems of education, employment, and consumption, thus shifting material transactions to the rationally managed and standardized contexts, and promoting the ideal of seeking relationships and happiness in these same contexts (Gorsuch 1996; Kamp 2002).

In contemporary Beshbulak, some Kyrgyz critique ritual exchanges in terms that reflect Soviet-era discourses about morality and rational economy. They see rituals as wasteful or "irrational" and attempt to limit their commitments, choosing greater self-sufficiency and fewer rituals. One woman resists the constant socializing of Kyrgyz because she says it seems uncivilized, but this reflexive comment does not change the fact that she does enjoy participating in social events. Others limit exchanges that prioritize kin relations at the expense of personal choices. One man refused bridewealth (*kalïng*) when his daughters married because he felt material transactions might constrain a couple's happiness:

[My daughters] chose their husbands by themselves... I asked the *kuda* (the parents of the son-in-law) not to give bridewealth. ... I told them that the couple should simply be happy, I didn't want money for my daughters, I only wish for their happiness. ... I think taking bridewealth is bad: it suggests you forced the person to marry or sold her. If the people who took my daughter gave me money, it implies that they can use my daughter as a slave. It should be free and clean. They should marry for love, and I do not want a bridewealth.

This view of bridewealth payments is an unusual ideological resistance to Kyrgyz tradition, which is otherwise strongly upheld because people feel that without the transfer of bridewealth neither the bride nor her parents will be respected. Another attitude that originates in Soviet discourses is the sense that patrilineal clan (*uruu*) identity and solidarity are problematic because they lead to nepotism and bias. Post-Soviet politics and schooling in Kyrgyzstan have generally led to more positive views and a renewed embrace of clan identities and activities. However, continuing appreciation of Soviet "rational" economic planning can be seen in the widespread wish that Kyrgyzstan's government would do more to manage the market by guaranteeing stable commodity prices so producers can predict what they will receive for their harvests, and by establishing state enterprises such as a juice and canning factory that would serve as a reliable buyer of local produce.

The analysis of self-sufficiency reveals how Soviet efforts to rationalize both economic and social lives involved disrupting traditional, local, and particularistic socioeconomic relations and replacing them with bureaucratic, ideologically standardized ties to the state and its rituals (Lane 1981; Keller 2001). The strong Soviet state restricted economic and social activity, and its planners strove to manage production and gain control over surpluses to use in building an ideal society. They attempted to prevent people from using resources in village-level ritual activities such as feasting and life-cycle exchange practices. Most traditional practices were restricted and scorned as backward. The Soviet state's management of people's symbolic and material lives led most to see themselves as Soviet citizens with political and economic commitments to state projects, and to adopt to varying degrees the state-imposed modern, rational ideologies and practices.

## Post-Soviet Economic Self-Sufficiency and Interdependence

In Beshbulak, as all over Kyrgyzstan, the dissolution of the Soviet political and economic system has resulted in a radical shift from reliance on state institutions and management toward greater self-reliance and self-sufficiency, but as Humphrey also found (1998), people continue to need access to markets, so at least in Kyrgyzstan, people have developed new enterprises and commodity products oriented toward market trade. Specialized production within the planned and integrated Soviet economy was no longer possible after 1991 and the state has been reduced to providing only basic infrastructure and services. Villagers now provide more diverse private services than were allowed during the Soviet period, when professionals were trained and authorized within state institutions. Currently, local clinics supported by NGO grant funding provide a mix of Soviet-style medical care along with some imported technology and drugs, but private doctors also diagnose illnesses and prescribe and dispense drugs from home offices. Spiritual healers suppressed by the Soviet state as irrational and unscientific are now widely accepted as providers of medical care and ritual services. The Soviet government severely restricted religious activities but in post-Soviet Kyrgyzstan there are mosques in almost every village, with prayers conducted by mullahs or imams who also provide spiritual services at household and community rituals, and sometimes work as healers as well.

By any measure, economic self-sufficiency and autonomous decision making about production and resource allocation have increased in the post-Soviet period: each household controls more private resources, especially land and animals, and makes more decisions about how to use these resources. In addition to the 0.15 hectare garden plots allowed during socialism, most households in Beshbulak received private plots of 1 to 2 irrigated hectares when the collective farm holdings were distributed to villagers (0.25 hectare per household member). Since state farm equipment and technical systems were no longer reliable and accessible, and Soviet market networks had broken down, local farmers experimented with new crops such as dry beans that require less technology and implemented simpler, domestic production techniques for existing crops and animals. Garden crops became much more important for subsistence, and many people planted apples and other fruit trees that give crops suited for market sales and canning. They abandoned the growing of tobacco because of declining markets and wheat because it was difficult to harvest and thresh without complex machinery. During the late 1990s and the 2000s farmers adopted the current mix of potatoes, fruit trees, garden vegetables, and sunflowers for subsistence and sale, maize and fodder crops for animal feed, and dry beans as a cash crop. These are produced and processed with a combination of rented harvesting, threshing and winnowing machinery, simple, sometimes makeshift, private equipment, and extensive hand processing.[15]

Dry beans are mostly exported to Turkey through local buyers, while potatoes, apples, and sunflowers are sold directly and through buyers for regional consumption. Apples and potatoes have to be sold within a couple of months of harvest while beans retain their value better because they do not decay or dry out, and thus provide a useful reserve that can be sold when cash is needed; they serve as an investment vehicle as well. Buyers of beans have to offer a fairer price to persuade people to sell because there is little risk of storage losses: people decide to sell when prices are high or they need money. Beshbulak farmers attribute much of their increasing prosperity since the late 1990s to bean production, but beans are not important for subsistence because few Kyrgyz eat them. Animal production for the market remains important, but only 15 to 20 percent of Beshbulak households regularly sell animals, while more than 80 percent raise some sheep, cows, or goats for milk products and meat for feasting rituals and gifts (Light 2015).

In addition to the broader range of local products and services to choose among, local transactions are more diverse than those of town markets: many exchanges do not involve cash, but cooperation, reciprocity, and gifts. Minor services such as healing do not have specified prices but are given in expectation that some gift or money will be given. Healers usually describe their skills as gifts, emphasizing that they did not intentionally learn them but were granted them spiritually and are obliged to help others regardless of material return. However, other services such as barbering also are done without a fixed price. In many community settings, open self-interest and profit maximizing such as bargaining over fees can negatively affect people's reputations. This cuts both ways: if someone does ask for a fee, it should be reasonable, and the customer should not bargain overtly.[16]

In the 1990s, when markets, transportation, and cash were limited, people raised mostly subsistence crops but also depended on barter and a variety of market trade activities to replace Soviet distribution systems. Animals, fuel, vodka, and staples such as wheat, sugar, and oil became important currencies for trade, barter, and gift exchange as people shifted from state-operated to private market activities. People experimented widely with market-oriented production in the 1990s although prevailing poverty and restraints on open pursuit of profit within community relations meant only a few activities were successful.

Unlike many villages in Kyrgyzstan, Beshbulak no longer has collective farm operations or joint productive activities except within a few families in which male siblings from separate households cooperate in herding.

Most households can farm their private plots with household labor but depend on mutual aid and hired labor when planting or harvesting, while the 15 percent of households that rent extra land depend more heavily on day laborers to expand production. Working together reduces the stigma and unpleasantness of farm tasks. Field work is considered the most unpleasant and is almost always done in groups: few people tend crops alone. This contrasts with herding, which is not only usually done alone, but often in remote areas, and sometimes even by children beginning around age ten. Herding is not labor-intensive and is felt to demonstrate independent skill and responsibility while agricultural labor is more strenuous and requires less skill. Working in a field for pay also suggests hierarchical relations between wealthy landowners and the working poor and reminds people of low-status work on the collective farms in the Soviet period. Herding was traditionally done on horseback and held a higher status during the Soviet period and before.

Both traditional and novel forms of village mutual aid expanded after the Soviet period.[17] Along with increased ritual life and the limiting of local market relations, mutual aid practices have helped limit economic differentiation and social fragmentation in the village. Everyday production involves a variety of cooperative activities among friends and kin, as well as more carefully calibrated reciprocal relations with neighbors. Groups of neighbors organize collective rotation for pasturing animals in a practice known as *kezüü* (cf. Werner 1998: 605). Friends and kin come together for cooperative work events known as *ashar*, which can involve anything from food processing to house-building. Groups of young male classmates cooperate in harvesting for each of their households. Crops are processed at home by kin and friends. Preserving fruits and vegetables is generally done by women in *ashar* work groups. Male agnates prepare for feasts by working together on slaughtering and butchering animals, while in-married *kelin*s (literally 'brides') cooperate in cleaning the inner organs and preparing the meat and other dishes.

## Sharing and Cooperation

Tension between the economic independence that people are expected to demonstrate by producing their own subsistence and the production of additional food and income to support ritual sharing in the community can emerge when people ask for help with household needs. Nonetheless most households participate in the moral economy in which sharing takes precedence over household economic independence and accumulation of resources.

Decisions about what is shared, how resources and help are asked for, and who shares with whom depend on the people, things, and social events involved. The hierarchy of value of social networks means that the least solidarity and sharing is shown to fellow villagers, and successively more is shown to neighbors, colleagues, friends, classmates, and agnatic and affinal kin. When a community member asks for small amounts of money or foodstuffs such as bread or flour the request is almost always granted. Charity often takes the form of earmarking small donations and unneeded materials to needy households. Neighbors often borrow household items from one another and are willing to share food. However, mutual aid with community members and neighbors is usually limited: people share labor or productive resources such as animals only within mutual aid relationships with friends, classmates, and kin. Assistance with production and in organizing feasts is usually reciprocated and younger kin are often given money when they help with work.

People carried out similar sharing and cooperative work relations during the socialist period, but the Soviet system allowed people also to offer resources they controlled within the collective farm, such as machines, construction materials, fuel, or fodder. Such sharing of resources and the collectivist spirit of socialist labor led to strong ties among work colleagues in brigades on the collective farm. The Soviet criticism of local practices of sharing and mutual aid within ritual contexts (seen as non-Soviet, irrational, or displaying ethnic chauvinism), offers an ironic contrast to the strongly ritualized sharing and cooperative work encouraged within the context of collective farming and work units. These collegial bonds continue to be important more than twenty years after the end of the Soviet system, in part because they reflect nostalgia for Soviet-era organization.

Beshbulak ideas about mutual aid seem more limited than what is found in villages in postsocialist Russia. Machines in Beshbulak generally are not loaned to others without contractual payment according to an accepted local standard. In the Ural Russian village where Douglas Rogers worked people felt obliged to share their farm machines and seemed unable to negotiate other terms. Rogers describes a Russian family who tried to avoid sharing their mini-tractor by harvesting without informing their usual mutual aid partners, but the partners came anyway and had to be allowed to help, and the family subsequently felt obliged to lend the mini-tractor to them for their harvesting (Rogers 2005: 70). In Beshbulak, few people share equipment because operators generally go wherever they will be paid: a piece of equipment is recognized as an investment with which a person should be able to make a living and thus is not an integral part of someone's farming activities. Only in one case that I know of was the use of a cultivator, operator, and fuel donated by a wealthy affine (*kuda*), and eventually reciprocated by giving a cow as a birthday gift.

More generally, Miller and Heady (2003) describe the pressures brought to bear on people in a Russian village who seek to separate themselves from local community interactions in order to pursue independent success. In Beshbulak, households generally conduct their productive activities relatively independently, but share the results of production through rituals. Cooperative work generally results not from social pressure but from desire for sociality and tends more toward celebration than efficient production.

## Ritualized Social Transactions

Some established forms of sharing and aid do not depend on specific existing relationships, but are social opportunities in the community that can be exploited through the ritual acts that make these more compelling than simple requests for help. To obtain money or a valuable gift one can perform *tartuu*, in which a good deed, performance, or well-crafted item, given with marks of respect to someone who is well-off, should be reciprocated with something of greater value. Lower-value spontaneous exchanges or sharing of good fortune are more common: someone conveying good news about a new marriage or birth will announce *süyünchüü* ("good news") and expect a small monetary gift in return. When someone returns from shopping in the market town they may be asked for *bazarlïk* ("of the bazaar") gifts by those they meet. When someone wins a prize, buys a new car, or opens a new shop the neighbors expect him or her to give a party to celebrate and share his or her good fortune: in such cases guests also bring gifts so the exchange is relatively balanced, and the collective celebration recognizes and validates the good fortune through social activity.

Good fortune should be shared and recognized: when a woman views a new bride she places a *jolluk* scarf on the bride's head as a gift and gives a small amount of money (known as *köründük*, "for seeing") to the mother-in-law, and when seeing a new baby such money is given as well. When dowry is delivered the woman who helps display the dowry is allowed to take one item from it and when someone is honored with a gift of formal clothing, the person who helps put it on is given a small monetary gift. These gifts marking social transactions include everyone within the material flows of community life: interaction and gifts are inextricable from communal relations and people should not be refused when they ask for something. Despite occasional jokes about these practices, Kyrgyz rarely avoid giving when expected or requested to do so.

Kyrgyz recognize and appreciate such prestations as transactions that are both ethnically specific and distinct from market transactions. They allow for flexibility and resilience in Kyrgyz socioeconomic transactions, and offer alternatives to the supposedly rational practices of market economies that are increasingly part of everyday life in Kyrgyzstan: local society continues to shape life around many existing economic practices rather than simply adopting those from outside (see Light 2015 for further examples).

Kyrgyz villagers negotiate community expectations around the constant giving of gifts, sometimes trying to get social agreement about limiting gifts such as clothes that are not likely to fit or carpets that are not needed (Beyer 2009). As described above, resistance to waste or excessive gift-giving may result from "rational" or "modern" values, often based upon principles learned as part of socialist ideology. Nonetheless, most villagers uphold expectations about sharing and gift exchange to prevent others from taking offense. Attendance at rituals when invited and giving and receiving gifts are serious obligations: ritual sharing and commensality show mutual respect and maintain community ties. Household self-sufficiency in production and consumption is expected and usually goes unremarked upon, but participation in community give and take is highly valued and receives strong positive feedback. Proper performances in the many categories of exchange prevent closure of the household economy into itself.

## Household Ritual Economies

Thrifty and disciplined management of household resources provides for household subsistence needs while also producing the material and labor reserves needed to hold ritual feasts. People in the household prioritize the production of animals used in feasting and the work needed to hold feasts. They work to prepare, serve, and clean up at feasts of agnatic kin and go as contributing guests to those of affinal kin. In addition to material resources and labor, the time commitment to feasts and other household ritual activities must also be provided by the household economy. In this section I provide more details about the relation of household economy to ritual practices.

Kyrgyz households consist of either nuclear or extended families, and sometimes as many as three married couples reside in the same compound. Marriage is generally patrilocal, with the bride initially moving into the home of the man's parents. When they have children, couples usually move into a house of their own, usually either a nearby homestead or a separate building in the same compound. The image of an extended household living around a shared oven or fire is still important, and they can be identified as a *tütün* (smoke) even though the present physical form includes several buildings around a courtyard with more than one cooking and living space. Male children eventually move into their own home after marriage, but the youngest son continues to live at home, cares for his elderly parents, and eventually inherits the home. Even after moving out, male and unmarried female children remain closely connected to their natal home and work with their parents to organize ritual events and assist with household work. Kyrgyz households are fairly permeable, with kin and friends often joining as temporary members when coming to a community for work or simply to help with household projects such as childcare or building projects.

In the Soviet period, Kyrgyz families averaged more than five children per couple but this has declined with the declining emphasis on hero-mothers and the loss of the Soviet-era child subsidies. For an average family with two employed parents, annual household income on the Beshbulak state farm in the 1980s averaged 1,800 rubles from wages, and a further 400 rubles from child support payments and pensions, and 300 rubles from sales of animals and other products to state market institutions (a ruble was officially equal to 1.50 USD). Bonuses, prizes, and awards might be worth as much as 500 rubles or more in some years but averaged only 50 rubles. Access to subsidized resources including transport, foodstuffs, electricity, fuel, and water provided by workplaces and local governments added to the stability and security of income (data from interviews, surveys and data in Tsentral'noe 1984). People describe the later Soviet period beginning in the 1960s as comfortable and characterized by a favorable balance of income and expenses, more and better quality housing, better child subsidies, increasing consumer goods, and easy access to education and medical care.

During my research in 2009–2010, Beshbulak households were directly producing roughly two-thirds of their subsistence food and supplementing this with income from a range of activities: through raising crops and animals an average household of five to seven people (with two to four children and perhaps a grandparent living at home) generates an annual cash income of 500–1,200 EUR from beans and/or potatoes, 100–300 EUR from fruits and vegetables, 200–300 EUR from wages, and 100–200 EUR from selling animals. A small shop selling household goods, gasoline, milk, eggs, and meat can generate another 200–400 EUR, and part- or full-time work in transport, textile production, network marketing, construction, ritual services, or healing may bring in another 200–500 EUR income after expenses.[18] These activities depend on the time and capacities of household members: the average household relies on sales of crops and one or two sideline businesses or wage work, resulting in an income of 1,500–1,800 EUR per year. Additional contributions may come from young adults living and working in Bishkek or abroad. Industrious and ambitious families that rent fields and hire workers can produce larger harvests of around five tons of beans or fifteen tons of potatoes, or maintain a larger flock of sheep and sell twenty to thirty animals per year. Such additional production results in another 1,000 EUR in annual income for a total of 2,500 EUR, although the additional work of producing and marketing these crops may cut into other sideline activities. Households with less land, fewer animals, poorer harvests, debts, fewer able-bodied people, or retired on small pensions may be forced to live on as little as 400–600 EUR per year and rely heavily on gifts and charity.

In addition to consuming the food it produces, the average household spends around 150–200 EUR per year per person for purchases of food, clothing, utilities, medical care, transport, and other basic needs. Thus, after covering subsistence needs a household of six people may have 300–500 EUR left over from the income described above. This surplus cash is usually spent on ritual activities, conveniences that can provide income such as automobiles or farm equipment, consumer goods such as televisions or refrigerators, entertainment, university education, or special medical care.

Ritual feasting is basic to household economic life and depends primarily on a stock of animals. The household's own events and its donations to those of others involve significant animal consumption, but this creates and maintains reciprocal relations with other households which in turn make contributions to one's own costly events. These circuits of delayed reciprocity are the social glue of the community and define trust relations and ties of mutual obligation. Life-cycle events, rituals and feasts, gifts, contributions, and eventual reciprocity are the long-term cycles that situate a household within ongoing social relations. Around births, deaths, and marriages the cycle of gifts and reciprocal obligations never balances out exactly, but continues as a long-term ebb and flow yielding significant returns on one's gifts as well as the all-important sense that the household is linked to others to whom it can turn for help when needed.[19] Table 4.1 shows the typical value of resources and cash used and received for the more important ritual feasts organized by households.

Table 4.1 reflects the fact that events tend to center on a single transition or transfer: in the cases of dowry and bridewealth, these involve giving money, animals, and objects that are related to the lives of the new couple, or recompense the parents for the loss of their daughter. In the cases of deaths, circumcisions, births, birthdays, and weddings, human beings undergo transitions, and while gifts or contributions may be large, they are not the central event, but instead are ways to mark the central event of the ritual to share in the activity of celebration or mourning.

Another way to understand the cases in table 4.1 is to categorize feasts in terms of numbers of guests and amount of resources consumed. When

**Table 4.1. Costs of Major Rituals (estimated total contributions in cash and kind, in EUR), compiled from interview and survey data.** These numbers include the value of material contributions such as animals, but not labor. Typical values for dowry and bridewealth gifts are included under the "donations and transfers from allies" heading.

| Ritual feast | Contributions and gifts from guests, not including central gift if any | Value of central gift | Cost to hosts including value of animals and gifts to guests | Animals consumed: sheep, cows, horses | Donations or transfers from allies other than main donor | Net effect of contributions |
|---|---|---|---|---|---|---|
| Wedding in home | 100 | 0 | 350 | 2,0,0 | 150 | Expense to household |
| Wedding in café | 400 | 0 | 1,000–1,500 | 5,0,1 | 400 | Expense to household |
| Transfer of *achuu basar* (preliminary bridewealth) | 100 | 200 | 100–150 | 1,0,0 | 0 | Expense to guests, gain to household |
| Transfer of dowry | 50 | 500–1000 | >200 | 2,0,0 | 0 | Expense to guests, gain to household |
| Transfer of bridewealth | 200 | 1,200–1,500 | 400–600 | 3,0,0 | 0 | Expense to guests, gain to household |
| Decade birthday | >500 | 0 | >500 | 3,0,0 | >500 | Gain to household |
| Circumcision celebration | 100 | 0 | 150 | 1,0,0 | 150 | Expense to household |
| Celebration of child's birth | 100 | 0 | 350 | 2,0,0 | 150 | Expense to household |
| Minor commemorative meal | 100 | 0 | 150 | 1,0,0 | 150 | Expense to household |
| Funeral | 500 | 0 | 800 | 3,0,1 | 500 | Net gain to hosts |
| Major commemorative meal (*ash*) | >1,000 | 0 | 1000 | 3,1,1 | >1,000 | Net gain to hosts |

analyzed from this perspective, we can divide household ritual feasts into four general categories:

- Small feasts require resources worth from 25–100 EUR, with part or all of a sheep and other foods served to at most twenty guests. These are minor celebrations for local kin and neighbors such as for winning a prize, acquiring a new car, or an annual death commemoration.
- Middle-range feasts involve resources of 100–200 EUR in value, with up to fifty guests of kin and neighbors served two to three sheep and a variety of other foods, including some delicacies bought from the market.[20] Such feasts include sacred meals for blessings (*kuday tamak*), larger annual death commemorations, and celebrations of a new baby or a son's circumcision, or delivery of dowry.
- Large feasts are worth from 300–700 EUR, with up to 150 guests served in the home, but often in several shifts or by serving guests in neighboring homes as well. These usually require slaughtering a large animal such as a horse or cow, or three or more sheep and significant market purchases of foods, and if it is a celebration include musicians and other entertainment and a videographer recording the event. Such events include funerals and the one-year *ash* commemorations, weddings, bridewealth deliveries, and large shop openings.
- Very large feasts at cafés cost at least 1,000 EUR, and allow more than 200 guests to be served several courses prepared from at least one cow or horse as well as several sheep. These are almost always celebrations of life-cycle events in more prosperous families, including weddings, new homes, decade birthdays, and circumcisions, with different events often combined to justify the larger celebration. There is musical entertainment, dancing, a videographer and a *tamada* master of ceremonies who organizes the many parts of the celebration and provides amusement for the guests. Café events can take six hours and include two or three courses of food interspersed with entertainment and prestations.

Only prosperous households with income from more than their own farm fields can afford a café feast, so the increasing presence of cafés in Kyrgyzstan reflects the nascent social divisions resulting from intensified household production. Cafés and *tamada* masters of ceremony—a position that developed during the Soviet period from the *tamada* who directs wine drinking in Georgian feasts—are part of an expanding market in ritual services that enable better-off households to hold more refined and professional events while preserving local and ethnic characteristics. Café events are somewhat exclusive in the sense that only some people can afford them, but the workers who prepare the event are agnatic kin of the hosts—the café owner provides equipment but not food or staff—and older guests are generally invited because of kin ties rather than being selected for their wealth or success. In addition, the host of a café feast usually donates money for a game of *kök börü* (buzkashi) at the local field in which young men from the area compete for prizes. Such a game represents another way for households to share resources with the wider community when they have good fortune.[21]

The ability to hold feasts is a central measure of what I term the social sufficiency of the household, and results from intensified production beyond subsistence needs as well as thrift and discipline to avoid consuming this additional production. A further feature of feasts is that they are so frequent that they contribute significantly to household subsistence. Household consumption includes leftovers that guests and workers take home from feasts, including meat, fried breads, and sweets, and most of the meat consumed in many homes comes from such leftovers.

The social sufficiency of the household depends on careful management of resources for planned events, as well as helping others with their sudden needs such as funerals, or drawing on others when necessary for the household's own unforeseen rituals. Planned events should be recognized as appropriate to the occasion and to what the household can afford, the food and animals it has or can obtain, and the people it can supply or bring in to do the work. A household that holds a wedding at home rarely seeks financial help from others, but does rely on kin and friends to prepare and serve food at the event and to carry out ritual activities.[22] Guests usually bring small cash gifts that cover some costs, as well as small gifts for elders and others honored among the host's agnates. Honored older guests generally bring little but contribute *bata* blessings and prayers.[23] One wedding feast I participated in was followed a week later by a feast held exclusively for ten older couples to seek further blessings from them for the new couple and the groom's parents. This extra feast was held during the day and without music and dancing in order to be more relaxing for the elders. It cost roughly 30 EUR for food in addition to a sheep that was slaughtered from the household's herd.

## Annual Ritual Expenses

A household of four to six people only needs to spend around 20–25 EUR on food in an average month, mostly on flour and oil, and dairy products bought cheaply from neighbors if the household does not produce its own. A mid-sized ritual event worth 300 EUR may cost as much as one year's expenses for food and a large one approaches the amount a household spends each year for entertainment, transport, and clothing as well. Thus, household thrift and self-sufficiency in these other areas are important sources of savings to provide for social sufficiency and support the ritual economy.

The average household hosts one medium or large ritual event each year and contributes many gifts when attending others, resulting in an average cash expenditure on rituals of 200–300 EUR per year in addition to the consumption of five sheep. This easily goes higher when there are numerous events: a prosperous household made up of one successful professional mother, two married sons, their wives, and two children owned two horses, one cow, and twenty sheep and goats, as well as 1.8 hectares of land. In one busy year they had a total income of about 2,800 EUR and spent around 1,500 EUR in cash and animals worth around 700 EUR for rituals. One thousand EUR were spent on a large event they hosted at a café and the rest was spent on participation in ten medium and large rituals at which they contributed a variety of gifts, including three animals (a sheep, a two-year-old horse, and a cow) that they raised themselves.

Commitment to rituals involves time and labor. Major rituals require extensive planning and discussions to coordinate food, gifts, entertainment, and the work and contributions of participating kin. Smaller rituals also involve work over several days to prepare the food and the space for guests to sit and socialize. To host twenty-five to forty people at a mid-range event such as a circumcision celebration requires making baked and fried breads and salads, and preparing the meat of one or two sheep to be served on eight to fourteen platters of noodles. This involves the work of at least five family members and kin or friends to prepare the house, cook, serve, and clean up, with a total commitment of seven to ten person-days of work.

A household that hosts one medium or large ritual event each year and helps others in five similar events commits at least fifteen to twenty person-days. In addition, minor hospitality events require annually another five to ten person-days of work. To fully analyze the time needed for ritual activities would require calculating the time needed to generate income to cover the costs and to tend animals, process milk, and grow and preserve the fruits and vegetables consumed in rituals. A further complication in these calculations is that domestic food production enables the thrift that allows more household income to be spent on feasts. A rough estimate of all of the different activities suggests that one-third to one-half of a household's annual labor is expended on ritual events, including ordinary hospitality for visitors, each year.[24] The average adult also spends ten to fifteen days as a guest at rituals each year. These are conservative figures because I am not including feasts for rotating savings associations or holiday meals prepared in common by multiple homes during Ramadan or the Nooruz spring equinox festival.

## Conclusion

Ritual feasting is costly and time-consuming but is indispensable for linking Kyrgyz into the vigorous networks of their economic and social life, and few households want to remain aloof and avoid the production of a domestic surplus. Neither markets nor capitalism nor political power and taxation motivate production and organize consumption as thoroughly as the demands of commensal rituals in the village of Beshbulak. These patterns are widespread in Kyrgyzstan: people travel long distances and bring large gifts to participate in feasts in far-flung parts of the country. Many people who have moved to Bishkek for work or study remain closely involved in local events and frequently make the eight-hour journey to Beshbulak to join family, friends, and classmates in feasts; only those with inflexible working hours or who are willing to be seen as socially detached come less often.

This chapter has explored the complex balance in household economies and suggested that one way to understand them is by examining the economic and ritual cycles that connect household production, social activities, mutual aid, and consumption. Self-sufficient subsistence production enables the household to participate in the social life revolving around life-cycle rituals, feasting, and large transfers of resources during ritual events. Household subsistence production sustains household members but the rituals also distribute resources and reproduce households themselves by establishing marriages and motivating the mutual aid that contributes to farming. Feasting itself produces leftovers that make significant material and symbolic contributions to household subsistence.

Neither Sahlins nor Wolf envisioned a central role for feasts and social rituals in producing links among households nor the importance of such links for economic life. Sahlins in particular held to his argument that intensified production depended on political power motivating people to produce more than they needed for subsistence. In her analysis of a postsocialist collective farm in the mid 1990s, Humphrey (2002) suggested that managers may organize ritual events to sustain successful collective production, which suggests that political and economic power depends on sponsoring ritual activities in order to promote productive activities. Humphrey thus describes an intermediate stage between the political power of the Soviet period and the complete dissolution of collectives found in many post-Soviet contexts: post-Soviet managers are politically and economically weak and have to rely upon ritual to coordinate cooperative work and sharing. In the case of Beshbulak, ritual produces strong reciprocating ties among households that motivate intensified production, but households manage their own production and commit to ritual activities without direction from a leader, while negotiating collectively to decide about appropriate contributions to agnatic or classmate activities. In the absence of Soviet economic and social management, households have taken over both the planning and carrying out of their own production and provision of subsistence as well as organizing shared participation in complex and costly ritual activities.

Household production and allocation of time, money, and other resources reflect the high value attached to ritual events. Accumulating animals for rituals is more important than selling them for cash or consuming them at home but the fact that some households do specialize in producing animals for market sales shows that ritual use is not exclusive. The limited use of animals for domestic consumption or market exchange points to partially overlapping spheres of economic activity, shaped through a variety of influences and continuing to change over time in response to Beshbulak villagers' decisions about resources, constraints, strategies, and goals.

Rituals are vital for mutual recognition and sociality in the Kyrgyz community and for maintaining important social relations. In addition to generating material exchange and shared commensality, guests are expected to participate in feasts to recognize and share in a household's good and bad events, and even to help improve the household's fortune by participating when it holds a *kuday tamak*. Guests are welcomed because they give blessings to the host through commensality, prayers, and good wishes (*bata*). Ritual feasts produce the *sacra* of mutual recognition essential to constituting the community (cf. Gudeman 2001: 30–36; Robbins 2009). Shared participation in feasts produces a kind of spiritual mutual aid or sacralized social relations. Material resources, particularly meat, are turned into symbolic resources, through cooperative raising, slaughtering, cooking, and serving animals.

By limiting his analysis to the political and economic, and drawing on the research of Alexander Chayanov, Marshall Sahlins (1972) concluded that the *domestic mode of production* responds only to subsistence needs, but in Kyrgyz communities households are committed to mutual aid and commensal exchange that stimulate production earmarked for rituals that is little used for subsistence or market sales. Ritual commensality provides a *community mode of production and circulation* of shared symbolic and material benefits generated from the surplus produced by households. Most Kyrgyz households intensify production and participate in more rituals to realize collective benefits rather than maximizing free time or investing in greater personal or household accumulation. Producing and exchanging this surplus links people into modes of community exchange that are relatively isolated from the rules of market exchange.

**Figure 4.1.** Map of Nathan Light's Field Site.

Nathan Light, currently a guest researcher in the Department of Linguistics and Philology at Uppsala University, Sweden, received his Ph.D. in Folklore from Indiana University. He has taught anthropology, folklore, history and sociology at the University of Toledo, American University-Central Asia, Uppsala University, and elsewhere. His publications include the volume *Intimate Heritage: Creating Uyghur Muqam Song in Xinjiang* (2008) and numerous articles on Central Asian society, culture, and history.

## Notes

1. Beshbulak, like the river Karatash, introduced below, are not the real names: I preserve the anonymity of the village and individuals because people there trusted me with confidential information that could be damaging if they were identified. On the other hand, it is a pleasure for me to thank Judith Beyer, Svetlana Jacquesson, Paolo Sartori, and Vladislava Vladimirova for many helpful discussions related to this chapter.

2. Both crops and animal production also offer "profit" in the form of returns larger than one's material and labor input, but these do not exploit others or reduce their income. See Light 2015 for discussion of Beshbulak practices in relation to loans and repayment. I do not consider here investment into education and subsequent professional opportunities within the state apparatus and other institutions, because villagers have to move away in order to pursue such activities (cf. Engvall 2011).

3. Marshall Sahlins (1972: 170) points out that interactions among social entities such as clans hold society together, not through fusion into a whole, but by creating

ties among segmentary groups. But to fully understand how interlocking relations work in Kyrgyz society, we have to go beyond corporate segmentary groups
and identify the many ways multiple group memberships and solidarities are important in Kyrgyz communities, and the many different productive activities and
rituals in which people come together. Nancy Tapper (1991) describes the more
independent and self-sufficient Maduzai Durrani households in Afghanistan, with
marriages controlled strictly by the head of household. These marriages do provide
cross-cutting ties that serve as resources for resolving conflicts among groups in
the society, but the relative autonomy of groups leads to more frequent feuding.
This also relates to Keith Hart's (1986) assertions that the "presence of society"
facilitates haggling: in Maduzai relations, there can be considerable haggling over
important gifts such as bridewealth but conflict also starts easily because there are
few institutions to limit it. People readily default to open aggression when negoti-
ations break down or one party feels injured by another. This suggests that other
social factors, including shared commitments to avoiding conflict and maintaining
ties, shape social interactions and determine whether people act to promote personal gain, public reputation and honor, or collective harmony.

4. Public announcement of local commodity prices facilitates comparison and limits
   bargaining: buyers post the prices they are paying for different kinds of dry beans.
   Only prices paid for beans are announced like this although some shops also have
   signs announcing prices they charge for flour and meat.

5. People do not always help others hold feasts, but their stories of doing so shows
   that it is a strongly held ideal in the community. Self-sufficient subsistence is important, but so is generosity in helping others, motivated by belief in their good
   faith desire to return to self-sufficiency.

6. In other parts of Kyrgyzstan, the production of home-grown food is even more
   important for hospitality as suggested by an example from the fieldwork of Scott
   Radnitz (2010: 47–48). A wealthy professional villager who was more committed
   to developing political and economic ties to Bishkek rather than within his own
   village nonetheless hired people to raise two cows and vegetables at his village
   home in southern Kyrgyzstan in order to be able to offer "home-grown" food to his
   guests.

7. The term fund should be understood to include accumulation of both money and
   in-kind resources. I prefer to describe feasts as involving ritual and ceremony,
   because Kyrgyz feasts are ways of marking rituals and the commensal sociality of
   the feast has spiritual effects. Ritual feasts are not merely social recognition of a
   life-cycle transition but also enhance the spiritual meaning of these transitions and
   produce blessings.

8. Wolf argues that the ceremonial fund can be depleted, resulting in damage to local
   social organization. But Kyrgyz seem so attached to maintaining their ceremonial
   fund of animals that they resist using them for subsistence, preferring to survive on
   meager rations. Animals also provide useful resources such as milk, wool, or dung,
   and can be sold, but are primarily reserved for ritual.

9. Enrique Mayer (2005) acknowledges that surplus production can arise alongside
   subsistence production but does not consider that the surplus can be reserved for
   a "ceremonial" or ritual fund.

10. Although this can be compared to reserving a separate formal room or "parlor" for guests in some European contexts, most Kyrgyz households have multiple guest rooms that are sparsely furnished. Using household reserves of equipment and bedding they can be converted into spaces for eating or sleeping.

11. The domestic production for subsistence and of a surplus intended for rituals is clearly distinct from Sahlins's concept of surplus production resulting from political hierarchies. I suggest that feasting within reciprocal social relations even works as an "anti-politics machine" (Ferguson 1990) and creates a social space that is relatively free of contention and competition because people set aside disagreements for the sake of generating the positive sociality treasured by Kyrgyz under the term *intimak* (on the Maduzai ideal of household unity known as *entepak*, cf. Tapper 1991: 102). In Kyrgyzstan more politically salient feasts do occur as Werner (1999) describes for Kazakhstan, in which wealthy households give feasts and receive valuable gifts from wealthy political and economic allies, but these were not common in Beshbulak and even if people did participate in such a feast they felt little obligation to offer political support. In her dissertation, Aksana Ismailbekova (2012) describes a hierarchical patron-client situation in which political power is developed through a patron's support of kin, workers, and local residents, but rural areas of Kyrgyzstan rarely have the level of trade or industry necessary to support such patronage. A successful Bishkek entrepreneur who grew up in Beshbulak has invested extensively in the village and attempted to generate a political following but has not been able to mobilize much support. His investments mainly lead people to support him in making further investments, rather than supporting his political activities.

12. In general, collective farms included more ethnic Kyrgyz, while state farms included more Russians. Beginning in the 1940s wartime deportees such as Germans, Tatars, Meskhetian Turks, Karachays, and Chechens were also incorporated into the state farms. State farms received greater aid from the central government and residents enjoyed a better standard of living. Because of their closer linkages to central economic planning and technical and social services, state farms also became identified as more civilized and rationalized communities with better access to education and consumer goods. There are no systematic comparative studies, but Soviet collective farms were generally more monoethnic, more weakly committed to state ideologies, and stronger in preserving ethnically marked social and ritual practices (e.g., Beyer 2009).

13. Tsentral'noe 1984: 111–124. These statistics probably undercount privately held animals and meat production and overcount the collectively held animals, since there was a common practice of mixing private animals with the collective herds. Some slaughtering was probably done in secret in order to avoid state controls. See Volin (1967) for details of the general Soviet shift toward larger collective farms.

14. The Soviet state sought to manage people's life stages as well as their status or value within society, and institutions that valued people through social relations, or granted status without recourse to socialist principles, threatened the state's regulation of social identities and human values.

15. Village farm technology and processes deserve study as part of a detailed material history of changing farm practices in Soviet and post-Soviet Kyrgyzstan. The

changing equipment and innovations in crop processing (as in other household tasks, hospitality, etc.) offer important insights into local economic life.

16. This complicates Keith Hart's contention that contexts of greater social distance lead ceremony to dominate over negotiation, while socially closer individuals can haggle more (1986: 648). Colleagues, friends, or neighbors are loath to haggle or seek benefit at another's expense and generosity tends to dominate in most village settings because reputation is more important than savings. Many Kyrgyz avoid haggling even in markets, viewing haggling as an ethnic marker of more urbanized traders, such Uzbeks, Tajiks, or Russians.

17. Many of these practices existed during the Soviet period but now enjoy renewed appreciation. The changes in attitudes about and prevalence of traditional mutual aid deserve a separate study because traditionality itself has become a resource villagers use to persuade others to share or help. People feel obliged to contribute when something is framed as traditional.

18. Highly appreciated professionals such as musicians or masters of ceremonies for ritual events can earn as much as 5,000 EUR per year. It is very difficult to calculate annual income or profit accurately for many endeavors because they often involve interest-free loans of capital from kin. Thus someone driving a taxi or tractor may make some profit, but only because they are not returning interest on the investment. Well-off kin and friends thus subsidize opportunities for someone to demonstrate his or her self-sufficiency, although the enterprise would not be successful with a market-rate loan.

19. This can be compared to Parry and Bloch's (1989) ideas about long-term and short-term transaction orders, but I suggest that shorter-term transactions begin with less commitment, while long-term transactions indicate in advance a willingness to work toward a strong trust relation. A feature of long-term cycles in Beshbulak is that reciprocation does not involve increasing debt, and hence in a market context where monetary loans would bear interest, the giver actually forgoes a market return on capital but benefits from the social return of the ongoing relationship. Beshbulak villagers do try to reciprocate animals or other large gifts with a return gift that is a bit more than the original: this increment does not increase over time but is meant to display appreciation and goodwill. Such gift exchanges may be identified or even given as money, but because currencies change in value, the underlying obligation is specified in terms of animals, cartons of foods and drink, or standard sets of bedding in the case of dowry. It can also change to align with changing standards for particular ritual gifts (bridewealth, funeral gift, etc.) People should repay gifts with an equivalent animal or item, or its value on the present market, regardless of how much later, unless the standard gift for such a ritual has changed significantly over time. Gifts are also adjusted according to how much the household can afford, how close the people have remained, and how much appreciation the household members want to show.

20. For larger rituals people go to the market town an hour away to find wholesale sellers and buy large quantities of flour, rice, oil, vegetables, fruits, nuts, sweets, and animals if they do not have their own. Most materials for smaller ritual events are produced within the community, including preserved fruit and vegetables, milk products and animals, and some purchased staples such as oil and flour. Small

quantities of nonlocal products such as dried fruits, nuts, and sweets are important elements of most ritual hospitality that generally can be bought at local shops.

21. *Kuday tamak* held to receive blessings and community feasts held at the local mosque are good examples of avoiding the status markers of private professionally organized feasts. Simple food is served, all neighbors and community members are welcome, and there is no entertainment or videotaping. These inclusive feasts reflect the belief that egalitarian social participation results in spiritual benefits, while displays of wealth in café feasts show greater respect and honor to guests and improve the reputation of the host as well.

22. A common story about wedding feasts reflects the pressure created by investing time and resources. A boy may tell his family that he is getting married, indicating that they should prepare a feast. He and his friends take responsibility for bringing the bride, often through a kidnapping that the bride is not expecting (Kleinbach 2003; Kleinbach, Ablezova, and Aitieva 2005). If the kidnapping fails or the kidnapped woman refuses to stay the boy may try to kidnap someone else simply because the feast is already prepared.

23. See Light 2015. The term for honored elders (*aksakal*, literally "white beard") applies also to women over the age of sixty.

24. This can be compared to the 20 to 27 percent of working time committed to work on festivals found by Chayanov for peasant households in imperial Russia (cited in Sahlins 1972: 90). Unfortunately, his analysis does not report the time spent working to provide the resources used in the festivals, nor does Sahlins recognize that such expenses should be understood as a motivation for intensified production.

## References

Barth, Fredrik. 1967. "Economic Spheres in Darfur." In *Themes in Economic Anthropology*, ed. Raymond Firth, 149–174. London: Tavistock.

Beyer, Judith. 2009. *According to Salt: An Ethnography of Customary Law in Talas, Kyrgyzstan.* Dissertation, Martin Luther University, Halle-Saale, Germany.

Bohannan, Paul. 1955. "Some Principles of Exchange and Investment among the Tiv." *American Anthropologist* 57: 60–70.

Edgar, Adrienne Lynn. 2004. *Tribal Nation: The Making of Soviet Turkmenistan.* Princeton: Princeton University Press.

Engvall, Johan. 2011. *The State as an Investment Market: An Analytical Framework for Interpreting Politics and Bureaucracy in Kyrgyzstan.* Dissertation, Uppsala University, Sweden.

Ferguson, James. 1990. *The Anti-Politics Machine: "Development", Depoliticization and Bureaucratic Power in Lesotho.* Cambridge: Cambridge University Press.

Gorsuch, Anne E. 1996. "'A Woman is Not a Man': The Culture of Gender and Generation in Soviet Russia, 1921-1928." *Slavic Review* 55, no. 3: 636–660.

Gudeman, Stephen. 2001. *The Anthropology of Economy: Community, Market and Culture.* Oxford: Blackwell Publishers.

Hart, Keith. 1986. "Heads or Tails? Two Sides of the Coin." *Man.* New Series 21, no. 4: 637–656.

Humphrey, Caroline. 1998. *Marx Went Away—But Karl Stayed Behind.* Ann Arbor: University of Michigan Press.

———. 2002. *The Unmaking of Soviet Life: Everyday Economies after Socialism.* Ithaca, NY: Cornell University Press.

Ismailbekova, Aksana. 2012. *"The Native Son and Blood Ties:" Kinship and Poetics of Patronage in Rural Kyrgyzstan.* Dissertation, Martin Luther University, Halle-Saale, Germany.

Jacquesson, Svetlana. 2010. *Pastoréalismes: Anthropologie Historique des Processus d'Intégration Chez les Kirghiz du Tian Shan Intérieur.* Wiesbaden: Reichert.

Kamp, Marianne. 2002. "Pilgrimage and Performance: Uzbek Women and the Imagining of Uzbekistan in the 1920s." *International Journal of Middle East Studies* 34, no. 2: 263–278.

———. 2008. *The New Woman in Uzbekistan: Islam, Modernity and Unveiling Under Communism.* Seattle: University of Washington Press.

Keller, Shoshana. 2001. *To Moscow, Not Mecca: The Soviet Campaign against Islam in Central Asia, 1917-1941.* Westport, CT: Greenwood Publishing Group.

Kleinbach, Russell. 2003. "Frequency of Non-Consensual Bride Kidnapping in the Kyrgyz Republic." *International Journal of Central Asian Studies* 8, no. 1: 108–128.

Kleinbach, Russell, Mehrigiul Ablezova, and Medina Aitieva. 2005. "Kidnapping for Marriage (ala kachuu) in a Kyrgyz Village." *Central Asian Survey* 24, no. 2: 191–202.

Kushner, Pavel I. 1929. *Gornaia Kirgiziia (sotsiologicheskaia razvedka).* Trudy nauchno-issledovatel'skoi assotsiatsii pri kommunisticheskom universitete trudiashchikhsia Vostoka imeni I. V. Stalina, vypusk II. Moscow.

Lane, Christel. 1981. *The Rites of Rulers: Ritual in Industrial Society—The Soviet Case.* Cambridge: Cambridge University Press.

Light, Nathan. 2015. "Animals in the Kyrgyz Ritual Economy." In *Economy and Ritual: Six Studies of Postsocialist Transformations,* ed. Stephen Gudeman and Chris Hann, 52–78. New York: Berghahn Books.

Loring, Benjamin. 2008. *Building Socialism in Kyrgyzstan: Nation-making, Rural Development, and Social Change, 1921–1932.* Dissertation, Brandeis University, Waltham, MA.

Mayer, Enrique. 2005. "Households and Their Markets in the Andes." In *Handbook of Economic Anthropology,* ed. James Carrier, 405–422. Cheltenham: Edward Elgar.

Michaels, Paula. 2003. *Curative Powers: Medicine and Empire in Stalin's Central Asia.* Pittsburgh, PA: University of Pittsburgh Press.

Miller, Liesl, and Patrick Heady. 2003. "Cooperation, Power, and Community: Economy and Ideology in the Russian Countryside." In *The Postsocialist Agrarian Question: Property Relations and the Rural Condition,* ed. Chris Hann and the "Property Relations Group," 257–292. Münster: Lit.

Northrop, Douglas. 2004. *Veiled Empire: Gender & Power in Stalinist Central Asia.* Ithaca, NY: Cornell University Press.

Parry, Jonathan, and Maurice Bloch. 1989. "Introduction: Money and the Morality of Exchange." In *Money and the Morality of Exchange,* ed. Jonathan Parry and Maurice Bloch, 1–32. Cambridge: Cambridge University Press.

Radnitz, Scott. 2010. *Weapons of the Wealthy: Predatory Regimes and Elite-led Protests in Central Asia.* Ithaca, NY: Cornell University Press.

Robbins, Joel. 2009. "Rethinking Gifts and Commodities: Reciprocity, Recognition, and the Morality of Exchange." In *Economics and Morality: Anthropological Approaches*, ed. Katherine E. Browne and B. Lynne Milgram, 43–58. Lanham, MD: Alta Mira Press.

Rogers, Douglas. 2005. "Moonshine, Money, and the Politics of Liquidity in Rural Russia." *American Ethnologist* 32, no. 1: 63–81.

Sahlins, Marshall. 1972. *Stone Age Economics.* New York: Aldine de Gruyter.

Tapper, Nancy. 1991. *Bartered Brides: Politics, Gender and Marriage in an Afghan Tribal Society.* New York: Cambridge University Press.

Tsentral'noe statisticheskoe upravlenie Kirgizskoi SSR. 1984. *Kirgizstan k 60 letiiu obrazovaniia.* Frunze: Izdatel'stvo Kyrgyzstan.

Volin, Lazar. 1967. "Khrushchev and the Agricultural Scene." In *Soviet and East European Agriculture*, ed. Jerzy F. Karcz, 1–21. Berkeley: University of California Press.

Werner, Cynthia. 1998. "Household Networks and the Security of Mutual Indebtedness in Rural Kazakstan." *Central Asian Survey* 17, no. 4: 597–612.

———. 1999. "The Dynamics of Feasting and Gift Exchange in Rural Kazakstan [sic]." In *Contemporary Kazaks: Cultural and Social Perspectives*, ed. Ingvar Svanberg, 47–72. New York: St. Martin's Press.

Wolf, Eric. 1966. *Peasants.* Englewood Cliffs, NJ: Prentice-Hall.

# 5

# "They Work in a Closed Circle"

*Self-Sufficiency in House-Based Rural Tourism in the Rhodope Mountains, Bulgaria*

DETELINA TOCHEVA

Studying house-based rural tourism in the south-central Rhodope mountains in Bulgaria in 2009–2010, I found that the most successful families in this relatively new business were said to be "working in a closed circle."[1] If it was in a way true that these families mobilized their members almost fully, there were multiple connections and dependencies on external actors, relationships, and systems that permitted them to be successful in their domestic enterprise. For the local people, the "closed circle" was the best model of economic organization for an entrepreneurial house. Thus, while the few families said to be really "working in a closed circle" were an exception, the study of this exception allows more general insights. The "closed circle" raises a series of questions about the contemporary relevance of the metaphor and about this specific model of domestic organization located at the intersection of the home and the market. I approach this metaphor of self-sufficiency as "an act of redescription" and remodeling (Gudeman 1986: 47). A focus on metaphors used for the economy in general (Gudeman 1986) and for the domestic economy in particular (Gudeman and Rivera 1990) can greatly contribute to an understanding of the ways in which domestic economies operate and interact with larger economic domains. But what does a metaphor of closure say about a domestic livelihood transformed into an entrepreneurial venture in the era of global connections and prevailing interdependence? What does the metaphor convey and conceal about internal relations and relations to the broader economy? I examine the intricacies between a vernacular model of self-sufficiency, household entrepreneurship, gender relations, differentiation within households, and participation in the capitalist market.

In the expression "working in a closed circle" (*rabotia v zatvoren tsikal*), the Bulgarian term *tsikal* means "loop" or "circuit" and semantically pertains to the sphere of physics and industrial production. Used in the domain of rural tourism in the Rhodopes, it refers to a specific type of production *and* to human relationships. Thus, translating the expression *zatvoren tsikal* as "closed circle," which describes at the same time a circular process *and* a connected and limited group of people (rather than "loop" or "closed circuit"), is a good compromise. This phrase and the active form "to close the circle" (*zatvariam tsikala*) are encountered also in other regions in Bulgaria. In the 1990s, "closing the circle" was used by postsocialist collective farm leaders to speak of a productive objective they were trying to meet. They wished to produce with the assets of the members and only for these members in order to limit market exchange to a minimum, considering that they would be losers in any such exchange. In another case, the expression was used by collective farm members to illustrate their wish to make not only rough produce (milk, meat), but final products (cheese, sausages) in order to sell high-value commodities directly.[2] In both cases the unit of reference was the collective. There were no references to collective production in the case presented here, and the villagers did not draw a connection between socialist production and their newly coined ideal of a familial "closed circle."

In rural tourism in the Rhodopes the unit referred to as a circle is the household. "Work in a closed circle" is understood to be the key to entrepreneurial success. "Working in a closed circle" refers to three interrelated ideas: (1) domestic production using only local resources—land, fodder, animals—without external inputs generates "clean" agricultural produce, free of polluting substances; (2) limited dependency on external actors and institutions, such as private employers, the state, and hired labor guarantees better management and efficiency; but this limited dependency also involves participation in market exchange and state mechanisms of redistribution; and (3) self-provisioning through household labor, with all the inequalities and hierarchical relationships it implies, leads to business success. In other words, the local idea of the "closed circle" places value in some households' ability to participate in the market through marketing some part of their domestic economy thanks to the mobilization of all energies within the limits of the house, that is, of nonwage labor.

On the one hand, household production and management testify to a clear preference for fully familial entrepreneurship that excludes the possibility of turning into a standard company, and hence can be seen as a resistance of the domestic domain against market forces. On the other hand, receiving tourists in the rural houses, an activity that Mary Bouquet in her study of family farms in northwest Devon, England, called "the partial commercialization of the domestic domain" (Bouquet 1982: 229), can be interpreted as an unambiguous inroad of the market into the home. Such contradictory analyses of the same phenomenon belong to what Norman Long characterized as the trap of "either/or propositions" that attempt to answer the question whether nonwage labor and family cooperation in capitalism are (1) "a transitional phenomenon that will eventually wither away," (2) a form of resistance, or (3) "functional" and "convenient" to the very workings of capitalism (Long 1984: 1).

In some cases, an either/or response is appropriate. June Nash (1994) has argued that considering subsistence production and nonwage work together at times of economic crisis allows insights into the mechanisms of social reproduction in the context of global expansion of capitalism. This approach is certainly supported here. But if in Latin America she detected forms of collective consciousness and mobilization against global capitalism, the Bulgarian villagers with whom I worked do not view their practices of self-provisioning as permitting them to resist or to defeat the market. Neither do they feel that their domestic economy is threatened with disappearance. In other words, what I see is neither resistance nor invasion. Rather, the metaphor of the "closed circle" points toward a particular model of relationships with the market and with state redistribution,[3] relationships that valorize a certain kind of domestic self-sufficiency. I argue that an analysis of a vernacular metaphor of household sufficiency and an examination of the empirical realities to which it refers allow insights into a more complex relationship between a house economy and larger economic domains.

Usually, anthropologists tend to consider the idea of domestic self-sufficiency as a misleading representation imagined by early social theorists who attempted to depict the household economy's remote past and drew the picture of peasant societies in a stereotypical manner, untouched by large-scale production, or even exchange. In fact, some of the early theorists were more subtle. For example, Gerd Spittler shows that Karl Bücher, who coined the phrase "the independent domestic economy" and who was criticized for the unrealistic assumption of a self-sufficient domestic unit, was in fact misread: "… Bücher only means that the domestic economy is designed to supply the needs of the group. This does not exclude the possibility of disposing of surpluses and alleviating temporary shortages with supplies from outside. The unequal gifts of nature are also balanced through exchange between domestic economies or tribes (tribal trade). Labor in common (such as bidden labor) is organized as a rule not within but between domestic economies" (Spittler 2008: 93–94).[4]

In Spittler's interpretation, for Bücher, "the aim of the domestic economy is to be as self-sufficient as possible" (Spittler 2008: 94). Following on Spittler's reading of Bücher, self-sufficiency should not be defined as a withdrawal from exchange in general, and from the market and redistribution in particular through total self-provisioning. The analysis should focus on the multiple ideas and realizations of self-sufficiency that point to local knowledge about how to reach a balance between in-house collaboration and production, and external multi-leveled involvements. Thus, the question to ask is rather what are these different ideas and practices of self-sufficiency and how do they occur in a given sociopolitical and economic situation at a given moment in history?

For the Rhodope villagers "a closed circle" is a condition that has to be reached, not an original point of departure or a pristine state of the domestic economy. The expression started to be used in rural tourism in the period of implementation of market economy and while the ever-diminishing welfare state has gained renewed importance for making a living after the demise of socialism. This model of self-sufficiency does not mean "creating a loop from production to consumption to production," though there is a strong idea that the closed circle "marks independence and the borders of the group" (Gudeman 2001: 43). The new realities depicted as a "closed circle" are attained in order to foster a certain form of market participation, not to hinder it in a search for isolation.

The "closed circle" is a model for success in a specific entrepreneurial venture. It encapsulates a definition of the non-expansive entrepreneur, observant of a template of connection and closure. Analyzing entrepreneurs under the changing sociopolitical circumstances of northern Norway in the 1960s, Fredrik Barth used the following classical definition: "an entrepreneur is someone who takes the initiative on administrating resources, and pursues and expansive economic policy" (Barth 1963: 5). Although I share Barth's opinion that entrepreneurship has to be approached in its relation to social change, his definition proves problematic in the case of the Rhodope villagers insofar as the ideal of the household "closed circle" sets limits to the notion of expansion, for the work effort and the assets mobilized are practically and ideally limited.

Hence, an intrinsic tension characterizes the ideal Rhodope household-entrepreneur in rural tourism. On the one hand, "working in a closed circle" stresses self-provisioning and limitation of the productive energies to the household members. On the other hand, the increasingly global market of rural tourism requires a deep, multi-leveled involvement with a myriad of actors outside the household. The metaphor of "the closed circle" points to people's awareness of the fact that a certain kind of closure is best suited to help local families reach efficiency in the market. This may be viewed as instrumental means-end behavior. However, it is not purely instrumental, nor is it focused on individual profit maximization or on the pursuit of a hedonistic concept of happiness. Local comments on those households who have successfully engaged in rural tourism by "working in a closed circle" also point to hard toil, restless life, and mental overstrain, and hence undermine such explanations.

In what follows, first I introduce the economy of two villages, which I refer to using the pseudonyms Belan and Radino, and I briefly depict the domestic economy. By referring to "work in a closed circle" the villagers gauge the household's degree of economic success in rural tourism and its inner relationships. I present the motivations for limiting dependency on the outside, as expressed by a member of one the two most successful local households. Then I turn to the intra- and extra-household relationships, to the internal tensions and differentiation, and to the practical relevance of a smaller unit of reference encompassed within the "closed circle."

## Background

The field research took place between July 2009 and April 2010 and was augmented by four additional trips, the longest of which lasted a month and the shortest a week. Belan and Radino, the two villages where I worked, formed one administrative territorial unit at several points in the past, but now they are officially separate villages. All in all around 500 inhabitants, predominantly of Muslim origin, live there, or 227 households according to the figures of the mayors' offices.[5] In comparison with the 1980s, the population has significantly declined: from around a thousand, it had dropped by half. Roughly a hundred out of the 500 registered inhabitants do not live in their village on a permanent basis; these are wage workers, high school youths who spend the week in the town and students who study at the universities of the large cities. Middle-aged and older inhabitants form a majority. The primary school has around 30 children, while in the 1990s there were around 200. But empty streets and quiet yards in the fall and winter sharply differ from the lively environment found in the spring and summer. These seasonal variations are determined by a move to the home village in the summer for dozens of people who live in towns and cities, and by the usual arrival of grandchildren who spend weeks with their grandparents during the summer. Another reason for the changing atmosphere is the seasonal influx of tourists in quest for relaxing holidays in the mountains, country food, and hiking.

The villages are located close to the border with Greece, in the south of the central part of the Rhodope mountains. During socialism, this area was under strict surveillance, with capitalist Greece on the other side. External visitors were denied access most of the time, while locals needed special permits in order to move even between the two villages. The situation has been reversed since the fall of socialism in 1989. Out-migration sharply increased, especially since the painful economic decline of the region caused by the dismantling of the state-run farms, the closing of small state-owned industries, and the decreased availability of public jobs. Thus, tourists are more welcome than ever.

In the nineteenth century, the Rhodopes were usually depicted as a backward mountain region, inhabited by a mixed Muslim and Christian population, engaged in agriculture and animal husbandry (mostly sheep) with low productivity, very low educational levels, and houses far below the urban standards of that time. In fact, different trades and handicrafts have developed in the Rhodopes. Historians of the nineteenth and early twentieth centuries emphasize that the Rhodope population was integrated within different economic, social, and Ottoman institutional networks (Brunnbauer 2003: 189–191). Muslims more strongly depended on agriculture and sheep breeding, Christians on trade, crafts, and masonry. Overall, the local economy was related to larger economic conditions, such as the demand for wool for the Ottoman army in the nineteenth century. Neither the village communities nor the households were self-sufficient in any significant way. Writing about the nineteenth-century households in the same area where Belan and Radino are situated, Ulf Brunnbauer concludes that "[t]hey were not isolated monads and, in many cases, did not act autonomously but rather within the networks in which they were integrated. In the case of *Pomak* [Muslim] households, kinship and the village community were the main mechanisms of social integration; Christian households had an additional network, professional organizations that linked them to the wider, and eventually to the global market" (Brunnbauer 2002: 335).

Despite this integration into larger networks and the strength of educational and patriotic movements in the Central Rhodopes after the retreat of the Ottoman Empire, the image of material backwardness and lack of economic efficacy was overwhelming, probably due to the devastation of the region by four successive wars in the first half of the twentieth century. The vast projects of socialist modernization in the 1950s and 1960s radically changed life in the area. A few villagers, of Christian and Muslim origin, even occupied high military and administrative positions in the region and in the capital. In these villages, the new state policies introduced electricity and running water, built paved roads, and provided urban facilities that were becoming the norm in other parts of the country. The socialist regime supported kindergartens and schools, and typically opened small industrial plants in the countryside. In the 1970s and 1980s, clothing factories employed thousands of women in the Rhodopes, while the state-owned company for public transportation was the prominent employer of men. But the institution that employed most villagers and that now, in the eyes of the locals, perfectly epitomizes village life in the last decades of socialism is the state-run collective farm with its large number of cattle, sheep, and land cultivated wherever it was physically possible, "even on the worst slopes."

Socialism offered employment opportunities outside of the domestic sphere; having a job was compulsory. Socialist collectivization in the 1950s decisively changed the nature and the prominence of the domestic economy. Yet, domestic agriculture and animal breeding have never been interrupted in these villages. Every house also sustained itself through work on small plots and care for sheep and cows; there was hardly a house without a stable under socialism. House-based agriculture and animal breeding, whether they were turned toward production for sale or to be consumed within the household, have continuously secured local livelihood. The differentiated involvements of the members of the domestic unit (usually two to three generations), in articulation with employment outside of the home, are a key to understanding the role of domestic production (Creed 1998). The crisis that followed decollectivization in the early 1990s, coupled with the hyperinflation in 1996–1997, resulted in a massive out-migration and in an increased reliance on home produce, not only for those who stayed in the village.[6] Hence, by 2009–2010 house-based production was surely not new; the novelty was the opening of the houses to tourists, an activity that involves a sale of hospitality, agricultural produce, and a way of life.

The house economy in the area is mixed, combining multiple sources of income and self-provisioning. A general feature is that village houses have always been owned by those who live in them. At one extreme would be elderly couples or single persons who can afford to live on their old-age pension, do not keep animals, and barely cultivate their land. At the other extreme are households with complex livelihoods, such as a household with three to four generations, with one or two couples based in the village, employed there or commuting daily to the town, with one or two old-age pensioners, all involved in domestic farming and agriculture. Such households add more or less steady incomes to domestic foodstuffs, the combination of all these helping them make a living for themselves and for those (grown up) children and grandchildren who live in the city. Like village inhabitants, city dwellers are faced with alternating periods of paid work and unemployment, with delayed payments being recurrent in the private sector. The village houses produce milk and meat, potatoes, beans and other vegetables that they may sell or consume, without being able to anticipate this. Foodstuffs usually go to the city, while cash may circulate in both directions. Even the few villagers who work in Greece, Spain, the United Kingdom, Austria, Canada, Alaska, or elsewhere tend to come back home and rely on home-grown food for a few months, whether they bring home money or not. Occasional tourism in some houses further complicates the picture. In addition, partaking in a "bed and breakfast" service, tourists often wish to taste the local cuisine (home-produced meat, dairy products, vegetables) and buy sacks of potatoes and kilograms of beans to bring along in the city. Some ride horses. All these provide additional income. The houses that receive tourists more regularly and officially have established ways of organizing their internal and external relationships and managing labor, money, and food. Between these two extreme forms of house economy, those who live on their pensions and those who combine a variety of income, lie a whole range of different variants.

Local tourism is a business entirely run by families. It is officially encouraged by the state through EU funds, but the few cases of locals who tried to enroll in such programs proved disappointing. Some became heavily indebted to banks as a result for example of officials not having approved their project for EU funding at the latest stage of the procedure when the construction of an extension of the house was already completed. These experiences discouraged further engagement. Rural tourism (*selski turizam* translates also as "village tourism") is a seasonal activity and no family makes a living from tourism alone. This activity heavily depends on household agricultural produce, private houses, nonwage labor of family members, and personal connections. The families most successful in tourism, those said to "work in a closed circle," also receive steady income from salaries and pensions.

The first house in the villages to receive tourists, officially registered in 1999, belongs to the Kamenov family from Belan. Their case is discussed below. The Kamenovs share their fame as the most successful in this business in the area with the Lanov family from Radino. To give an idea of the magnitude of tourism, for a population of about 500 inhabitants altogether, in summer 2011 there were fourteen officially registered guesthouses (two of them were registered as hotels). At least six additional houses have been receiving tourists on an informal and irregular basis over the past few years. In addition, in 2011, there was one hotel and at least four houses that were in the process of construction/renovation with the intention to open the next summer. A family owning a large plot on a hill with barbecue equipment for tourists was building solid bungalows in order to offer overnight accommodation. Even those who do not receive tourists in their houses are involved in this activity in some ways. A few people lent their horses for horse-riding excursions. A large-scale farmer sells lamb, sheep milk, and cheese to the houses receiving tourists, as well as to tourists directly. Villagers sell their potatoes, beans, and occasionally milk and meat to tourists.

The villagers own their houses and most of them receive tourists in the house in which they also live. A couple of guesthouses belong to external people, well-known to the locals, who rent them out to tourists and rely on some villagers to provide the tourists with food and services. Some guesthouses and two hotels are adjacent to, or located near, the house of the owners.

Through tourism, the local people not only open their houses, but also feel connected to the rest of the country and to the global world through foreign visitors. The house and a way of making a living have become marketable goods. The success of some houses has deeply reshaped local hierarchies and altered earlier patterns of domestic economy. This restructuring of hierarchies and power relationships is also a source of animosity and conflict.

## A Metaphor to Gauge Quality, In-House Relations and Business Success

Speech about the "closed circle" is widespread in the area. "Work in a closed circle" implies production of high-quality food. It is also a measure used to gauge business success by describing this success as stemming from a unique pattern of in-house relationships. It is presented as an alternative to fading job opportunities and to dissatisfaction with external workers. The metaphor is used internally and does not belong to the discourse of self-presentation to tourists.

### A Vernacular Quality Label

People associate home-produced food with purity. Although only two families are considered to be "really working in a closed circle," the metaphor appears in a much larger rhetoric of cleanliness of food present in the countryside as in the world. Thus, this global rhetoric supports the local idea of purity. Locally, ordinary people and politicians alike use the metaphor in this sense. For instance, the mayor of a neighboring village told me that "work in a closed circle" was valorizing because this gave the villagers the possibility "to offer their own produce in their small dining room, local dishes, no GMO [genetically modified organisms]. It is not expensive and it is interesting for the tourist to see, to taste real things." A woman whose family had recently transformed the third floor of their house into a tourist facility with three rooms and a dining room told me that she used "90 percent of [her] home produce—milk and dairy products, meat, vegetables, tomatoes, cucumbers." These are in fact produced with the active participation of her parents-in-law, who occupy the ground floor of the house. This house often receives groups who are accommodated elsewhere, but come there for lunch or dinner. The woman opposed "fear" of additives in food in the large cities to trust in the "clean" local home-produced food:

"Our aim is to use the bio, the homemade, and this is precisely what the tourists look for. Because if you take the food in restaurants, in big cities, sometimes the meat is clean, sometimes it is with additives, and this is what people fear. Here at least I can guarantee that the meat is clean, veal or game." The absence of considerable quantities of chemical fertilizers and pesticides has been increasingly characteristic of local domestic agriculture since the closing of the collective farm by 1992, through which many were able to receive such products for their personal needs. It is largely claimed that the decline in the use of chemicals and concentrated fodder for cattle and sheep was clearly an outcome of the high market prices that replaced earlier opportunities for cheap provisioning. As a consequence, domestic farming and agricultural produce has indeed become "cleaner." But an application for an official organic or ecological quality label seems unaffordable. Only the Kamenov house is a member of the international Slow Food organization that defends ecological standards. Most tourists trust word of mouth recommendations in which the cleanliness and quality of food figure prominently. The locals actively incorporate the "organic" discourse in their marketing strategies, in particular because they know the expectations of their tourists who come imbued with ideas of "bio," "eco," and "clean" food. But they do not necessarily speak to the tourists of the "closed circle."

### *"Everything Swirls": The Need for Nonwage Workers*

Although all villagers who produce on their plots and keep their own animals proudly claim that they consume "clean" produce, not all of them are said to "really work in a closed circle." The ideal version of "the closed circle" implies not merely house-based "ecologically clean" production, but also one that draws on the mobilization of all household members. Thus, the purity of foodstuffs resonates with the way in which household relationships become harnessed for the sake of business objectives. There are two households, the Lanovs and the Kamenovs, respectively from Radino and Belan, that are said to really work in a "closed circle."

The woman quoted above commented on the Lanovs, her neighbors in Radino: "They realize the closed circle. They produce everything starting with vegetables. This is the best, when you make one closed circle. This is the best, but this means a lot of work." Another woman from Radino spoke of the same family. Her own house for tourists works in a different way. She lives in the town with her husband and their two sons who go to college. The family owns a sawmill in the vicinity of the town which they consider to be their main source of income. Their house in the village has been thoroughly refurbished. They rent it to tourists and for events such as weddings, and rarely stay there themselves. The tourists are allowed to bring their own food and cook it there. Nevertheless, the owners are always ready to provide food if asked. In the outskirts of the town where they live most of the time, they keep sheep. They cultivate potatoes and common vegetables on their land close to the town as well as in the garden surrounding their village house. The family offers home-grown produce: "I don't have Coca-Cola or Fanta. I take milk and yogurt from my neighbor. We try to use countryside food as much as possible. Here we have a garden with salads, onion, and everybody helps."

If the tourists ask them to roast a lamb, they take one of their own or buy it from the neighbors. When I asked if this was a "closed circle," my informant replied by pointing to all the "clean" things they were able to produce as evidence of their family working in a "closed circle." Then she turned to the idea of self-provisioning with work, which is also referred to by the metaphor:

> But one cannot think only of money. If you take [produce] from the neighbor, he will receive some money too. One cannot think only in a closed way.... By 2006–7 we employed the neighbors on a working contract [to receive our tourists]. But we have less work to offer now. We are in [the town] all the time.... While the Kamenovs are here all the time. I did not spin up things in the way in which the Lanovs and the Kamenovs did.... The Lanovs are like this: the mother cooks and makes slippers.[7] Everything swirls. The grandfather works wood, makes wooden things. And they are all here.

Nonwage work of household members is preferred to hiring other people. It is usually claimed that not paying wages and splitting the profit among the household members is a key to making more money in this business. Yet, as this informant pointed out, not all can afford to operate in this way. One has to be there, to be available, and not only to own accommodation facilities and home foodstuffs. All household members have to be devoted to "spinning up" the business.

One may argue that the possibility to "work in a closed circle" directly depends on the domestic cycle (Chayanov 1986 [1924-5]). This is surely part of the explanation, but it needs two qualifications. First, we are dealing with a society where, despite high rates of unemployment since the middle of the 1990s, salaried work has been the norm from the 1950s onward; hence, a Chayanovian type of peasant household cannot be found and the developmental cycle approach needs to take into account this circumstance (see Leonard and Kaneff 2002). Second, the two local successful households have many members by local standards. There are a few other extended households in the two villages, but the simple nuclear families, or the nuclear families living with one elderly parent, outnumber by far the complex ones.[8] Households that remain complex over more than ten years (as in the case of the Kamenovs) and whose members are often present in the village in order to participate in receiving tourists, such as the Lanovs and the Kamenovs, are atypical. They do not reproduce socialist or earlier models. Indeed, during the second half of the nineteenth century, "[a] complex household organization was, … in most cases, only a short-term solution in the household cycle, the length of which depended on the dynamics of the household, demographic realities, and the availability of land" (Brunnbauer 2003: 188–189). Under socialism, the nuclear and slightly extended house-holds (three generations, and/or collaterals) were the norm. In postsocialist Bulgaria, households as large as the Lanovs and the Kamenovs constitute rather a minority. The latter need their many members to stay together because they have become an entrepreneurial unit, and not the other way around. For them, specific circumstances made useful the availability of workers. And it was not the mere availability of workers that guaranteed success in rural tourism, though this was a precondition. How they en-gaged in rural tourism and why they felt the need to "close the circle" is discussed below.

### *The Lanov Family Business*

Constraints and choices led the Lanovs and the Kamenovs to work within the limits of the household. I briefly examine the first case and then I fo-cus more thoroughly on the second case. The Lanov household comprises eleven members belonging to four generations, all involved in one way or another in the family business (figure 5.1). They own a house that has been adapted to receive tourists since 2007. But their main asset is what they call a "tourist complex," an area in which they offer accommodation and catering. This major activity was launched officially in 2005. They receive 3,000 to 4,000 tourists per year according to the grandfather's estimation. The grandfather presents the beginnings as an incidental idea; he had no-ticed that tourists would stop to rest on his (restituted) land during their hiking trips. This is how he and his friend came up with the idea of building some equipment. Technical support from friends and the making-do sys-tem helped accomplish the basic works in the beginning. Yet, village gossip claims that he had acquired a starting capital of around 20,000 EUR from the sale of his father's old house. One has also to pay attention to the con-text of declining job opportunities and the slippery market for agricultural produce. The family used to produce annually up to 70 tons of potatoes between the beginning of the 1990s and 2002. When the prices for pesti-cides went up and the market became far more competitive, the related in-come declined. In the meanwhile, jobs had become unreliable and salaries

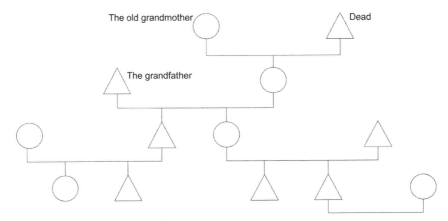

**Figure 5.1.** The Lanov Family.

and wages were an insufficient source of income. In this context, tourism seemed to offer a good supplement. It became more lucrative to sell one's own produce to tourists instead of exporting it directly to the market. By 2010, the business was officially run by the son; his wife is the only person among the eleven members to have a salaried job in the town. She is however in charge with keeping accounts for the family. Three persons receive old-age pensions. Since the Lanovs have started receiving tourists each year they keep around ten sheep and fifteen lambs, two cows, and two or three calves. They produce around 400 kilos of beans, around two tons of potatoes, and many vegetables. Their own meat and vegetables are usually not enough. This is why "we buy from our neighbors. We try to use everything from the Rhodopes, everything must be natural." Yet, the Lanovs heavily depend on external suppliers for additional vegetables, pork meat, and drinks. Their circle is by no means closed.

The grandfather explained why the household preferred to rely on its members. In the summer 2009, they employed two local persons to help when the influx of tourists made the situation unmanageable. These workers were given a very high salary by local standards, and lunch and dinner as an extra. But they wanted more money, started lying, and refused to work, after which they were fired. Now recourse to external helpers was limited to occasional short-term participation of trustworthy neighbors. I asked the grandfather about his opinion about programs for regional development and support to mountain areas, especially for rural tourism, loudly advertised by the government. He spoke of past attempts to set up an application for one such program. The complexity of the procedure was amazing, the number of papers requested was discouraging, and different individuals' expectations about receiving bribes definitely disappointed them. "It is better to stay within family business," he stated, confirming the general reluctance to apply for official programs usually found in the area.

### Why Do the Kamenovs Prefer to Work on Their Own?

The enterprise of each successful family involves a myriad of external connections for supplies, the mobilization of networks of trust, and dependency on state redistribution and private employers. Nonetheless, members of these families reproduce the discourse of a turn inward when they reflect on their business. This implies limiting the circle of work provisioning to the household members and opening this circle in many other respects. I will first give voice to Alex, from the Kamenov family, who explained why the Kamenovs prefer to produce as much as possible and why service to tourists and work related to the family business in general have to be limited to the "closed circle" of nonwage workers.

The Kamenovs have formally engaged in rural tourism since 1999. There are ten of them (figure 5.2). The retired parents have two married sons. Alex, the elder brother, and his wife have a son who got married but has no children yet. The younger brother and his wife Mina have two sons who are still at college. Though the third generation is usually out of the village—the young married couple lives in the neighboring town and the two brothers study in other regions—they go back home when possible and fully participate to helping in the periods of intensive work, such as haymaking, potato harvesting, or chopping firewood. The Kamenovs' two houses share a yard and all animal keeping and agricultural assets. These are the most visited among the houses for tourists in Belan, with more than 3,000 tourists per year.[9]

Rural tourism was an entirely new endeavor; the family had no entrepreneurial experience before socialism. Alex, the elder of the two middle-

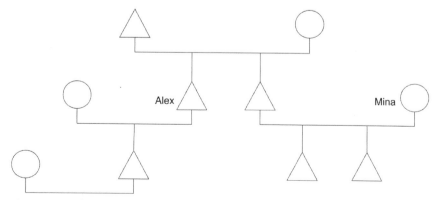

**Figure 5.2.** The Kamenov Family.

aged brothers, is said to be the backbone of the Kamenovs' tourist business. Trained as a teacher, he is still teaching at the village school where he assumed office as a director a few years ago. According to him, cutoffs in the public sector and unreliable private employers oriented the family toward this new endeavor. With the massive layoffs in the very beginning of the 1990s, the three women lost their jobs, while his brother was only employed part-time by the border police: "This kind of livelihood [salaries] started to fade away and we began to look for an alternative." In 1994 they opened the first private grocery store in the village and became the owners of the first private truck. "We started to manage, so to say, individually." Alex was part of all groups that tried to establish connections with stronger organizations with the objective of developing rural tourism. The idea that the family had to get by somehow was on his mind: "In 2000, but already in 1999, our region was severely affected by the crisis, which meant mainly unemployment resulting from the complete closing of factories and workshops." As a school teacher, Alex attended municipality meetings at which he heard about the expansion of rural tourism in areas in Western Europe that had been deindustrialized and were situated in attractive natural environments. At one such meeting, a woman spoke of France and of the conditions necessary to start developing rural tourism there: "One does not need serious investment or even land when one has a house, free rooms, a yard, a farm, and especially if one has already some other extras, such as a small shop and marketing opportunities. I started to actually think about our assets in these terms." Alex decided "to experiment" and established the first association for tourism with a lawyer from the neighboring village. Therefore, his house was the first officially registered in the village. Since that moment, Alex has become the key figure of all initiatives, associations, and projects related to tourism, which also raises conflicts with other villagers.

The Kamenovs have already employed external people to help them. The outcome has disappointed them: "If we offer some people jobs as cooks or as hotel maids, then they say 'Oh no, we don't want to work for 300 leva [150 EUR]'. Or when they come they sit, they twiddle their thumbs and wait for someone to tell them what to do. I have to go to check their work behind them, to correct and to make a remark." Former employees told me that for them the work was too hard and the employers' expectations almost impossible to meet. After having employed a few local women during several summer seasons, they stopped. Over the past two years, the Kamenovs have employed occasionally only customers indebted to their grocery store as a way of paying back their debt.

The withdrawal to the household circle is presented as the result of economic policies and dissatisfaction with external workers. Hence, self-sufficiency in terms of self-provisioning with labor was not the Kamenovs' starting position; previously they had employees. Yet, their current self-provisioning with nonwage work means only a partial inward turn. There are rather balances between self-provisioning with labor, produce, and other resources, and vital multi-leveled external relationships and flows. The Kamenovs' "closed circle" functions with internal tensions generated by the unequal power positions of the different house members.

## Looking Inside the Kamenovs' "Closed Circle"

Turning inward in some domains is experienced as protective against external uncertainties; it can even be seen as a precondition to success. I wish to demonstrate, first, that the modalities of this inward turn imply a specific idea of a dynamic balancing between opening and closure. More specifically, "working in a closed circle" is seen as the best way to engage with the larger market; it is not an attempt at isolation. Indeed, the Kamenovs' "closed circle" is in fact a relatively open one. Besides certain degrees of self-provisioning with food and labor, they operate a masterful balancing between inflows and outflows, between internal and external connections and commitments. But this "circle" is also the locus of tensions and inequalities. I wish to show also that a pattern of gender relationships, differential circumstances of house owning, and individual external status and connections play a crucial role for intra-household differentiation. The way in which the Kamenovs operate the "closed circle," that is, how they harness their energies, is determined by the adoption of broader patterns of gender[10] and seniority and, paradoxically perhaps, by their individual status and connections outside of the house. Finally I demonstrate that the "circle" encompasses smaller, distinct economic units of belonging.

## Self-Provisioning with Food and Labor

The Kamenovs have reached impressive levels of self-provisioning with foodstuffs. Service to tourists is taken over by household members. There is a common belief among villagers engaged in rural tourism that offering domestic produce to guests is the prerequisite for making profit. As Alex put it: "This is where profit comes from, otherwise you don't earn anything." The strong local idea that self-provisioning through nonwage work secures domestic subsistence by limiting outflows of cash extends to the sphere of tourism; domestic produce would limit the expenses and would bring profit. Indeed, the Kamenovs produce a lot compared to other village houses; Alex claimed that 99 percent of what they offer to tourists is domestic produce. Practice, however, points to knowledgeable and skillful management of, on the one hand, productive energies inside the house and, on the other hand, inflows and outflows of cash and produce.

The Kamenovs keep animals together: each year, they have usually two calves, two cows, eight sheep and more than a dozen lambs, more than thirty rabbits, three horses, and chickens. They cultivate around 0.5 hectares of potatoes, part of which they sell, and another part of which they eat and cook for tourists. They produce and offer milk, yogurt, and some dairy specialties. This is hardly enough to feed all their tourists, so that meat, vegetables, fruits, and drinks regularly come from other villagers or from the outside. The Kamenovs know well their suppliers with whom they have established long-term relationships. A local large-scale farmer sells lambs to all guesthouses and the Kamenovs figure prominently among his best clients. The Kamenovs advertise their food as homemade, locally produced, or bought from a trustworthy supplier to stress its purity.

The Kamenovs invest a huge amount of labor to keep the agricultural and farming activities going. The grandmother likes to say that "laziness has been eliminated from the Kamenovs." Other villagers acknowledge the Kamenovs' hard work, too. Each of them participates in different ways in the daily care for animals, but also in haymaking, wood chopping, and agricultural activities. All of them stress this full participation. However, the allocation of tasks follows some gender lines. Laundry and room tidying are chiefly female activities, which means in practice that they are done by the two wives of the second generation, and occasionally by Alex's young daughter-in-law when the young couple is back to Belan. While everyone participates in the kitchen in certain ways, specialties are prepared by the grandmother, who is proud of her three-year experience as a cook in socialist times in a prestigious restaurant in Bulgaria's second largest city. Alex's brother's wife Mina also often cooks. Alex's wife milks the cows twice a day. Mina makes herself available during the day for any purpose, because she is in a way in the house, since she works in the family shop located on the ground floor of Alex's house. In the evening, all must be there to serve food and take care of the guests. This intensive daily collaboration implies a feeling of permanent togetherness. This is perhaps one of the reasons why the Kamenovs often present a homogenizing discourse about themselves by emphasizing that they have their meals together, share efforts, and manage to overcome conflicts and tensions that, as all of them claim, sometimes do occur between them. Nonetheless, everyone has a different position within the family business and not everyone is equally dis/satisfied with his or her position.

## External Participations, Internal Inequalities, and Different Units of Belonging

Two intertwined factors need to be analyzed to highlight how the Kamenovs' "closed circle" works in practice: their connections and involvements beyond the household and their internal differentiation. The harsh economic crisis, especially unemployment since the 1990s, has continued to afflict a significant part of the population. The withering of a livelihood based on salary was pointed out by Alex as the initial reason for the family to look for alternative ways to make a living; neither employers nor the welfare system could be trusted anymore, he claimed. Nonetheless, if one looks at the circumstances of the house members over the past few years, nothing evidences mistrust in state welfare. Nor do they retreat from allegedly dying-out salaried work. The Kamenovs earn money from jobs and pensions and use the state welfare system, skillfully combining these assets with their tourist business. The general level of salaries and pensions is rather low in the region. The two are nevertheless very much appreciated. While salaries and pensions provide the Kamenovs with some money and entitle them to public health care and social benefits, tourism brings more significant income. Everyone's specific relation to external employers and external engagements have influenced internal relationships within their "closed circle." Gender and seniority play a role as well. Profit from food offered to the tourists is split between the two couples of the second generation. Each couple puts together money earned through salaries and pensions. There are no significant differences in the level of the salaries. The pensions are slightly lower than the salaries, but close to the general level in the village. Ultimately the three nuclear families of the household spend and save separately from each other.

While the grandmother was unemployed when the family opened their shop, she has retired since then, so that she and the grandfather receive old-age pensions. The grandmother claimed that they could use their "full pensions." Usually, elderly people use their pensions to pay the bills for the basic monthly needs such as electric, water, taxes, and telephone. All families appreciate having a pensioner in the house because the old-age state-provided pension means the house is able to meet those expenses. The Kamenovs' grandmother referred to her and her husband's pensions as "full" in the sense that they do not pay any bills. How has this exceptional situation become possible? In all houses receiving tourists, electric, water, and other bills related to housekeeping are considered together, that is, there is no separate accounting for the house members' consumption on one side, and the tourists' consumption on the other side. As the old couple helps receive the guests—the grandfather takes care also of the sheep and cattle; the grandmother cooks and helps in the kitchen—the grand-mother considers they deserve not to pay bills as a counterpart. The bills are paid from the overall income from tourism. This places the old couple in a privileged position among other retired villagers. Every summer the old Kamenovs go for two weeks of vacation to the seaside or elsewhere. This practice began during socialism for all categories—workers, school-children, pensioners—and was generalized in the 1970s. Other retired vil-lagers have abandoned the custom since the crisis of the 1990s.

Alex is the director of the school, in addition to being the president of the local association for tourism, a deputy head of the committee of the village house of culture (*chitalishte*), and a member of several local and regional associations. These commitments to public life directly contribute to enhance his control over decisions at the village level, which allows him to advertise the family guesthouse and to bring average tourists as well as well-heeled guests, such as politicians and businessmen. Alex's wife is the head of the shirt-making factory of the village, which employs around thirty women. Alex's brother is an officer in the border police. All three receive a regular salary. Alex's brother's wife Mina has the most unsteady income. She took over the grocery store.

This store was initially established in the name of Alex's wife, but since she found a stable job in the shirt-making factory, unemployed Mina became the shopkeeper. Four other grocery stores were created in the meantime. Enhanced competition coupled with out-migration meant decreased sales. Mina's two sons left to study and Mina and her husband have been provid-ing for them to allow them to study in good schools. In contrast, Alex's son has a job in the administration of the regional town, though he and his wife are not completely independent from the income of their parents. Mina's income is her profit from the shop. Commodities from this shop are usually taken for free by the whole family. As they eat together every day, taking for free foodstuffs and other items from the shop seems to them justified. As the grandmother put it: "We take cheese, bread, everything from the shop. In practice, it feeds us," in addition of course to what they produce by them-selves. Mina is supposed to keep the accounts for the grocery store in a way that would allow her to keep a "salary" for herself too. But, as she confides to close friends, there are months when she ends up not making any money for herself. As each one keeps money income from salaries and pensions for him- or herself, Mina and her husband are the most disadvantaged. She is the only one without a regular income from the outside. Thus, belonging more than the others to the "closed circle," in addition to facing high costs for her children's studies, puts her nuclear family in an unfavorable position.

Not only does the practice of taking commodities from the store without paying engender differentiation, but it fosters another inequality deriving from another line of division within the Kamenov household. The latter stems from a traditional regional pattern of house ownership that privileges older sons for a period of time. This model of seniority means that older sons who get married would move to a new house, while the youngest one would stay with his parents even when he gets married and has children (see Brunnbauer 2003: 188–189). He is the one who would inherit the parents' house. This model is more or less followed in practice. The Kamenovs did stick to it. The Kamenovs have two houses. The first one was built in the 1960s by the old couple and by their parents. This is where Alex and his brother grew up. In 1984, still a just married young man, Alex built his own house on the large plot next to his parents' house. This is where he and his wife live now and where the grocery store is located. The older house belongs to the old parents, who occupy the ground floor. Alex's younger brother and his wife Mina live in this house too. Their rooms upstairs are also used to accommodate tourists. Usually, tourists are accommodated at Alex's house, but when it is full the tourists are accommodated in the old parents' house, in the rooms of Mina and her husband. This is why in the high season Mina and her husband, and their children when they are at home, stay in the house of Mina's mother, located in the same village. The two couples of the second generation divide into equal shares profit made from food offered to the tourists, but each couple keeps whatever comes from the overnight accommodation, depending on the house in which the tourists are accommodated. This means that Alex and his wife make more money from accommodating tourists than Mina and her husband. In addition, the two sons are unequally established within the household, the elder brother owning his own house, the younger one having to move constantly, in the summer, between the house of his parents and that of his wife's mother, since the couple spends the night in this latter house but works and takes meals with the other Kamenovs.

Alex's son receives a salary, but he and his wife are supported by Alex and his wife. Alex's young daughter-in-law is still enrolled at the university and his son's salary is relatively low. Village gossip reports that when the young couple leaves to go to the town at the end of the weekend, their parents and grandparents give them bulky bags of food and other things. Although Mina's sons are equally loved by the family members and are offered food and money too, being relatively young and pursuing their education, they do not earn any money. The different situations of the third generation, in addition to the unequal income from tourism, place the two couples of the second generation in fairly different positions. It is therefore little surprise that when in a conversation with Alex I asked whether their family (without specifying whom I meant) had savings, he answered "Yes," which is a noticeably rare answer in the village. In a conversation with Mina, she responded

"No" to the same question and even added "We have debts." Both declared that tourism was their major source of income. But each spoke of his or her nuclear family. Within the household circle of shared work effort, spending and saving belong to the distinct domain of the nuclear family. If the unit of reference of the metaphor of self-sufficiency is the household, this metaphor leaves aside the simultaneous practical relevance of the nuclear family as an economic unit and the advantages and disadvantages related to each member's structural position. All four nuclear units within the Kamenov household are in a different economic situation. The imbalance between the two couples of the second generation is enhanced by Alex's outside image as the Kamenovs' leader. Alex has a reputation for being a smart businessman and an all-powerful school director who uses his erudition and connections to extend the power of his family and profit from tourism.

The Kamenovs have a strong presence in the village; they are members of the folk dance club and the tourist association that some earlier members say they have left in order to escape from the over-dominant position of the Kamenovs. Their participation is remarkable; no matter how tiring the workday has been, they never miss a folk dance rehearsal or some public meeting related to the life of the village. Their house is the only local house member of the international Slow Food organization; they are the first family to work with a travel agency for alternative tourism; they have received high level politicians and prominent businessmen; in summer 2010 they offered a horse-riding excursion to the American ambassador and to a former Bulgarian minister of Foreign Affairs during their private visit to the Rhodopes. Alex has close relationships with local- and national-level politicians, which has actually proven to be of benefit not only to the family business, but also to the school. Alex has good relationships with other houses for tourists, when he is not in conflict with them. He is able to make a connection between his tourists and the locals who can offer entertainment such as live music, cave visits, canoeing, or rock climbing. These connections and ability to mobilize wide networks are admired by some villagers; others, however, dislike him for his authoritarian behavior and his roughness toward simple people, as well as sometimes toward Mina, his own wife, and his daughter-in-law.

The Kamenovs' "closed circle" is marked by tense relationships inside and outside. It functions according to patterns of gendered roles and seniority within the household. In addition, the individual status and connections of everyone outside the house determine to a large extent the Kamenovs' internal relationships and status inequality. Looking at their overall economic model, the Kamenovs appear to be virtuosos of astute balancing between external involvement and in-house collaboration. All external connections and participations in community life and beyond contribute to the success of their family business. But they pay a high price, suffering from physically and mentally exhausting workdays and the resentment of many villagers.

## Why a Closed Circle?

The current era of a bewilderingly complex global economy has not erased the centrality of the domestic economy. There are numerous models of domestic livelihood that go together with deepening economic uncertainty and competition. Amid such multiplicity, the vernacular emphasis on household sufficiency under a local form of neoliberal capitalism attests to the relevance of an ideal of self-sufficiency in this context of uncertainty and instability. This recent emphasis also indicates that the importance of household sufficiency is historically contingent, not evolutionarily determined. The implementation of a template of self-sufficiency is not opposed to market participation; to the contrary, in this case study, it has proven a convenient facilitator of market participation, without however meaning that the domestic economy is turning into a standard enterprise.

While the metaphor stresses closure, other discourses and practices point to a variety of forms of openness. Indeed, other local discourses and practices emphasize flows, connections, exchange, and external involvements. Tourism itself is locally practiced as a form of opening one's own house to external visitors. These two aspects have a dialectical relation. They can be seen as the two sides of the coin of the domestic economy.

But why, then, has this metaphor of self-sufficiency gained such prominence? My answer is that the metaphor reveals where people place value. "Having connections" (*da imash vrazki*) was the most appreciated thing in socialist times; in Bulgaria the expression was widespread and pointed to the understanding that informal relationships beyond the household were able to provide not simply access to things and services, but also status and good life. Comparatively, it is a striking shift that contemporary Rhodope villagers state that "closing the circle" is the best way to come to terms with the local form of market economy. This does not mean that external connections are disregarded. But people choose to stress metaphorically the other side of the coin. Indeed, "working in a closed circle" locates value in internal cooperation. The model sets limits to market participation, for this house-based enterprise cannot grow once it has reached the cultural and physical limits of domestic work and collaboration. If the "closed circle" is so celebrated locally, this is not because the people cannot imagine working in another way; actually many work in other ways. One of the most important implications of the model is to help people regain a feeling of control precisely at the moment when they are engaging with the dynamic, unpredictable market of rural tourism. Representing the ideal entrepreneurial domestic economy as a "closed circle" creates the possibility to frame it as a fully controllable domain in opposition to external uncertainties. Thus, this feeling of control is projected onto the realm in which the people strive to participate, which is the otherwise uncontrollable market. Production in a "closed circle" also generates "clean" food as opposed to food "with additives" available beyond the "closed circle." Then, in another register, it is the cradle of purity. The efficiency of work and the quality of produce, described as two areas of closure, taken together guarantee the best possible participation in the market.

Figure 5.3. Map of Detelina Tocheva's Field Site.

**Detelina Tocheva** received her Ph.D. in Social Anthropology from the École des Hautes Études en Sciences Sociales with a study of child protection in Estonia. Her first postdoctoral project, also based at the Max Planck Institute for Social Anthropology, concerned post-Soviet Russian Orthodoxy in northwestern Russia. She has published numerous papers on these subjects in journals such as *Anthropological Quarterly* and *European Journal of Sociology.*

## Notes

1. This chapter continues the analysis begun in Tocheva 2015, which provides more background information about the main locality researched, together with detailed acknowledgments.
2. For these personal communications I am grateful to Gerald Creed and Aliki Angelidou, respectively.
3. I am grateful to Mihály Sárkány for pointing out to me the importance of state redistribution, an element that I had already stressed but not to the degree it deserved.
4. This is a fairly different reading from the way Sahlins used Bücher's idea (Sahlins 1972: 76, passim) to claim that the domestic mode of production in primitive societies was the cause for "underproduction" and that only external political forces would incite the domestic units to produce above that level (Ibid.: 41–148).
5. These figures mean that there is an average of two persons per household. They reflect the way in which the mayor's office defines a household. An elderly person, though living with the family of her married son or daughter and their children, is usually considered as a separate household. The same goes for a child who is grown up and earns a salary, even though he or she still lives with his or her parents.
6. Ghodsee (2010) examines the socially and economically devastating effects of postsocialist privatization in a nearby area of the Rhodopes where the socialist regime had developed mining. Privatization in the Rhodopes, as elsewhere in the country, took the form of large-scale elite-driven embezzlement that undermined entire sectors of the economy (see Ganev 2007).
7. "The mother" in question is in fact the oldest grandmother in the Lanovs' house. She is known as a skillful seamstress, able to make beautiful slippers sold to tourists.
8. In addition, new patterns of mobility, mainly related to temporary employment, make it difficult to trace the boundaries of the village households. Many families own or rent an apartment in the nearby town; some of their members commute weekly, or even several times per week.
9. None of the family members was able to give me exact figures, but they claimed they had surely more than 3,000 visitors annually.
10. In the Devon case study by Mary Bouquet, the practice of taking tourists in the farm houses was entirely controlled by women and had led to a rise in their status within their own houses as well as in the local community (Bouquet 1982, 1984).

# References

Barth, Fredrik. 1963. "Introduction." In *The Role of the Entrepreneur in Social Change in Northern Norway*, ed. Fredrik Barth, 5–18. Bergen: Norwegian Universities Press.

Bouquet, Mary. 1982. "Production and Reproduction of Family Farms in South-West England." *Sociologia Ruralis* 22, no. 3–4: 227–244.

———. 1984. "Women's Work in Rural South-West England." In *Family and Work in Rural Society: Perspectives on Non-Wage Labour*, ed. Norman Long, 143–159. London: Tavistock Publications.

Brunnbauer, Ulf. 2002. "Families and Mountains in the Balkans: Christian and Muslim Household Structures in the Rhodopes, 19th-20th Century." *The History of the Family* 7: 327–350.

———. 2003. "Descent or Territoriality: Inheritance and Family Forms in the Late Ottoman and Early Post-Ottoman Balkans." In *Distinct Inheritances: Property, Family and Community in a Changing Europe*, ed. Hannes Grandits and Patrick Heady, 181–205. Münster: LIT.

Chayanov, A. V. 1986 [1924-5]. *The Theory of Peasant Economy*. Manchester: Manchester University Press.

Creed, Gerald W. 1998. *Domesticating Revolution: From Socialist Reform to Ambivalent Transition in a Bulgarian Village*. University Park: Pennsylvania State University Press.

Ganev, Venelin I. 2007. *Preying on the State: The Transformation of Bulgaria after 1989*. Ithaca, NY: Cornell University Press.

Ghodsee, Kristen. 2010. *Muslim Lives in Eastern Europe: Gender, Ethnicity, and the Transformation of Islam in Postsocialist Bulgaria*. Princeton, NJ: Princeton University Press.

Gudeman, Stephen. 1986. *Economics as Culture: Models and Metaphors of Livelihood*. London: Routledge & Kegan Paul.

———. 2001. *The Anthropology of Economy: Community, Market, and Culture*. Malden, MA: Blackwell.

Gudeman, Stephen, and Alberto Rivera. 1990. *Conversations in Colombia: The Domestic Economy in Life and Text*. Cambridge: Cambridge University Press.

Leonard, Pamela, and Deema Kaneff, eds. 2002. *Post-Socialist Peasant? Rural and Urban Constructions of Identity in Eastern Europe, East Asia and the Former Soviet Union*. Basingstoke: Palgrave.

Long, Norman. 1984. "Introduction." In *Family and Work in Rural Society: Perspectives on Non-Wage Labour*, ed. Norman Long, 1–29. London: Tavistock Publications.

Nash, June. 1994. "Global Integration and Subsistence Insecurity." *American Anthropologist, New Series* 96, no. 1: 7–30.

Sahlins, Marshall. 1972. *Stone Age Economics*. New York: Aldine de Gruyter.

Spittler, Gerd. 2008. *Founders of the Anthropology of Work: German Social Scientists of the 19th and Early 20th Centuries and the First Ethnographers*. Berlin: LIT.

Tocheva, Detelina. 2015 "Kurban: Shifting Economy and the Transformation of a Ritual." In *Economy and Ritual: Studies in Postsocialist Tranformations*, ed. Stephen Gudeman and Chris Hann, 107–136. New York: Berghahn Books.

# 6

## "Being One's Own Master"

### Reciprocity and Technology among Transylvanian Forest Dwellers

Monica Vasile

Self-sufficiency is a central value for the producers and traders of timber in the Apuseni Mountains of Transylvania, Romania. Economic realities, however, show these producers and traders' many forms of dependence on others. In this chapter I examine how their notions of independence and "mastery" (*a fi stăpân*) interweave with production and commercial practices. Their example contrasts with many anthropological descriptions of peasant societies, where households work as relatively closed units of subsistence (see Chayanov 1986 [1924–5]; Sahlins's (1972) concept of the domestic mode of production). Gudeman and Rivera (1990) focus on the house as a primary locus of production and consumption in Latin America, using the metaphor of the base. In the Transylvanian highlands the metaphor of a stream or flow seems more appropriate, in the sense that people flourish as a result of their flexibility, creativity, and continuous movement. What matters is the process of their work rather than their accumulated assets. These villagers seek out connections to different markets. They are accustomed to trading sawn wood for cereals and to selling animals in local markets, and they did so even when the private sale of such household products was severely punished by the socialist state.

Other anthropological studies have challenged the image of the smallholder as isolated and removed from market dependence (Netting 1993). African rural households are not rigidly bounded or self-sufficient (Guyer 1981). However, these studies have failed to examine the emergence of such "myths" and the ways in which cultural ideas of self-sufficiency translate into economic action. Village life in the Apuseni Mountains poses continuous dilemmas, e.g., about how much debt to take on, when and how much help to seek from others, and when to offer to pay for help without infringing on the affective nature of relationships. Both autonomy and relatedness are valued. While too much dependence can be called debt and regarded as demeaning for the dependent party, too much autonomy is a denial of sociability. Striving to attain an ideal self-sufficiency, the dwellers from the Apuseni eventually created a postsocialist compromise, reconciling in their own way the universal tension between the values of community and those of the market (Gudeman 2008). I shall explore this tension as it is played out in the context of work relations, emphasizing the subjectivities of economic independence.

By subjectivity I mean "the ensemble of modes of perception, affect, thought, desire, fear, and so forth that animate acting subjects" (Ortner 2005: 31). What are the subjective forms of self-sufficiency? Why is it given such emphasis when economic exchange, dependence, and debt are so prominent in people's everyday lives? People often referred to the idea of "being one's own master" (*să fii propriul tău stăpân*), meaning they preferred to avoid external work relationships and to use their working time for the house. In contrast to Aristotle's notion of flourishing, well-being in the Apuseni Mountains presupposes the pursuit of self-interest and money-making. People did not only aspire to achieve subsistence, but also to have money and to own expensive equipment that enabled them to process timber at home. To lay claim to mastery is to obliterate past times of oppression and shortage and to signal a leap forward that reformulates relations of mutual dependence. With the demise of the socialist state, Apuseni timber traders have experienced a great increase in prosperity, and with it an increased sense of self-sufficiency and mastery. Altogether, people feel they are "moving forward" (*a merge înainte*), and ascribe the change to their own individual initiative and risk-taking.

To address the ways that "social formations shape, organize and provoke" economic subjectivities (Ortner 2005: 31), the chapter lays out chronologically the harsh history of the Apuseni dwellers during the presocialist, socialist and postsocialist periods, by examining narratives, practices, and the contexts that produced them, with an emphasis on local experiences of work and trade relationships.

## Presocialist Dependence: Feudalism, Grain, Debt

Under the Habsburg Empire in the eighteenth and the nineteenth centuries, parts of the Apuseni Mountains were owned by Hungarian noble families. However, the densely forested area around the village of Urși[1] was in the "fiscal domain" owned by the Aulic Chamber in Vienna (Csucsuja 1998). Serfs were required to contribute labor days and quotas of wood for the mining industry (Prodan 1979). Under Empress Maria Theresa (1717–1780) they enjoyed forest use rights and commercial privileges, but their situation worsened under her successor, Joseph II (1780–1790). The heavy quotas of wood that he imposed led to massive peasant rebellions in 1784,[2] and eventually to the abolition of serfdom in the region. In the early nineteenth century, in the guise of land reforms, the authorities took steps to prevent commercial forestry and levied high taxes on forest use. The peasants rebelled again in 1848, and although this revolution failed, small-scale commerce thrived in the following decades with the introduction of water-powered sawmills. These were later superseded by steam engines and as a result, large capitalist enterprises outpaced small local producers of timber (Csucsuja 1998: 140). At the beginning of the twentieth century, the peasants of the Apuseni Mountains were again severely impoverished.

After the dismantling of the Austro-Hungarian Empire, in 1918, Transylvania was allocated to Romania, and nationalist ideas came to the forefront. Inspired by the Russian agrarianists, the ideology of the interwar period celebrated peasants who produced for the nation (Madgearu 1999) and "national exchange" between urban industrial areas and rural agrarian areas, which were supposed to sustain each other in symbiosis (Manoilescu 2002). Romania's comparative advantage was imagined as linked to its status as a "predominantly agrarian country" (*ţară eminamente agrară*). Two elements were considered central for the establishment of viable peasant households and eradication of historical backwardness. The first related to guaranteeing peasants' ownership of "work property" (*proprietatea de muncă*), and supported the development of the family-labor farm (see Madgearu 1999).[3] Second, it was considered necessary to extend credit to peasants, so that they could improve their farming activities with capital investment. Locally owned peasant banks (*bănci populare*) and credit cooperatives (*cooperative de credit*) were established in almost every village of the country.[4]

The villages of the Apuseni Mountains, scattered at high altitude in unfavorable ecological conditions, were renowned for their poverty (Ciomac 1933; Ciomac and Popa-Neacşa 1936; Papahagi 1925; Suciu 1929). For example, Tache Papahagi noted: "Good householding is rare. Poverty dominates. One can find numerous houses without any cattle or without any animal to carry heavy burdens (*animal de povară*). Pastoral life is non-existent" (Papahagi 1925: 16). Neither households nor villages were self-sufficient. Although villagers practiced limited agriculture, it was estimated that households produced only one-quarter of the grain they consumed (Suciu 1929: 20).[5] They obtained the rest primarily through barter and timber sales in the plains.

During the interwar period, all households made their living through some engagement with wood-cutting or working. In 1927, there were a total of 790 households in the commune of which Urşi is the largest village. The heads of 390 households worked independently as wood workers and traders (*ciubărari, şindrilari, scândurari*), making and selling wooden barrels, roof tiles, and planks. The remaining 400 worked as waged lumberjacks (*tăietori de lemne*) for foreign logging enterprises (Suciu 1929: 39, 50). The same source tells us that approximately one in six households had a horse and a cart, and one in sixty households had a water-activated sawmill (*firez*). The village elite comprised those (fewer than 20 percent of household heads) who owned horses, carts and sawmills. More than half of those making a livelihood as timber workers and traders did not own even a fraction of the necessary means of production. These poor villagers were called *pălmaşi* because they worked "with their hands" (i.e., without draft animals or machinery). Most had to pay other villagers for logging, transport, and milling services. Often the traders sold their wooden products from door to door far away from their home areas.

Petru Suciu, who collected household budgets in the village in 1928, described the poorer households as covered with "debts and hunger" (Suciu 1929: 96).[6] The condition of debt was omnipresent and humiliating, as popular verses indicate:

Throughout the world, throughout the country
The young men from Gîrda[7] are unique:
Heavy dancers, heavy drinkers
Indebted to the whole tavern;
To me, to you,
Nobody knows.
To pay back, I work to death—
Yet I get ever deeper into debt.

(Papahagi 1925: 61)

## Socialist Redistribution: Food Requisitions in the Mountains

The years of hardship continued during the first decades of socialism. Due to low quality land, distributed on steep slopes unsuitable for agriculture, Urşi was not collectivized and people retained ownership of their land. The elites of the village also did not suffer a great deal, as in other parts of the country.[8] Harsh livelihoods were rendered particularly precarious by food requisitions, known as quotas (*cote*), which poisoned social relations by giving rise to false declarations and accusations of betrayal on the part of fellow villagers. Such compulsory deliveries to the state followed precedents in the Soviet Union and were enforced in Romania between 1948 and 1956, in tandem with initial efforts at collectivization (see Kligman and

Verdery 2011; Beck 1979; Kideckel 1993; Verdery 2003). The system was a means to ensure that the new industrial population would have adequate food supplies, and it also worked to reduce status differences between peasants (Kligman and Verdery 2011: 117). The produce requisitioned varied according to the ecology of the region, and higher amounts were demanded from peasants with more land. Failure to deliver the produce stipulated resulted in crippling fines and imprisonment. Despite these sanctions, peasants still tried to evade quotas and the task of collecting them was "so unpleasant that collectors might collude with the peasants to reduce their obligations" (Kligman and Verdery 2011: 113).

Although their natural environment was unsuited to agriculture, the villagers of Urşi were required to deliver annually one pig of at least 100 kg, and some were additionally required to supply eggs. The collector of quotas was the local sales clerk of the socialist consumption cooperative, which replaced the earlier private shops.[9] His position and role in "giving bread to the people" also gave him tremendous power over all his fellow villagers (Sampson 1987: 130). He was responsible for the allocation of staples, fodder, household tools, and other basic products that were otherwise unavailable. He managed people as he wished; as people recall "when he whistled once, 40 men would come to help him with work." Boltaşu, as he was nicknamed after the old names of village stores (*boltă*), could demand work from fellow villagers or sexual services from women in return for turning a blind eye to irregularities in the delivery of quotas. He could afford to be arrogant as no one else, a "despot," as people called him; however, his self-image was quite the opposite: he considered himself to be generous because he provided luxury foods for weddings and would put in a good word for people who had trouble with the police.[10]

The system of food requisitions is remembered with bitterness as an attack on self-sufficiency and the social fabric of the village. Across Romania, the attempt to subsume household self-sufficiency to the ideal of national self-sufficiency resulted in the destruction of a household food base that was already vulnerable. In the Apuseni Mountains, the erosion of local livelihoods was particularly acute. Villagers went hungry, despite continuing to take risks by trading timber illicitly. Money gained through trade was sometimes used even to buy the agricultural produce that people were required to deliver as *cote* to the state.

## Socialist Dependence 1: Forest Brigades and Illegal Trade

During the early decades of socialism, villagers migrated long distances to find work in the southern Carpathians, and children as young as eleven had to carry out hard physical work at home. They recall eating frugally, fasting several days per week, and on occasion having to beg their neighbors for grain to bake bread. Unlike the agricultural and animal husbandry collectives established elsewhere, in mountain villages such as Urşi, work was reorganized in the form of state-run forestry enterprises called brigades (*brigăzi*). Despite the ban on private commerce, many still practiced it to supplement their wages from the state. Villagers had to become skilled in making social connections to circumvent rules by striking illegal deals with foresters and other officials.

The first jobs in the new state forestry enterprises set up in the 1950s involved long-distance commuting. This work left men with memories of misery and hardship. Mitu was sixty-six years old in 2009 and considered to be a middle-range householder in the village. During the communist period, he used to work for the state and trade on the side:

> I started to work for the state when I was 14, in '57. They came here with buses and spread us out across the valleys; we could choose where to go. I went with my father and other people from here to work in the mountains of Sebeş [to the south, see map provided at the end of the chapter]. We were three men working together, felling trees and cutting them to some standard; harsh work, just like working in prison. We were living there in barracks, 25 men in one building, no sheets, no pillows, no hygiene, we had nowhere to wash... imagine the smell in those barracks, the hair from your nose would fall out from the stench. The food ration was 4 loaves per week and one kilo and a half of fatback, and you had to pay, it was not for free. I left the village in February and came back in April, for Easter, for one week. I brought home some money; actually, more fleas than money... imagine I did not have a haircut for 3 months...

When forestry enterprises were established locally in 1960, Mitu's life became easier. Then he could remain at home because buses carried the workers into and out of the forest every day. Yet, Mitu recalls feeling like an "old man" after ten years of forestry work, when he was called up for military service at the age of twenty-four. He chose not to work for the brigade when he left the army:

> ...I sold timber here and there for two years. I worked with another guy; we paid drivers, state drivers, to take our merchandise; we had a small arrangement with the forester for a cart of wood, and from that deal we actually filled two trucks; after two years, we thought it was getting risky, it was kind of obvious for anybody how we were making our money; so we got employed again, and what we were supposed to get done in one month, we strove to get it done in two weeks, working like crazy, so that the other two weeks we could work for ourselves, we continued our private business. I had my own horses and cart, I sawed the logs at the brigade's sawmill, bribing the miller there, and went to villages in the plains to sell it. Along the way, we would barter [wood for cereals] or, if we got money, we would then buy cereals, fish;

where you made a deal, people would let you sleep in their stables, or in summer, we slept in our carts under the stars.

Trade was only possible by circumventing rules, bribing policemen, and traveling "from village to village, like the gypsies," because in the officially designated marketplaces controls were strict. The brigade bosses would complain that employees from the Apuseni Mountains were the worst workers, because they were always heading off home to make hay or loading their carts with "state trees" for illicit trade. Bosses were themselves local people, and they felt obliged to cover fellow villagers against the controls of superiors, marking their absences as "days of work" (*să facă pontajul*).

Around 1980, shortages required the introduction of food rationing. Consumption was regulated by vouchers (*cartele*) that were supposed to ensure a sufficient daily intake of calories, calculated on "scientific bases." This was the period in which President Ceaușescu was determined to eliminate the country's external debt. Some mountain inhabitants, particularly shepherds, benefited from this obsession with self-sufficiency at the level of the nation, as their dairy products commanded high prices on the black market (Stewart 1998).[11] Forestry workers lost out, as the exchange value of their wood fell. When recalling these years, people would often begin their stories with calculations of food as an indicator of their poverty: how much bread and fatback they had per day, or how much they had in their bag when they went away for a week:

> In the '80s the shortages of food began. On the road across the country with my goods, I had some bread from home, but it was never enough; I realized the shortage one day when I went to the store to get some bread. The shopkeeper told me, "I cannot give you any, it is on voucher, you can't buy without the voucher"... a lady was there, she gave me her voucher, God help her if she's still alive. Otherwise we had to beg the bakers; even with those damned vouchers, the bread was just never enough.

## Socialist Dependence 2: The Work of Women and Children—Collecting Berries and Tending Animals

If men had to combine state work with private business as ingeniously as they could to feed their families, women had to be innovative too in order to sustain household activities and, if possible, make extra money on the side. I gathered lively accounts of harsh lives during socialist times. For example, Lena was born in 1946, into a family that was neither wealthy nor poor. Her father worked in the forest "with his hands" (*cu palmile*) to fell trees with an axe for the state forestry brigade. He came home on Saturday, and on Sunday evening he was off to work again. Her mother raised eight children and did all the work in and around the house. Lena remembered with a sigh how she used to go with her mother to collect berries, which were a source of extra money as well as a valued food:

> Around here the women made money with blueberries. We sold blueberries at the collection booths. At 5 in the morning, my mum would wake me up; I remember I was 12 years old. And we went up into the hills, in the wet grass at dawn, to reach the meadows with blueberry bushes. We sold 10, 15 kilos per day, even 20, depending on how much we could collect, my mum and I.[12] We would save the money, not spend it immediately, you know; on Wednesdays and Fridays we would fast, we hardly ate anything at all, only blueberries with a bit of bread; on the meadow there, mum would rest next to a spring and eat, and for us, the kids, she would put a bit of sugar on the blueberries.

In the Apuseni Mountains women did a lot of farming work, which elsewhere was carried out by men. They mowed, made haystacks for winter provisions, carried heavy loads, and kept the garden and barns. During summer, Lena's mother and her children lived in their hut on the alpine pasture, about seven kilometers from the village, where the cows could graze freely on the family plot. However, there was always work to be done back in their village garden, where they cultivated a small plot of rye and potatoes, so the children over the age of seven were often left alone in the hut. As she went up and down the hills, Lena's mother would load infants into hemp bags (*desagi*) which she carried on her back, while slightly older ones would walk beside her, holding onto a corner of her dress. The older children stayed at the high pasture to tend the pigs, poultry lambs, and cattle. Lena recounted all this in a sentimental tone: "Mum had to climb the hills up and down all by herself, with heavy loads, she would not have dreamed that one day a car would take her up the hill. ... we would watch her cross the field as she walked down the hill, getting smaller and smaller, my little brothers jumping all around her. Then, all day long my brother and I would watch a small point on the horizon where my mother was supposed to appear, climbing back up the hill... all day and every day our eyes were trained on that point... is mummy coming?" Lena's memories focus on the care and concern that her mother had for Lena and her siblings, but she also told me of the conflicts experienced by women during the early decades of socialism. Persistent food shortages engendered many family conflicts that women had to resolve. In the beginning of her marriage, Lena's mother lived with her mother-in-law, with whom she always quarreled over her supposedly wasteful habits. As Lena recounts: "My grandmother was a bit of a bitch. She would always reprimand my mum, because she was not thrifty enough with food for us. Mum had feelings for us; of course, a mother cannot bear to see her children hungry. She hid us behind the barn to feed us. There were hard times, not enough food for everyone."

## Contemporary Self-Reliance: Technology and Market Opportunities

After the fall of socialism, people who practiced petty commerce during communism became aware of a range of new opportunities to make money. Commercial links with Western Europe, countrywide nationwide construction boom and pervasive legal chaos made for a propitious environment for the timber traders. Accustomed to frugality, they did not rush to enlarge their houses or buy expensive furniture but invested in productive equipment first. Forests and the state forestry enterprises were partly privatized, enabling villagers to buy machinery cheaply or simply to grab it.[13] In addition to trucks and other equipment, two men from Urși managed to buy two professional sawmills from the collapsing state enterprises and installed them in the village. By 1995, approximately one in three households bought their own mills and timber was being processed day and night. When their own trucks were insufficient, they rented trucks in other communities to carry their goods to weekly markets, or to sell through private networks.

The commercial possibilities captured the attention of young men, aged around twenty in 1995. Daniel, for example, borrowed money and sold his apartment, without the approval of his wife, to raise initial capital. He went abroad and bought three German trucks, kept one, and sold the other two. He used the proceeds to enter the timber business. He reckoned that in just one year he made six times more money than the value of the apartment he sold. He described his business as a risky undertaking, but "since everybody around was successful, how could you not have the guts to do it? That moment was golden." Daniel later left the village and by 2010 he owned a large sawmill in the town of Sebeș (see map at the end of the chapter). Like other young men of his generation, he felt the lure of easy money. As he described it, they felt that "prosperity was in [their] own hands" in a way that had not been possible for their fathers under socialism.

After 1995, almost all villagers engaged in the production and trade of timber. Unlike other forest regions with a history of collective property rights, Urși did not experience the formation of a mafia-type economy, and material improvement was open to all, influenced by the maintenance of entrepreneurial trade interests during socialism.[14] Villagers aspire to own all the means of production necessary for cutting and processing timber, and transporting it to market. To be fully self-sufficient one would need to own a chainsaw; a tractor or horses and a wagon to bring cut wood from the forest; a sawmill; and a truck for the final journey to market. In 2010, I counted only five families in the village who met this condition (out of

124). Members of these families think of themselves as "having everything," because "having the production technology means not depending on others, thus not giving away money." I found that one house in three owned a horse, one in six owned a sawmill (which was half the number said to exist in 1995), and one in ten a truck. Those who focus their work in the village level tend to own both a sawmill and horse, but they have to strike deals with truck-owning neighbors to transport and sell their merchandise or wait for dealers to come to the village. Some own a truck and a sawmill but no horses. The final stages of the transportation and marketing chain have become more risky and rewarding because laws grew stricter after the chaos of the early 1990s.

In practice, most households, including the above-mentioned five which meet the technological preconditions for self-sufficiency, engage with other households, either family or neighbors. About half of these contacts involve paid work, while the other half is classified as "reciprocal help" (*ajutor reciproc*). To hire someone to work for money is not easy, and the daily rate is significantly higher than in other regions of Romania (about 35 EUR in 2009).

Inter-household relations are also essential in other activities outside the timber sector. For example, since rain can ruin the hay harvest, it is vital that each household recruits enough people to mow and turn the hayfields in a single day. Mutual aid is the preferred solution, but if this is not possible, day-laborers are hired from outside the village. When this occurs, there is a strong preference to pay them according to the area harvested instead of offering a day-rate. Being by the day is said to encourage laziness and the consumption of more food, which the owner of the hayfields is obliged to provide. The laborers, for their part, accept this system, which allows them to earn sums far higher than the standard rate for day labor (as high as 150 EUR for two days of work).

The survey I conducted in 2009–2010[15] showed that 95 percent of the surveyed households were involved in one way or another with the market, either by selling in marketplaces or directly to customers (see table 6.1). More than half of the households combine regular income (wages or pensions) with additional sporadic income from the market. Twenty-eight percent of households live solely by selling produce or their labor. Such casual labor may involve pulling wood out of the forest with horses or sawing timber for neighbors. Some villagers work irregularly as smiths, car mechanics, masons, or house painters. All of these services are in demand in the village. Pensions generally derive from employment in the forestry sector during socialist times, but their average value is low (100 to 150 EUR per month).

**Table 6.1.** Sources of Household Income.

| | | |
|---|---|---|
| Regular income | 72% of surveyed households—at least one regular income in house: | |
| | Wages | 28% |
| | Pensions | 62% |
| | Both wages and pensions | 10% |
| Selling products | 95%, of which: | |
| | Sell timber | 78% |
| | Sell mushrooms | 44% |
| | Sell blueberries | 67% |
| | Sell pines for Christmas trees | 33% |
| | Sell animals | 78% |
| Regular income plus additional market income | 56% | |
| Barter timber for cereals (to feed animals) | 66% | |

N = 30, approx. one-quarter of all village households in 2010.

Although the villagers are opposed to waged labor ideologically and declare that stable commitments to employers are undesirable, the survey showed that six households had at least one member in employment (as a forester or driver, or in a local institution such as the school, church, or local administration).[16] When asked to specify the most important source of household income, twenty-three people (70 percent) declared "the wood" or "the merchandise", meaning the timber trade, as suggested in table 6.2. In addition to these revenues, many households pick and sell blueberries and mushrooms (67 percent and 44 percent). Such work is talked about as a low-class occupation and usually associated with Gypsies who come every summer. Despite the negative connotation, the well-developed market and network of intermediaries make this gathering a rewarding practice.[17]

**Table 6.2.** Average Annual Household Income, 2010 (in EUR).

| | |
|---|---|
| Sale of timber | 4,000 |
| Wages | 2,000 |
| Sale of mushrooms | 1,500 |
| Pensions | 1,200 |
| Sale of blueberries | 1,000 |
| Sale of animals | 800 |
| Sale of pines for Christmas trees | 300 |

The figures in table 6.2. indicate the average income obtained in each sector, but no household is active in all sectors. It should be noted that the seasonal activities of mushroom and blueberry picking (when combined, as they are usually are) generate more than an average annual wage. In addition, in 2009 60 percent of all households (according to the agricultural registers, and 78 percent according to my survey) sold at least one large animal at the weekly fairs.

A part of the food consumed is bought from shops. For example, in the case of one family that owns two cows, two pigs and fifteen chicken (the Trif family detailed below, see table 6.3.), roughly two thirds of the food consumed is home produced (according to my evaluations in terms of money value). An average family slaughters one pig (at Christmas) and one calf (at Easter) per year. Potatoes are grown mostly to feed the pigs, two tons being considered a good annual yield. Most villagers also cultivate small vegetable garden, but the produce is seldom sufficient for the year.

## Prosperity: Diligence and Reciprocal Help

The Trif family, which hosted me, is among the ten wealthiest families in the village. Their position is bolstered and symbolically expressed by the position of their land at the heart of the village.[18] The family 'head', Dumi, was a forestry brigadier during the socialist regime and built up connections he could continue to use even in retirement. Their house, built on two levels, is large and functional, although its furnishings are quite basic. Their success reveals local values of diligence, thrift, and hard work. To illustrate, I will detail the family's activities, as I recorded them one early spring day in 2010:

> The lights go on shortly after dawn, and the whole house is freezing. The six of us huddle together around the hissing pots and pans on the stove. Everybody grabs a cup of hot milk and a piece of bread in the cold house. After feeding the pigs a hot "breakfast" and taking the cows to the meadow, Mona, the 22-year-old unmarried daughter, opens the store (functions also as village pub), which is a registered family-business. Tourist accommodation upstairs is rarely occupied. Gina, Mona's mother, loads the washing machine and puts the pots on the stove to cook lunch and dinner, and runs over to the house of George, her brother-in-law, to make sure he will come later in the morning to help her with his horse to spread manure and ashes to fertilize the hayfields. Meanwhile, Dumi, and his younger, unmarried son Sivu, 24, set off to the forest at a great pace to cut down and haul in the logs. The day was cold and grim, grey clouds hanging overhead. Dumi and Sivu arrive back home around midday with a load of logs covered in melting snow onto the back of a borrowed truck; they eat frugally, and then unload the logs in a hurry at the sawmill in their yard. They prepare the logs and the sawmill starts buzzing. Gina lends them a hand because for several days now they are trying to finish an urgent order for sawn

timber from an old customer of theirs, the priest from a neighboring village. The family makes at least 8000 EUR from its sales of wood in the course of a year. Today the men continue long after dark, but Gina has to leave them at dusk to take care of the animals. At around seven, the cold is creeping up on the workingmen, so they stop sawing for today and they can enjoy a hot meal that Gina serves them. Later on, Sivu goes out for a beer with his mates in the neighboring village, an occasion for him to show a bit off with the red VW Golf he purchased last year, while Dumi joins his daughter in the loud village pub, to chat and play some cards.

Gina explained her approach to life: "We can live well here, but money does not fall from the sky. We have to strive to keep going, do this, do that, always something, and not to lay back." The Trifs have stable incomes, including Dumi's pension and the small salaries earned by Gina and Sivu, plus an income stream from timber and the bar, but they supplement these sources with additional activities. Before Christmas, the sons went to the forest and cut down young pines to sell as Christmas trees. They took fifty trees, three days in a row, to the marketplace in the city of Turda (see map at the end of the chapter), spending the day there to sell them, at −15°C. In summer, the children intermittently collect and sell mushrooms, stressing the "fun" of it, rather than the "need" for money, because they are embarrassed to be associated with the low-class image that pickers have acquired in recent years. I calculated that this household makes at least 23,000 EUR per year in cash, from which they spend at most 7,000 EUR for daily life (including expenses for timber production and furniture); the rest is available for "big investments" (see table 6.3. below).[19]

**Table 6.3.** Annual Budget of the Trif Household (2010, in EUR, excluding extraordinary purchases).

| Monetary income (22,400) | | Monetary expenditure (6,750) | |
|---|---|---|---|
| Sale of timber | 8,000 | Electricity (for sawmill) | 1,300 |
| Salaries (Gina and Sivu) | 3,600 | Wedding attendance (approx. eight times per year)[20] | 1,200 |
| Pension (Dumi) | 3,000 | Food | 700 |
| Store and bar profit | 3,000 | Clothes | 700 |
| Rent for summer festival | 2,000 | Fuel | 600 |
| Guesthouse | 1,500 | Cereals for animals | 500 |
| Sale of animals | 800 | Household equipment | 600 |
| Sale of Christmas trees | 500 | Work payments | 350 |
| | | Taxes and fees | 300 |
| **Value of self-provisioning (1,350)** | | | |
| Pork | 400 | Phone | 200 |
| Cheese/milk | 400 | Restaurants and going out | 200 |
| Vegetables (mainly potatoes) | 200 | Internet | 100 |
| Fruits/alcohol | 50 | | |
| Eggs | 150 | | |
| Chicken | 150 | | |
| **Total** | 23,750 | **Total** | 6,750 |
| **Surplus 17,000** | | | |

Despite their high level of disposable income, the family worries about borrowing money. Not long before I moved in with them, the family had paid a bribe of 3,000 EUR to secure a job for the older son, Radu, in the city of Oradea, two hours away. There, instead of paying a rent, they planned to buy him an apartment costing 40,000 EUR. They did not have the whole sum in cash and would therefore have to borrow around 10,000 EUR from three relatives. Gina worried about how to proceed with these relatives, "call them closely before Christmas to wish them happy holidays and ask for money in the same phone call? Oh, better not mix the two, better to call them right the next day, to get the anxiety out of the way." Shortly after Christmas, they bought the apartment and during the same year, the older son acquired a good secondhand car.

The Trifs consider that the key to their success is continuous diligence and careful calculations of social relationships. They do need help from others, yet they "depend on nobody." This means that they approach various people for help, engage in varying combinations of mutual assistance and hired labor, and attempt to cancel their debts quickly. The Trifs do not own a horse and cart, and often need help with transporting logs. To secure this help, they can ask either George, the husband of Gina's sister, with whom they exchange labor, to come with his horse; or they can approach Tibi, a family friend, to help them with his tractor. In the latter case, they must pay a fixed daily rate plus fuel costs. George is obliged to help them because his son goes to high school in a town where the Trif family owns a flat, and he is allowed to live there for free. In addition, George occasionally uses the Trifs' sawmill. Nevertheless, George is not always available to help. When the Trifs ask him, he usually accepts, but he sets his time conditions: "in two days' time" or "next week I am free." Since the Trifs want to have their work done "in the proper time," they often prefer to pay Tibi, or some other man available, instead of waiting for George.

Despite his inferior economic position, George can afford to be unavailable, and the Trifs respect his decisions. Although they do not pay George in cash, the Trifs say that he cannot be expected to work "for free," even if he is a close relative. Long-standing debts run in the background, but short-term debts are open on both sides, and both George's household and the Trifs are anxious to cancel them quickly. I once heard George say "I have to help them today because last week they let me do my timber at their sawmill." In the summer of 2009, George's main activity was picking mushrooms, which he enjoys: "mushroom picking is so much more relaxing and pleasurable than doing timber; and also it pays well; it is like finding money on the ground." He receives cash payment for his occasional work as a smith, and for some of the other families that he "helps" by lending out his horse. Kinship bonds do not exclude payment; George's father-in law has a pension and savings in the bank, so he gives money to George from time to time for the help that he receives.

The relationship between the Trifs and Tibi and his wife Maria is similarly layered with calculations of dependence and freedom on both sides. Sometimes the Trifs pay Tibi for the use of his tractor (one of the few in the village), but they also engage in "reciprocal help" (*ajutor reciproc*), for example, by driving Maria to the regional town to buy furniture or heavy house appliances. With her two young daughters, Maria helps the Trifs to harvest hay and potatoes. Instead of using the Trifs' sawmill, however, Tibi and Maria prefer to mill their logs at another villager's sawmill and pay the usual price. They do not want to "burden the relationship" (*să nu încarci relația*) with the Trifs. Besides, if they pay a neighbor when they need something done, they "feel free," "without further obligations." They had thought about buying their own sawmill in association with Tibi's brother, who is a well-to-do timber transporter, but they feared that getting together in this way would leave them with long-term debts to the older brother.

The Trifs also have work relations with several other houses in the village. When neither George nor Tibi is available, for example, the Trifs ask for Luca's help. Luca lives on a hillside some distance away from the main road, and does not have access to powerful enough electricity to run his own sawmill. The Trifs describe Luca as a diligent worker, but they do not engage him frequently because his services are not cheap. Usually, Luca refuses to take the payment the Trifs offer, saying "No, I don't accept the money, you were always very kind to me," but Gina insists on paying him and stuffs the bills into his pocket. After Luca has left she voiced her concerns to me: "he is expensive, but he does good work. If I don't pay him well, next time when I'll need him, he won't come."

The Trifs can also ask for help from Gina's youngest brother Florea, who earns money by working for others with his horse, yet the Trifs seldom ask him for help. Florea still lives with Gina's parents, and they support a powerful man in the village, the parliamentary deputy (son of the communist shopkeeper mentioned above), whom the Trifs have long regarded as an opponent. Moreover, Florea is generally said to be simple-minded, and not a good worker. As a result, he usually works for a lower rate of pay than normal for the Pentecostal family in the village; nobody else wants to work with them on account of their religious "weirdness," despite their being hard-working and quite successful. Another person whom the Trifs hire only exceptionally is Eli, their next-door neighbor. Once, when he worked for them for half a day with his horses and cart, Gina gave him one stack of hay that was surplus to her own requirements; after understanding that Eli needed more hay for the winter, she downloaded a second stack into his yard, for which Eli insisted on paying. Wanting to secure Eli's work indebt-

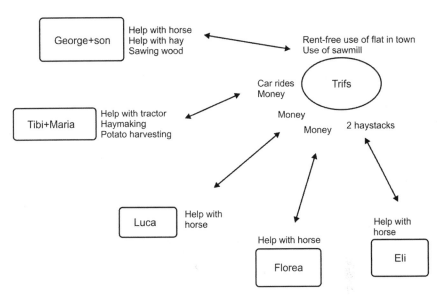

**Figure 6.1.** Work Network of the Trif Family.

edness, Gina refused the payment saying: "You'll help me some other day with the horses, I don't take the money."

As figure 6.1 shows, the highest rate of reciprocal help comes from George, who is a close relative and intimate family friend, and secondly from Tibi and Maria, who are also considered friends. Simply calling someone a friend (*prieten*) sets the parameters of exchange, but the valence of friendship seems rather different from that described by recent studies of Russia (Caldwell 2004; Ledeneva 1998; Pesmen 2000). In the Apuseni Mountains, friends are not bound together and saying 'no' is understandable and acceptable. Reciprocities in Urşi are balanced in the sense that people feel obliged to repay immediately, even if this means paying money. Friends can also refuse to help without offending the asker. The exchanges that transpire between the Trif family and those in their network occur as individual episodes of a "coincidence of interests" between both parties, but over time prove to consolidate the relationship.

## "Master of Oneself" and "Keeping Going"

People in the Apuseni Mountains value autonomy and equality in their social relations, as well as a certain stubbornness. In addition to "being one's own master"—hinting at self-made persons, independence, and individualism—they often speak of "keeping going" (*dă-i să meargă*)—suggesting relentless industry, mobility, fast thinking, and risk-taking. People like to draw parallels between their own acts of defiance against the state, struggles for freedom, or tax avoidance with those of Vasile Horea, the leader of the 1784 peasant uprising: "Here people do not like to obey rules; we are like this; Horea, he struggled with an empire for the sake of freedom." [21]

According to some anthropological accounts, the experience of socialism changed some aspects of people's relationship with work. For example, Gail Kligman and Katherine Verdery argued that communism modified the work ethic of Romanians "almost beyond recognition" (2011: 429). The changes introduced by collectivization and the bureaucratization of work "...struck a blow against ideas of the person based on identification with work. Collectivization reduced not only the commitment to work, but the self-directed initiative that had accompanied possession in rural ideology, for self-direction could no longer define the person, if direction came from the farm leaders [...] collectivization destroyed peasants' love of work..." (Ibid.: 432). But, the changed identification with work did not eliminate self-direction entirely. Kligman and Verdery also point out that everyday uncertainty was pervasive and required creative individual responses (Ibid.: 425). Other ethnographic accounts of socialist Romania acknowledge ubiquitous individual agency and self-direction, in spite of collectivization (Kideckel 1993; Beck 1979; Sampson 1987; Stewart 1998). My ethnography from Urși reveals non-collectivized mountain villagers able to maintain a high sense of self-direction. Various forms of cunning were necessary to evade the state in the forestry work environment. As a result, the 'new' socialist person had to be creative and shrewd. Those values pertaining to independence, self-direction, and self-sufficiency could come to the forefront again following the collapse of the socialist institutions. Apuseni dwellers look back and say "we made our own fortunes," with reference to both socialist and postsocialist periods.

In Romanian, to be *stăpân*, master, means to dominate others, but also to own (*a stăpâni*) and to be reserved or thrifty (*a se stăpâni*). The idea that one "has to be one's own master" (*să fii propriul tău stăpân*) is highly developed in Urși and manifest in various ways. Among other things, it involves having money, which implies "not being indebted to anyone" (*să nu ai datorii/obligații la nimeni*). Bad indebtedness refers to work obligations, not to money debts. Money loans (*împrumut*) from friends and relatives, which bear no interest, can under some circumstances be regarded positively. Local loaning is a recurrent practice, regarded as a means to advance, and to be ahead of others, as part of an ideology of "keeping things going." The opposite of taking loans would be to hoard money, in order to gather enough to make purchases. But, to save for too long is seen as stagnation.

Villagers think it is important for money to circulate. Money can work (*banul lucrează*) to the advantage of the borrower in the sense that it can be invested, or used to avoid paying unproductive rents. The questionnaire that I used indicated that large acquisitions, such as house, car, or horse, were typically made by borrowing large sums of money from friends and family. Smaller amounts, ranging upward of 100 EUR, were loaned on a weekly or monthly basis: "to cover needs, until you sell some logs." Indebtedness is pervasive, yet since almost everyone in the village is highly solvent, nobody can remember about a case of default.[22] Interest-bearing bank loans are strictly avoided.

Being indebted to work for others is feared more than monetary debt because it means lagging behind in one's own work. The question of who owes work to whom, what kind of work, and how much, is a crucial issue of negotiation among kin, neighbors and covillagers. To be a good householder means "keeping distance" and not allowing relationships to become burdensome. As shown in the description of the Trifs' strategies, while Luca tries to leave a small debt to Gina outstanding, she insists on paying him in order to avoid indebtedness, while at the same she herself tries to use money to pay her neighbor Eli an advance for hay, in order to secure his help with the horse at some future date.

To avoid work debts and spending money, villagers want to possess machinery, an option practically closed to them in the past. However, new equipment is expensive, while secondhand machines typically incur high running costs. Buying equipment in common makes people anxious, as I noted in the case of Tibi. Working regularly with a neighbor, for a fixed sum is a good solution, as Tibi's wife Maria declared: "I pay this neighbor and I have no further obligations to anyone." Another preferred strategy that does not create increased dependence is reciprocal help, provided it is carefully balanced.

Time compression attributed by social theorists to late capitalism (Harvey 1989) seems to have reached the Apuseni Mountains, yet the consequences here look less alienating. A common local expression that captures this ebullient spirit is "keep going" (*dă-i să meargă*), meaning to constantly move on, to be industrious, to ensure that work runs smoothly, as "water flows in a stream," as one of my informants put it. People utter the phrase "keep going" at the sawmill, in the fields, or during house work, as a kind of leitmotiv. Unlike the peasants of the southern Carpathians, who experienced exhaustion and stress after the fall of socialism (Fox 2011: 242), in the Apuseni I never heard people talking of stress. Certainly they often felt tired; however, tiredness after work expected to lead immediately to gain was perceived as fulfilling. Maria, often complained about working too hard, especially at the sawmill: "I had to mill a pile of trunks, see these boards? Tomorrow they come to get them; I had to do it all today, life is like this. Well, I did it, it is accomplished work, not wasted; but I am so tired, I feel like vomiting. Yet, there is no time to sit around, I have to go to the house now, milk the cows and cook. Come on, let's get it done quickly!" Not only for work, but also in trade, speed is perceived as essential. The fast circulation of money, as well as the capacity to make rapid decisions faster than others, is a daily virtue. Thinking and acting are seen as the result of calculation, but a kind of calculation that has "entered one's veins" and is carried out almost as a reflex. Traders should "feel" when to lower the price, how to adapt to every new customer, how to earn a little more money by cheating, and, in the event of the cheating being discovered, how to avoid losing face. The example of a villager, nicknamed "the student", who managed to buy the timber marketplace in Timişoara (see map below), the largest city in western Romania, is often quoted as an instance of "sparkling" business inspiration. One of his partners gave the student's recipe for success as follows: "He felt the moment, that's it! He was brilliantly smart for five minutes, and then he could sleep for one year. In those five minutes, his mind was a shining comet..."

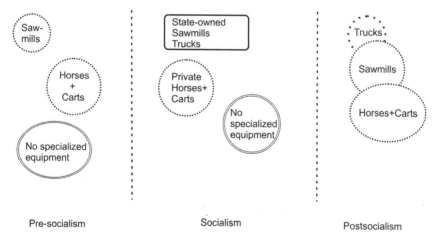

Pre-socialism          Socialism          Postsocialism

**Figure 6.2.** Village Hierarchy and Technology: 1) presocialist period: a small elite owned sawmills; the next category owned horses and carts, a large part did not own anything; 2) socialist period: most equipment was not owned privately, but used by a few privileged householders from state forestry brigades; some households owned horses and carts; 3) postsocialism: the most prosperous own trucks and sawmills; trucks are the most expensive items and transport to the market adds most value, though it is also high risk; others own only sawmills, or a sawmill and a horse and cart; the more equipment one has, the more prosperous one is held to be.

## Conclusion

The postsocialist economy of the Apuseni mountains is thriving. I have shown that this local economy is based on an array of entrepreneurial choices, yet in their narratives villagers emphasize self-sufficiency and the value of "being one's own master." To understand the prominence of these ideas it was necessary to begin in the era before socialism, when villagers were entangled in a variety of dependencies, notably with logging companies, sawmills, and money lenders. Poems in that period scorned indebtedness, which nonetheless was omnipresent. Far from any idyll of rustic self-sufficiency, 80 percent of the inhabitants depended on the better-off 20 percent for access to horses, carts, and sawmills in order to produce and sell timber throughout the country.

Socialism replaced the traditional ideology, which emphasized private property and entrepreneurialism, with its opposite: an ideology of centralization and collectivization, with the aim of making peasants into proletarians. In practice, a twofold movement ensued. The confiscation of the means of production and repression of the elites freed the majority of villagers from their former dependencies. Henceforth they had to work in socialist brigades and were subject to food requisitions, rendering them dependent on new elites. Over time, villagers learned how to take advantage of the system and devise new income-generating possibilities, yet they remained stuck within a system that discouraged private initiative and trade, and did not reward individual effort. Like other regions of Romania, the Apuseni Mountains were exposed to the caprices of the socialist state. Shortages ended with the fall of socialism, when privatization and favorable technological conditions allowed villagers to produce and transport their wares faster and make larger profits than ever before. Nowadays, timber-loaded trucks pass daily through the village of Urşi on their way to sawmills and markets. The road is dotted with collection booths for berries and mushrooms. All in all, the forests that had previously been the exclusive domain of corrupt foresters have become a source of prosperity and a sense of being *stăpân* (master) for almost everyone in the village. Contrasting themselves with earlier generations that could hardly meet subsistence needs, at present the Apuseni dwellers feel empowered and readily articulate narratives of increased self-direction and ideals of self-sufficiency.

The people highlight two material features in relation to "being one's own master": money and technology. Money means gain and circulating capital. It can take the form of debt, which can mean purchasing power, and it can mean payment for work. Money is by no means new to the area, though prior to socialism much of the timber trade was carried out through barter. The dynamic markets for forest products after the fall of socialism gave villagers the feeling that they could make money faster and more easily than ever before, leading them to value speed and movement. Individual effort and skill were now rewarded by the market and society. Not everybody in the village experienced gain and the sense of empowerment to the same extent, but for most families the immediate postsocialist years were a golden age. Economic crisis has reduced incomes significantly in recent years, but I found that villagers retained their new optimism and continued to praise the qualities of flexibility and of money as preconditions for mastery.

The second key element in local understandings of self-sufficiency is increased control of the technology required for the production and marketing of timber. Before socialism, most villagers had relied on others for access to mills and often to other equipment as well. During socialism, access required the cultivation of connections and bribes to state officials. Thus, the possibility to purchase one's own equipment meant a significant boost to the self-esteem of the postsocialist villager. I found that the fall in timber prices triggered by the economic crisis in 2009, coupled with the rising cost of new machinery, now subject to higher tax rates, had mitigated this earlier exhilaration. But villagers continued to highlight the importance of having one's own means of production in order to be free of debt and dependency. This autonomy was never absolute: Apuseni villagers remained connected to each other in loose networks involving both reciprocal help and paid work. Liberated from a rapacious state but bound to the new entanglements of the market, villagers declare that they feel freer than ever before. This is best illustrated in the way they negotiate their work relationships, balancing the necessity for relatedness against the anxiety of dependence and its most concrete form, indebtedness. Can the householder of the Apuseni Mountains be called individualist, or "disembedded" from society as a result of the efflorescence of the market? Rather than have recourse to a "tired theoretical antinomy" that cannot depict the "infinitely more complicated" notions of personhood that one finds on the ground (Comaroff and Comaroff 2001: 269), I have tried to show that both relatedness and autonomy are vehicles for securing material livelihood and well-being. The key issue is the extent to which involvement with others is perceived to hinder one's own flourishing in productive and commercial ventures. On the ground, this boundary setting can be harsh: people are not afraid to say "no" or to pay a friend in money. Yet, the distance set in this way is seldom an insuperable barrier; it is rather a legitimate device to make oneself understood in particular circumstances. The Apuseni dweller carries many of the hallmarks of short-term, neoliberal capitalist personhood, but these features are embedded in a rural society in which long-term bonds and identities remain strong.

**Figure 6.3.** Map of Monica Vasile's Field Site.

**Monica Vasile,** currently a Visiting Fellow at the Integrative Research Institute on Human-Environment Systems, Humboldt University, Berlin, holds a Ph.D. in Sociology from the University of Bucharest. Her first postdoctoral position was at the Max Planck Institute for the Study of Societies, Cologne. She has published numerous articles in books and scholarly journals, on topics related to forest commons, property relations, corruption, and environmental conservation.

## Notes

1. The name of the village is a pseudonym; so too are all villagers' names. Despite their distrust of outsiders, they opened up to my queries and helped me understand delicate local matters of work relations, money and trade. See Vasile 2015 for further background information about the Apuseni Mountains and detailed acknowledgments of the help I received in this project.

2. The revolt is known by the name of its three leaders, Horea, Cloşca, and Crişan. Vasile Horea was from a village near Urşi, which makes locals very proud of their history and ancestry.

3. Consistent with Western property theory, it was assumed that family farms would lead to more efficient agricultural production because peasants would have a great motivation to work their own land and that the establishment of family farms would impede rural-urban exodus.

4. Inspired by Russian agrarian economists, including Chayanov, Romanian scholars and politicians were critical of the negative effects of capitalism in the form of merchant capital and usury. It was alleged that these drained resources and made no positive contribution to the national economies of eastern countries. The alternative was grassroots cooperative marketing, with popular banks in which peasants would be given shares (Botea and Vârban 1999). In the region where I worked these peasant banks are remembered as failures because they were misused by local elites. However, when local elites were honest and oriented toward the "common good," the banks had the intended effects (e.g., the popular bank Gilortul, described in Focşeneanu 1998).

5. In 2010, I found only two cultivators of autumn-wheat (*grâu de toamnă*). The reasons for ceasing grain cultivation are varied: some allege that the soil is polluted due to gold mining in neighboring communities; others point out that as a result of socialism it became possible to buy bread and fodder in local shops, and they thus had no reason to continue to practice low-yield, time-consuming agriculture.

6. Debt and credit took various forms. For example, one producer and trader of wooden boards with five children owed three-quarters of his debts (amounting to the retail value of four carts of wooden planks) to fellow villagers and one-quarter to the popular bank, which had granted him credit in corn (Suciu 1929: 36).

7. A village close to Urşi.

8. Members of the elite strata of this village did not own large amounts of land or wealth as did elites in other areas of the country, and were thus not subjected to deportation or punishment. Only one family was deported to the plains; their descendants came back to the village after sixteen years.

9. In Romanian villages, the socialist consumption cooperative (*cooperativa de consum*) (not to be confused with the collective farms, CAP, which were at the center of the collectivization process) was the only place to purchase staple foods, fodder, working tools, and other necessary products; vegetables could be purchased in a separate state-owned shop, the *aprozar*. Villagers were members of the cooperatives and they delivered products that were sold in consumption cooperatives elsewhere. Villagers were paid small amounts of money for the products they delivered (according to locals' memory, four times less than the price on the open black market), which they could then use to buy goods in the cooperative.

10. Although "a man of the communists," people recall that he would not turn fellow villagers in. They believe that his moral shortcomings were punished by God: his wife died at the age of forty and two of his three sons died before reaching that age. In the postsocialist era, his surviving son became the most prominent political figure of the area and its representative in the national parliament.

11. Stewart describes how Romanian shepherds during socialism installed elevators to serve their three-story village houses, or had marble walled stables (1998: 70).

12. The total monthly sum was almost the equivalent of a factory worker's monthly wages, but outside the three summer months women had few opportunities to earn cash.

13. For more information about privatization of forests in Romania see for example Sikor, Stahl, and Dorondel 2009, and Vasile and Măntescu 2009.

14. For example, in the region of Vrancea in the eastern Carpathians, after the fall of socialism only a few locals managed to start private businesses. The majority of villagers did not develop individual enterprises; instead they found employment for low wages or as day laborers by the few business owners (Vasile 2006, 2007, 2009).

15. The questionnaire was applied to thirty households, i.e., one-quarter of all village households, chosen on a random route basis; every fourth household was included. For details of this survey in the comparative framework of the Economy and Ritual group, see Gudeman and Hann (2015: Appendix).

16. However, at least another six jobs were available in the village at the small timber enterprises that locals were unwilling to take; their owners were therefore obliged to employ Gypsies from the neighboring towns.

17. About a dozen households set up collection booths, where every summer evening, they collected each an average of 100 kg of boletes (funghi porcini), at an average price of 3–4 EUR per kg. Much of this produce finds its way to Italy and Austria. An unskilled picker who picks twenty days per month for three months makes at least 1,500 EUR. The collector adds 0.25 EUR per kilogram and makes approximately 500 EUR per month during the peak period.

18. When the first road was built (at the beginning of twentieth century) no one was willing to allow it to pass through their property and encroach on their hayfields. However, the grandfather of Dumi Trif finally agreed to allow the road to be built through the middle of his fields, as a result of which the church, the bar, and the House of Culture were all erected on his land. Other elite families were marginalized in this process.

19. People are secretive regarding their accounts. However, based on daily observations in this household, where I myself was living, I feel confident about these estimations. Here, as on other occasions, I found it necessary to correct the spontaneous declarations s.

20. Wedding attendance for most village families occurs three to four times per year. Because the Trif family has unmarried children, they attend twice this number. For details on wedding attendance, obligations, and money gifts see Vasile 2015.

21. A few events that people can remember in the village today boosted this type of historical awareness. For example, in 1984, the still-socialist state sponsored bicentennial celebrations of the revolt of Horea (mentioned in note 2) in which politicians and historians, playwrights, and local intellectuals all emphasized the harsh living conditions of serfs and their heroic character in resisting foreigners'

appropriation of wood, gold and other natural resources found in the area. The associations with resistance seem to have stuck, strengthening a sense of regional self-sufficiency, even though Katherine Verdery rightfully noted that the state's heavy-handed orchestration of the events also gave "the populace the visceral experience of their subordination" (Verdery 1991: 242), an imagined experience of humility and endurance, together with an overwhelming experience of the power of the state to subject and redefine history. During the bicentennial, the Communist Party labeled the revolt a national revolution on the part of oppressed Romanians on the periphery of the Habsburg Empire (Pascu 1984), even though other historians insist that it was a social revolt with no national content whatsoever (Prodan 1979).

22. I only heard about one case of default in a neighboring village, in which the creditor went with a couple of friends to the defaulter's house and seized a chainsaw to cover the payment due.

## References

Aristotle. 2012. *Nicomahean Ethics*. Translated by Robert C. Bartlett. Chicago: University of Chicago Press.

Beck, Sam. 1979. *Transylvania: The Political Economy of a Frontier*. Ph.D. Thesis, University of Massachusetts-Amherst.

Botea, Emil, and Mirea Vârban. 1999. *Băncile populare – cooperative de credit*. Bucharest: Gircom.

Caldwell, Melissa. 2004. *Not by Bread Alone: Social Support in the New Russia*. Berkeley: University of California Press.

Chayanov, A. V. 1986 [1924-5]. *The Theory of Peasant Economy*. Manchester: Manchester University Press.

Chelcea, Ion. 1932. "Câteva constatări asupa caracterului psihologic al moților, Societatea de mâine." *revistă socială economică* 9, no. 6: 77–79.

Ciomac, Ion Luca. 1933. *Probleme economice din Munții Apuseni și ai Maramureșului*. Cluj: Tipografia Națională.

Ciomac, Ion Luca, and Valeriu Popa-Neacșa. 1936. *Cercetări asupra stărilor economice din Munții Apuseni*. Bucharest: Editura Universul.

Comaroff, John L., and Jean Comaroff. 2001. "On Personhood: An Anthropological Perspective from Africa." *Social Identities* 7, no. 2: 267–284.

Csucsuja, Istvan. 1998. *Istoria pădurilor din Transilvania. 1848-1914*. Cluj: Presa Universitară Clujeană.

Focșeneanu, Eleodor. 1998. *Dumitru Brezulescu: O viață închinată țărănimii*. Bucharest: Vremea.

Fox, Katy. 2011. *Peasants into European Farmers? EU Integration in the Carpathian Mountains of Romania*. Berlin: Lit.

Gudeman, Stephen. 2008. *Economy's Tension: The Dialectics of Market and Economy*. New York: Berghahn Books.

Gudeman, Stephen, and Alberto Rivera. 1990. *Conversations in Colombia*. Cambridge: Cambridge University Press.

Gudeman, Stephen, and Chris Hann. 2015. *Economy and Ritual: Studies of Postsocialist Transformations.* New York: Berghahn Books.

Guyer, Jane. 1981. "Household and Community in African Studies." *African Studies Review* 24, no. 2–3: 87–137.

Harvey, David. 1989. *The Condition of Postmodernity: An Enquiry Into the Origins of Cultural Change.* Oxford: Blackwell.

Kideckel, David. 1993. *The Solitude of Collectivism: Romanian Villagers to the Revolution and Beyond.* Ithaca, NY: Cornell University Press.

Kligman, Gail, and Verdery, Katherine. 2011. *Peasants Under Siege: The Collectivization of Romanian Agriculture, 1949-1962.* Princeton, NJ: Princeton University Press.

Lampland, Martha. 1995. *The Object of Labor: Commodification in Socialist Hungary.* Chicago: University of Chicago Press.

Ledeneva, Alena. 1998. *Russia's Economy of Favours: Blat, Networking and Informal Exchange.* Cambridge: Cambridge University Press.

Madgearu, Virgil. 1999 [1936]. *Agrarianism, Capitalism, Imperialism: Contributiuni la studiul evoluției sociale românești.* Bucharest: Institutul de arte grafice "Bucovina."

Manoilescu, Mihail. 2002 [1940]. *Rostul și destinul burgheziei românești.* Bucharest: Editura Albatros.

Netting, Robert. 1993. *Smallholders, Householders: Farm Families and the Ecology of Intensive, Sustainable Agriculture.* Stanford, CA: Stanford University Press.

Ortner, Sherry. 2005. "Subjectivity and Cultural Critique." *Anthropological Theory* 5, no. 1: 31–52.

Papahagi, Tache. 1925. *Cercetări în Munții Apuseni.* București: Grai și suflet, Institutul de Filologie și folclor.

Pascu, Ştefan. 1984. *Revoluția populară de sub conducerea lui Horea.* Bucharest: Editura Militară.

Pesmen, Dale. 2000. *Russia and Soul: An Exploration.* Ithaca, NY: Cornell University Press.

Prodan, David. 1979. *Răscoala lui Horea.* Bucuresti: Editura stiintifică si enciclopedică.

Sahlins, Marshall. 1972. *Stone Age Economics.* New York: Aldine de Gruyter.

Sampson, Steven. 1987. "The Second Economy of the Soviet Union and Eastern Europe." *The ANNALS of the American Academy of Political and Social Science* 493: 120–136.

Sikor, Thomas, Johannes Stahl, and Stefan Dorondel. 2009. "Negotiating Post-Socialist Property and State: Struggles over Forests in Albania and Romania." *Development and Change* 40, no. 1: 171–193.

Stewart, Michael. 1998. "'We should build a statue to Ceausescu here': The Trauma of De-collectivization in Two Romanian Villages." In *Surviving Post-Socialism: Local Strategies and Regional Responses in Eastern Europe and the Former Soviet Union,* ed. Sue Bridger and Frances Pine, 66–79. London: Routledge.

Suciu, Petru. 1929. *Tara Moților. Regiunea industrei lemnului.* Cluj: Editura de ziare.

Vasile, Monica. 2006. "Obştea Today in the Vrancea Mountains of Romania: Self-governing Institutions of Forest Commons." *Sociologie Românească* 4, no. 3: 111–130.

———. 2007. "Sense of Property, Deprivation and Memory in the Case of Obştea Vrânceană." *Sociologie Românească* 5, no. 2: 114–129.

———. 2009. Corruption in Romanian Forestry: Morality and Local Practice in the Context of Privatization, *Revista Româna de Sociologie* 20 (1–2): 105–120.

———. 2015. "The Trader's Wedding: Ritual Inflation and Money Gifts in Transylvania" In *Economy and Ritual: Studies in Postsocialist Tranformations,* ed. Stephen Gudeman and Chris Hann, 137–165, New York: Berghahn Books.

Vasile, Monica, and Liviu Măntescu. 2009. "Property Reforms in Rural Romania and Community-based Forests." *Sociologie Românească* 7, no. 2: 95–113.

Verdery, Katherine. 1991. *National Ideology Under Socialism: Identity and Cultural Politics in Ceausescu's Romania.* Berkeley: University of California Press.

———. 1996. *What Was Socialism, and What Comes Next?* Princeton, NJ: Princeton University Press.

———. 2003. *The Vanishing Hectare: Property and Value in Postsocialist Transylvania.* Ithaca, NY: Cornell University Press.

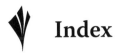

# Index